Preface

We live and work in a world that is becoming more internationalised and complex every day. The demand for up-to-date, worldwide and comparative reporting is therefore growing rapidly. Politicians, government officials, employers and trade unionists need to know about recent events and policy trends so that they can adjust their strategies and objectives accordingly. Students and teachers require relevant discussion and learning material, while the general reader may simply wish to be better informed. Labour specialists, finally, may seek to update their knowledge on the rapidly changing aspects of the world of work.

For this reason we have reviewed the periodicity and scope of the *World Labour Report*. While the previous four volumes were published at two-year intervals, this and future Reports will come out on a yearly basis. Instead of focusing on one theme, they will now cover the whole labour field, with recurrent chapters on: human rights at work; employment; labour relations; social protection and working conditions. An extensive statistical annex with key labour indicators is another feature of the new series.

The wave of democratisation which continues to sweep the world today is one of the key developments reviewed in this Report. It has brought about a strong improvement in human rights and labour relations. Freedom of association has now become the foundation of labour relations in many countries. And governments, employers and workers are increasingly working together in a tripartite setting. Nevertheless, many workers' and some employers' organisations are still seriously restricted in their freedom to organise and to negotiate.

The globalisation of the world economy and structural adjustment are another set of key factors currently shaping the world of work. Enterprises are relying more and more on the flexible use of labour to survive in competitive world markets. Widening income gaps between countries are heightening the pressure for workers to migrate. In the industrialised countries unemployment is rising. In many developing countries governments are pursuing structural adjustment policies by trimming their expenses and privatising their economies. Many developing countries also continue to suffer from widespread underemployment and a low return on labour. Thus, a rising proportion of the world labour force is working in the informal sector or employed under flexible labour contracts.

The advance of democracy, the struggle against poverty and the protection of workers are, in my view, the ILO's three main challenges for the coming years. The free development of a tripartite dialogue between governments, employers and workers will help the process of democratisation forward. Greater respect for human rights, such as the eradication of all forms of discrimination, will be another contributory factor. The struggle against increasing poverty has to be fought in both developed and developing countries. Finally, there is an increasing number of vulnerable workers, such as migrants and working children, who are in precarious employment conditions. More and more workers in the informal sector and the growing numbers of unemployed will need social protection. And all workers need better protection against new chemical hazards and, sometimes, against deteriorating environmental conditions.

This Report is the result of research and analysis carried out by the staff of the International Labour Office, and it may contain judgements that do not necessarily reflect the views of governments, employers or workers. The basic aim of this and future Reports is to satisfy the information needs of all actors and spectators of the world labour scene. But there is more. These reports also provide a unique opportunity to rethink the challenges that confront the ILO in the ever-changing world of work. I hope that this Report will enable us – with the knowledge of today's key developments – to help shape tomorrow's world of work.

20 January 1992

Michel Hansenne

World labour report 1992 5

Human rights at work
Employment
Labour relations
Social protection and working conditions
Statistical appendix

International Labour Office   Geneva

ISBN 92-2-107110-3

ISSN 0255-5514

First published 1992

Printed in Switzerland   HEL

Contents

Text tables

Text charts

Text boxes

Summary

This is the first of a new annual series of the *World Labour Report*. Each year the Report will devote a chapter to each of the following areas:

1. *Human rights at work*
2. *Employment*
3. *Labour relations*
4. *Social protection and working conditions*

A report as brief as this cannot claim to offer comprehensive coverage, so it will focus only on some of the more significant current developments, as well as on regions whose recent experience is of particular interest.

1. Human rights at work

This year the Report covers three human rights areas: freedom of association; child labour; and equal opportunities for women.

Freedom of association

Democratisation is the thread which runs through this section. Political transformation in Eastern Europe. The retreat of Latin America's military rulers. The progress of multi-party democracy in Africa. All are radically changing the lives of working people and their employers.

There is still some way to go, however, before working people can organise in freedom and in peace – hundreds of trade unionists were reported murdered in 1990 and 1991 and thousands more were imprisoned or sacked because of their union work.

Some of the most serious of human rights abuses have taken place in Colombia, as a result of the influence of the drug cartels. Since 1986 over 300 trade unionists have been killed and there have been ten attacks with dynamite on trade union premises. A similar climate of violence prevails in several countries of Central America. In El Salvador the premises of one of the trade union federations has been dynamited twice in recent years, killing nine people and injuring seven others. Many other trade unionists have also been murdered, or disappeared. And in the Philippines there have been many cases of human rights abuses connected with the operations of armed vigilante groups.

But the rights of workers and employers can also be directly threatened by government action. In Sudan, after the coup d'état of June 1989, trade unions were dissolved and their leaders imprisoned. Some have since been released but there are now reports of further detentions. The Chinese Government has also acted against trade unionists: many were killed, and others arrested in 1989, and many legislative provisions in China contradict the right of workers to set up organisations of their own choosing. Palestinian workers in the Occupied Territories have also been subject to severe government action – 1990 has seen a continuation of the summary arrests and detentions of trade unionists and their leaders.

Though it is more common for trade union organisations to be harassed, employers' organisations too can find themselves under threat. One long-running case started in Panama in 1987 when officials of employers' organisations were arrested for taking part in a pro-democracy demonstration and their premises were occupied. The case was only resolved in 1989 with the installation of a new government which released those arrested and returned their premises.

Though trade unionists in most countries may be free to organise, restrictions are often placed on particular groups of workers – typically those in the public sector. In Paraguay, for example, public sector workers cannot organise in trade unions or negotiate their conditions of employment collectively. And Thailand became the latest country to apply such restrictions when in 1991, following a military coup, the Government dissolved the state enterprise unions.

Governments may also legislate to restrict the ways in which trade unions can operate. This has happened in recent years in the United Kingdom. Current legislation includes, for example, provisions which make it unlawful for unions to indemnify union officials or members for any legal liabilities they incur on behalf of the union. These and other provisions have, in the judgement of the ILO's Committee on Freedom of Association, contravened Convention No. 87 on freedom of association.

While trade unions may be free to operate in most sectors of a national economy, some governments make an exception of export processing zones. Bangladesh, for example, exempts such zones from its Labour Code. The Government in Pakistan applies similar restrictions – though it is planning to lift some of these.

In the United States trade unions face a rather different problem. Some workers on strike have seen their jobs taken permanently by replacement labour: a practice which undermines their ability to strike – one of the essential means through which workers can defend their economic and social interests. The legislative authorities in the United States are currently examining a Bill aimed at abolishing this practice.

The elimination of child labour

Hundreds of millions of child labourers around the world work to support themselves and their families, often sacrificing their education, their health – and their childhood.

Asia has some of the highest numbers – up to 11 per cent of the labour force in certain places. Africa also has large concentrations: some countries have 20 per cent of their children working. And in Latin America, Brazil has seven million working children.

Child labour is not confined to developing countries, however. Millions of European children work in agriculture and in factories. And hundreds of thousands more work in the United States – the majority amongst immigrant communities working on farms.

Children work primarily because their families are poor. When survival is at stake everyone has to lend a hand, whether helping on the family farm, or working on a plantation, or selling chewing gum in the streets, or weaving carpets in sweatshop factories. They might not be well paid – child coffee pickers may only earn US$3 for a ten-hour day six days a week – but they can still provide a substantial proportion of family income.

The second major cause of child labour is that the clearest alternative – school – is either unavailable, inadequate, or just too expensive. Almost all children that are not in school can be presumed to be working in one way or another.

Among the most exploited children are those enslaved in bonded labour – of whom there are several million in South Asia. Child prostitutes, too, must be among the worst treated – prostitution is the fate of children all over the world, girls and boys, from a very young age.

Policies on child labour need to have two aspects. The first is to protect those children who are working – offering them health services, perhaps, or feeding programmes, or non-formal education. But the long-term aim must be to eliminate child labour. There are many steps which can be taken, including: improving and enforcing legislation; promoting school enrolment; raising public awareness of the dangers of child labour; and supporting the actions of communities and organisations who are helping child workers. But one immediate priority should be to remove children from the most hazardous workplaces: from the glass factories, from the coal mines, from the construction sites, from the garbage dumps and from the brothels – places for which they have neither the physical development nor the experience to cope.

Equal opportunities for women

More women are working outside the home than ever before. Many because they want to, others because they have to.

Sweden now has the highest gross participation rate of the industrial market economies (50 per cent of females are employed, or looking for work, compared with 56 per cent of males). And while most women are still concentrated in specific industries, such as clothing and footwear, things are slowly changing. In the United States, for example, women are now somewhat better represented among professional occupations such as architects and dentists. Legislative changes have played a part here, notably the ending in many countries of the exclusion of women from the police and armed forces.

In Eastern Europe and the former Soviet Union a high proportion of women work, supported by extensive public child-care facilities. But women still do not have the status they merit: in the former Soviet Union, for example, they hold only 5.6 per cent of high-level management posts.

In developing countries women officially make up a smaller proportion of the labour force (31 per cent) than they do in the industrial countries (40 per cent). But such statistics tend to overlook their work in agriculture and their participation in the informal sector which has increased sharply during recent periods of economic crisis.

Working women everywhere suffer discrimination: typically in pay (women still earn generally between 50 and 80 per cent of men's wages), and in promotion (many women are effectively put in a "mommy track" that assumes they will always make a limited contribution).

Sexual harassment at work is a further form of discrimination; 30 per cent of women surveyed in Belgium, for example, have experienced embarrassment and unease from uninvited sexual attention.

Tackling sex discrimination is a long and difficult task. Women have taken some of the most important steps, demanding their rights and achieving higher levels of education and training – despite the odds stacked against them. But legislation, on pay for example, has also played an important part. And affirmative action programmes have often succeeded where a more passive approach has failed to counter inertia or prejudice.

2. Employment

A recession which seems likely to continue in many of the industrial market economies. A radical shake-out of the underemployed in the Eastern Europe and the former Soviet Union. Continuing economic crisis in Africa. The employment picture in 1992 is hardly encouraging. But there are a few bright spots. In Latin America several countries which have been restructuring their economies may now have turned the corner. And in Asia the newly industrialising countries in particular continue to prosper.

Unemployment is rising in many of the industrialised market economies, and for the OECD countries the overall rate for 1992 is expected to be 7.1 per cent. Industry and construction are bearing the brunt of the job losses.

A notable change over the last ten years or so is that many countries now find it difficult to bring unemployment below 6 per cent. But there have also been important *qualitative* changes in employment. The closing of old industrial plants, shifts to the service sector, and the introduction of flexible production systems – all have helped fragment working life. And, as a result, jobs nowadays are less likely to be filled by permanent full-time employees; half or more of all new employment in France, Germany, the Netherlands, Luxembourg and Spain in the 1980s, for example, was for workers on part-time contracts.

Unemployment and the shift to part-time work have also increased poverty and inequality. The poor have now risen to 12 per cent of the population in Europe and to 13 per cent in the United States.

In Eastern Europe and the former Soviet Union unemployment is still remarkably low. Despite falls in production of around 20 per cent in 1990, unemployment (except in Poland) is still lower than in Western Europe. But the future is likely to be traumatic. Privatisation is not fully underway: the state sector still accounts for 85 per cent of employment in Czechoslovakia, for example. And since between 5 and 25 per cent of workers in many state enterprises may be underemployed they are in grave danger of losing their jobs. Unemployment in the long term could reach 15 to 20 per cent.

Africa's economic crisis continues. Real wages in sub-Saharan Africa fell, on average, by 30 per cent between 1980 and 1986. Urban unemployment is currently around 18 per cent and, given the prospects for slow growth in economies and fast growth in populations, this could rise to 31 per cent by the end of the decade.

Most new jobs will come from the informal sector, which currently employs an estimated 61 per cent of the urban labour force. And many of the new workers will be women, forced to move into the informal sector because their male partners have either lost their formal sector jobs or had their wages cut.

Rural Africa, where the majority of people live and work, has not been hit quite so badly. Agricultural producer prices have risen faster than wages and prices in general so some farmers may be better off, though those who rely on primary commodities have seen their incomes fall – producer prices fell by 54 per cent in Côte d'Ivoire in 1989, for example.

Asia outperformed every other region of the world in 1990, with the developing countries of the region achieving an average growth rate of 5.4 per cent. The star performers were the four newly industrialised economies (NIEs), Hong Kong, the Republic of Korea, Singapore and Taiwan (China), which in the 1980s accounted for half the manufactured exports of the developing countries.

Asia had to face the same hostile economic climate in the 1980s as any other region. But the more successful countries managed to find their own forms of structural adjustment, not just at the macro-economic level, but also through individual enterprises. Employers tended both to increase their level of technology and to require their labour force to be much more flexible – using more casual, contracted, or temporary employees, for example, and moving more towards pay systems based on the success of the enterprise.

Rural Asia did not share in much of this wealth, but poverty rates have been reduced in many countries including Bangladesh, China and India.

Latin America has just passed through what many people call the "lost decade" with GDP per capita 9.6 per cent lower in 1990 than in 1980. As elsewhere there has been a significant move to the informal sector which accounted for 25 per cent of non-agricultural workers in 1980 but now accounts for 31 per cent.

But there is some cause for optimism. Many countries managed to turn their economies round in the second half of the decade and now seem to be on more of an upward curve. Thus for Colombia, Chile, Uruguay and Venezuela the urban unemployment rate fell, after 1985, by between 3 and 10 percentage points.

Migrant workers

Two of the most significant trails for migrant workers in the 1990s will be in Europe and in Asia: from Eastern to Western Europe; and from the poorer to the richer countries of the Pacific Rim.

The upheavals in Eastern Europe have raised the prospect of a mass migration west in search of work. Many people already migrate seasonally (about 600,000 Poles work illegally in Germany during the peak agricultural season). But between 2 and 20 million people could now decide to move permanently. Such migration could bring benefits both to sending and receiving countries. But if the process is to be orderly and productive, a series of bilateral agreements will be needed.

In Asia many people have already moved from poorer countries like India or the Philippines to the richer economies like Japan or Singapore. Taking both legal and illegal migrants into account, some 300,000 workers move each year.

The more developed countries are, however, unwilling to accept large numbers of unskilled migrants. Japan fears the social and economic disruption they might cause, and the four NIEs are anxious to move up the technological ladder and argue that a ready pool of unskilled labour will delay the process.

But all face acute shortages of labour. Declining birth rates (there are now fewer babies in Japan than at any time since records began) and an unwillingness on the part of educated young people to take on "dirty, dangerous, or difficult" work mean that construction, manufacturing and services are having problems finding staff. Hence the large number of illegal workers: official estimates in Japan suggest 100,000, but there could be twice as many.

The receiving countries have redoubled their efforts to prevent illegal arrivals, with penalties which include deportation, fines and imprisonment in Japan and Taiwan (China) and caning in Singapore – for both workers and employers.

3. Labour relations

Labour relations, too, have been affected by the drive to multi-party democracy – whether being restored to a healthier state, as in Latin America, or introduced formally for the first time, as in many parts of Eastern Europe and the former Soviet Union.

Starting with the industrial market economies, however, the story is less of political change than of a swing in the balance of power *within* democracies – with employers seizing the initiative. Management has become more assertive. Technical innovation and high unemployment have helped them transform both their production methods and their relationship with the workforce. And trade unions have been put more on the defensive.

Trade union membership has fluctuated considerably in recent decades. After the rises of the 1960s and 1970s, unions in the OECD countries lost 5 million members in the 1980s, as the overall density rate dropped from 37 per cent in 1975 to 28 per cent in

1988. There have been signs in very recent years, however, that the figures have stabilised.

Still, unions do often have an impact beyond their own membership. Those in Spain, for example, may have recruited only 16 per cent of unionisable workers but the collective agreements they conclude are extended to cover 82 per cent of the workforce.

Bargaining methods remain quite diverse. Collective bargaining may be central (with national unions), or sectoral (across a particular industry). But increasingly the trend is to decentralise to individual enterprises.

And the agreements they reach are also changing somewhat. Unions, for their part, are more interested in qualitative improvements (such as job security and satisfaction) than they used to be, and employers have been looking for more flexibility from the workforce, hoping to agree on more flexible hours or to link pay to the success of the enterprise.

Governments have been taking a smaller part in collective bargaining since the mid-1980s. In some countries they do keep a close eye on the outcome but on the whole governments have allowed full freedom of negotiation to be established – partly because intervention in the past may have caused more problems than it has solved.

In Eastern Europe and the former Soviet Union, however, the trade unions have been the main actors – working with new governments to develop new forms of political and economic democracy and facing up to the idea that there *is* such a thing as "labour relations". Employers here have yet to emerge as a significant autonomous group.

Many new trade unions appeared all over the region from 1989 onwards, both to represent workers and to exert political pressure. Solidarity in Poland has now been joined by organisations like Podkrepa in Bulgaria, Fratia in Romania, and the new "workers' movement" in the former USSR.

The old "official unions" are still in place, though almost all have changed their names and declared their independence from the State. Of these, KOS in Czechoslovakia has been the most effective at transforming itself; elsewhere the official unions have lost many members.

Collective bargaining in the region is undergoing a profound transformation with new legislation which should gradually permit genuinely free bargaining – such as the Soviet Law on Enterprises (1990) and the Czech and Slovak Labour Code. And national tripartite bodies have been established. However, the position is still very fluid and few countries can really claim to have set the pattern for future labour relations systems.

In most developing countries governments tend to dominate labour relations. The trend here, though, may be for government control to slacken. In Africa, for example, governments are increasingly inviting unions and employers to participate more, or to resolve issues themselves. So tripartite labour advisory boards are being established (or inactive ones revived) to consider issues like minimum wages and health and safety. And ministries of labour which have become overburdened with disputes and workers' complaints are now looking for other ways to solve problems.

In Asia labour relations in the developing countries of the region depend first of all on levels of development. Union influence is growing in some of the poorer countries but declining in the more developed ones.

In the Philippines for example, union membership increased by 38 per cent between 1987 and 1989. And there were also significant rises in Bangladesh (27 per cent), Thailand (13 per cent) and Indonesia (16 per cent).

In the more developed countries, such as Singapore, the situation can be rather different. Trade union density may be high but unions are becoming less influential. Workers are better educated and their demands are becoming more sophisticated; they look for better conditions and shorter working hours and may consider trade unions a less important way of achieving such goals.

In the Republic of Korea, however, the unions have made significant progress since the process of democratisation started in 1987. The number of union members increased from 1 million in 1987 to 1.9 million in 1990.

One of the most significant trends in the developing countries of the region is the move towards the kind of flexible pay systems that operate in Japan. At present workers often get annual increments – 5 per cent in Malaysia, for example. But employers are finding this too rigid and expensive a system and are looking to models such as those of Singapore, where up to 20 per cent of the wage may be variable.

In Latin America governments, democratic or dictatorial, have always tried to keep firm control over labour issues. Not content with setting the general legal framework, they also try to determine how trade unions should work, what salary levels should be, and how disputes should be resolved.

Union membership is relatively low. Around 50 per cent of the labour force in Latin America is in the formal sector and around 30 per cent of this is unionised, though density rates do vary considerably from one country to another – highest in Argentina, Cuba, Nicaragua, Uruguay and Venezuela and lowest in Costa Rica, the Dominican Republic, Ecuador, El Salvador, Guatemala, Haiti, Honduras and Paraguay.

Employers' organisations in Latin America have increasingly been coming together in central federations – though these do not yet exist in Argentina, Brazil, Colombia, Ecuador and Uruguay. Such federations do not always, however, represent all sections of the economy. Most include neither public enterprises (which are often the largest employers in the formal sector) nor, at the other end of the scale, do they generally include the smallest companies. And they do not usually represent the interests of multinationals.

Most collective bargaining in Latin America is heavily controlled by the State, particularly at times of economic crisis. And this can determine anything from the form of negotiations right up to the final outcome. But another important development in recent years has been *concertación social* – the attempt to reach more general agreement on a package of social and economic issues. One of the most successful examples of this has been Mexico's Economic Solidarity Pact of 1987 which seems to have achieved many of its objectives, including reducing inflation and public expenditure and controlling salaries and prices. And there have been similar pacts signed in Venezuela (1989) and Chile (1990).

4. Social protection and working conditions

The Report this year focuses on three topical issues: social protection in Eastern Europe and the former Soviet Union; flexible working time; and preventing industrial disasters.

Social protection in Eastern Europe and the former Soviet Union

These countries need major changes in their systems of social protection – to cope with the pros-pect (and eventually the reality) of mass unemployment. How well they deal with the poverty and social disruption ahead may well determine how successfully they can move to a market economy.

Most have already made a start, setting minimum income levels to act as "safety nets" and establishing the basis of unemployment benefit. The payments may have to be quite low, given the budgetary restraints, but if they are set too low this could weaken the support for the reforms.

Pensions, too, will need to be reassessed. The entitlements of both today's pensioners and the older workers are now inadequate after many subsidies have been removed and inflation has reduced the value of fixed incomes. Some governments have made ad hoc adjustments, but pensions in future will probably have to be indexed.

In the long term most governments will want to move to a contributory self-financing pension scheme. But this will not solve the immediate problem, so younger workers will find themselves contributing both to their own future pensions and the current pensions of their parents and grandparents. Younger workers will have to demonstrate a high level of inter-generational solidarity if older people are not to face real hardship.

Flexible working time

One of the most significant changes in working life in industrialised countries is the introduction of flexible working time. Whether in the form of work-sharing, flexi-time, or hours averaging, or just compressing the working week, these new flexible approaches to working time are reshaping working life for millions of people.

Employers in the past have been unwilling to concede union demands for a shorter working week. But now that they can couple such changes with new flexible working patterns, they are taking most of the initiatives. "De-linking" working hours from plant operating hours allows them to make better use of capital equipment; to make output more flexible; to deal with complex staffing problems; to give greater customer satisfaction; and to increase productivity.

Trade unions tend to be suspicious of such schemes. They can see some advantages for workers in terms of flexibility, but they also point to the severe strain that flexible working time can place on both family and social life.

Preventing industrial disasters

Industrial installations are a potential source of hazard. Bhopal has become a symbol of what can go wrong. But while this may have been the worst non-nuclear major accident, there have been many other incidents. In 1989, for example, a chemical plant making polyethylene in Houston, Texas, exploded, killing 23 workers and injuring more than 130 others. And in Thailand, in 1990, an accident with a truck carrying liquid petroleum gas killed 91 people and injured more than 100.

Most countries have health and safety laws to protect workers and the environment under normal conditions. Now, however, the problems can be of a scale and type which few regulatory authorities could ever have envisaged.

New approaches to control are needed. The European Community (EC), for example, has adopted the Seveso Directive – in response to an accident in Italy which released clouds of highly toxic dioxin into the atmosphere. The Directive classifies installations according to degrees of risk and indicates what kind of notification manufacturers must give to the authorities. And all the countries of the EC have been incorporating the principles of the Directive in their own legislation and steadily updating their classifications. Germany has now classified 3,000 sites. Other industrialised countries have taken similar steps.

Developing countries have a more difficult task. They can have sophisticated and potentially dangerous technology on their territory, but may have neither the technical nor administrative capacity to supervise it. Even here though, some countries such as India, Mexico and Thailand have started to identify the most serious hazards and decide how to react to them.

In 1992 the International Labour Conference will consider new international instruments that can help countries minimise the risks from hazardous installations.

Chapter 1

Human rights at work

This issue of the *World Labour Report* highlights some of the clearest abuses of human rights at work, as well as the measures which can be taken to defend the rights both of individuals and of organisations (box 1.1). The three major human rights areas on which the 1992 Report focuses are:

1. *Freedom of association* – the rights of working people to organise themselves to promote their interests.
2. *The elimination of child labour* – the rights of young people to education and a childhood free from excessive work and exploitation.
3. *Equal opportunities for women* – the rights of women to equal pay for work of equal value, as well as freedom from all forms of sex discrimination.

Freedom of association

Many people find that the best way to defend their interests is to work together as a group. Trade unions or employers' organisations, cooperatives or community groups, all have worked to establish the right to operate and negotiate on their members' behalf.

But this can be a dangerous business. And trade unionists are a particular target. Complaints received by the ILO's Committee on Freedom of Association allege that hundreds of trade unionists throughout the world were murdered in 1990 and 1991, that several thousand were detained, and tens of thousands more sacked for their union work.

National political systems largely determine the ways in which rights can be exercised and the extent to which they will be respected. Truly democratic societies offer the most promising environment for freedom of association, and in 1992 the world is going through one of the most optimistic periods for many years. Political democracy is making steady progress throughout the world and having a profound effect on many aspects of working life. The disappearance of military rule in Latin America, the decline of the one-party State in Africa, and above all the retreat of the Communist Party in Eastern Europe and the former Soviet Union have transformed many aspects of the employment scene.

These political changes have all improved the opportunities for freedom of association. Many workers are now able to organise in ways which previously were dangerous or even impossible. Trade unions which had been a focus of opposition to authoritarian regimes – and often driven underground – now find themselves trusted partners with government. Indeed trade unionists, for their part, have helped trigger many of these political changes. From Uruguay to Zambia to Poland, strikes have been some of the most important steps towards multi-party democracy.

In Latin America, for example, many trade unions that were previously the object of government hostility are now negotiating freely with both governments and employers. And the changes in Eastern Europe and the former Soviet Union have also been substantial. Governments previously insisted that trade unions operate under direct government and party control. Legislation also forbade the formation of independent unions, and punished the normal exercise of rights of association with prison terms and compulsory labour. But most countries have now repealed the most restrictive legislation and abolished the leading role of the Communist Party in the mass organisations. Multiple trade unions are now allowed and several independent central trade union organisations have emerged. Many more workers now have the right to strike to defend their interests. The implications of this new environment for the conduct of labour relations will be covered in greater detail in Chapter 3.

1.1   Human rights – an international ideology

Human rights express a form of "natural law" higher than that of individual States. The need for such an international ideology has been felt since the nation State became the normal form of government. The phrase "human rights" may not have been specifically used but it was human rights concerns which led to the abolition of the slave trade, for example; which led to the foundation of the Red Cross. And it was a human rights philosophy which produced the League of Nations after World War I.

The International Labour Organisation was established in 1919 to defend the human rights of workers – to protect them and to try to improve their living conditions. The main tools it uses are a series of international Conventions. By 1945, when the United Nations was created, the ILO had adopted nearly 70 Conventions. The United Nations then began its work of codifying human rights principles, taking many of the ILO instruments as a source of inspiration. The Universal Declaration of Human Rights was adopted in 1948 and begins with the assertion that "All human beings are born free and equal in dignity and rights". Article 23 of the Declaration deals particularly with employment. Its basic principles closely resemble those of the ILO Constitution and several of its fundamental instruments.

The Universal Declaration of Human Rights is, however, only a statement of principle. To translate these ideas into a more binding form of international human rights law, two "covenants" were drafted in 1966. By ratifying these covenants, governments take on a legally binding obligation. The first is the International Covenant on Civil and Political Rights, which covers rights such as that to self-determination, and to freedom from torture and arbitrary arrest.

Governments ratifying this covenant (and 93 have done so) must immediately abide by it. The second is the International Covenant on Economic Social and Cultural Rights. Since this includes a duty for governments to feed, clothe and house their citizens (which may be beyond the means of poor countries), its requirements are only to be implemented "to the maximum of available resources". To date, 96 countries have ratified the second covenant.

Many of the labour rights established in principle in the United Nations Declaration and in the covenants had previously been codified into ILO Conventions which deal with the practical aspects of recognising and implementing such rights. Some of the most widely ratified of the ILO's 172 Conventions are those dealing with forced labour (Nos. 29 and 105), freedom of association (Nos. 87 and 98) and discrimination (No. 111). Other important issues such as protection for children, for women and for indigenous and tribal peoples are also covered both by the United Nations Declaration and covenants, and by specific ILO Conventions.

The ILO Conventions are one of the most effectively monitored sets of international standards. States which ratify a Convention have to report regularly on its implementation. These reports are scrutinised by a Committee of Experts composed of eminent jurists. The Committee can draw attention to any shortcomings, and also receive comments on a government's performance from workers' and employers' organisations.

Spain is currently the country which has ratified the greatest number of Conventions (123), followed by France (114). Further details on the number of ratifications are given in the Statistical Annex.

This section will concentrate on the rights and risks of association as currently experienced by workers' and employers' groups in different parts of the world.

Abuses of civil liberties

In human rights terms there are limits to what even democratic governments can achieve. People and organisations may still find themselves under attack from hostile groups operating outside the rule of law. Colombia has some of the worst problems – many of them arising from the influence of drug cartels. Over 300 trade union officials or members have been killed since 1986 and there have been ten attacks with dynamite on trade union · premises. Trade unionists are certainly not the only target, but their persistent championing of the rights of working people keeps them clearly in the firing line. The Government of Colombia is taking all the measures it can in very difficult circumstances. The director of the leading state security organisation, the DAS, has reiterated its determination to "dismantle the gangs of organised criminals who have murdered many people belonging to the Colombian trade union movement".

Brazil is another country where trade unionists have been murdered – particularly in the rural areas. In examining these cases, the ILO's Committee on Freedom of Association pointed out that: "a climate of violence and intimidation constitutes a serious obstacle to the exercise of trade union rights".

In Central America, a similar climate has been reported to prevail in El Salvador and Guatemala. In El Salvador the premises of the trade union federation FENASTRAS have been dynamited twice in recent years killing nine people and injuring seven others. And many other trade unionists have been murdered or have disappeared. Of the trade unionists who have been arrested and imprisoned, the Government responds that these have been for crimes or misdemeanours and do not constitute a concerted campaign against freedom of association.

In the Philippines, despite the democratic opening, it can still be dangerous for trade unionists to organise. And there have been many cases of human rights abuses. Most of these cases are connected with armed vigilance groups which operate with relative impunity. The Philippines Government points out that the increasing level of violence and criminality in the countryside stems from armed insurgents from both Right and Left.

Arrests of trade unionists and employers

But the rights of workers' and employers' organisations can also be directly threatened by government action. In the most severe cases governments have dissolved organisations using military force and have imprisoned officials.

Sudan has offered some of the most serious recent challenges to freedom of association. After the coup d'état of June 1989 the country's Constitution was suspended. Political parties and trade unions were dissolved, trade union leaders were imprisoned, strikes were to be punishable by imprisonment and in certain cases would warrant a death sentence. Ten doctors were arrested in November 1990 for participating in a protest strike; one was sentenced to death, though this was later commuted. The detained unionists have, according the Government, since been released, but allegations of further detentions have now been made. The decrees dissolving all trade unions remain in force.

The Chinese Government has also acted to restrict union organisation. In May 1989 an independent trade union movement, the Workers' Autonomous Federation, was created in several parts of China. Many of its members have been arrested and others were killed in June 1989. The Government argues that this was an illegal organisation. The ILO's Committee on Freedom of Association has concluded, however, that the constitutional and legislative provisions are in clear contradiction of the right of workers to set up organisations of their own choosing.

The Israeli authorities have also taken strong measures against Palestinian trade unionists in the Occupied Territories; 1990 has seen a continuation of the summary arrests and detentions of trade unionists and their leaders, as well as searches of trade union premises, confiscation of property and general harassment.

It is more common for trade unions to find themselves under threat, but employers' organisations, too, can have problems. One long-running case started in Panama in 1987 when the Government arrested officials of employers' organisations who had taken part in a pro-democracy demonstration. At the same time, officials of the Public Ministry took over the premises of the Chamber of Commerce and of the Trade Union of Industrialists of Panama. The prosecutions and the occupation continued over several years. In a protest against this continuing abuse of the rights of employers, some enterprises closed temporarily in May 1989 and a number (including McDonalds and Dairy Queen) had notices of sanctions served against them – under a decree promulgated earlier that year which required businesses to remain open during working hours unless otherwise authorised by law.

The issue was finally resolved when a new Government was installed at the end of 1989. The new administration freed the employers' leaders, restored their premises, and also revoked the sanctions against the enterprises concerned. It is also considering repealing the decree under which they were prosecuted.

Single union federations

Reports received by the ILO on more common restrictions on freedom of association in a number of countries show that the law allows only a single trade union federation – as in Egypt, Iraq, Mauritania and the Syrian Arab Republic. In Ethiopia, for example, the current law imposes a single trade union federation for workers and peasants. And the Government has in the past obliged trade unions and peasant organisations to disseminate its development plans as well as its ideology. Much of this policy has now changed, however. The new Government in Ethiopia bases its economic policy on a mixture of private, cooperative and state enterprise. The Government is working on a new Labour Code, though it has yet to finalise this.

Public sector workers

A further way in which governments can restrict freedom of association is by denying the right to organise to certain groups of workers. This typically affects civil servants and other public sector workers – in contravention of ILO Conventions which affirm that all workers, without distinction, should have the right to establish and join organisations of their own choosing. The Conventions do allow for some exceptions: they permit the exclusion of the police and armed forces, as well as restrictions on the right to strike for workers in certain carefully defined essential services. But many countries extend such restrictions to other public sector workers. In Paraguay, for example, public employees cannot organise in trade unions or negotiate their conditions of employment collectively. And strikes are forbidden in such areas as transport, basic commodities, and banking – many of which cannot be said to affect the personal health and safety of the population.

Thailand has been the most recent country to apply such restrictions. In April 1991, following a military coup, the state enterprise unions were disbanded, affecting some 200,000 workers. Unions were to be replaced by "associations" through which workers could press for improvements in wages and working conditions.

Elsewhere there have been some improvements for public sector workers. In Peru in 1984, for example, career members of the public service were granted freedom of association and the right to strike and the same rights were extended in 1987 to state employees in Guatemala.

Legislative restrictions on union freedom

Legislation may also be used to narrow trade union freedom of action in other ways – setting out the conditions under which strikes can be held, for example, or prescribing how the organisations are to be run. In the United Kingdom employment legislation has been modified by several Acts between 1980 and 1990. The legislation includes provisions which make it unlawful for unions to indemnify officials or members for any legal liabilities they may have incurred on behalf of the union. The legislation also has the effect of taking from trade unionists protection against common law liability for certain forms of industrial action. The ILO's Committee of Experts has concluded that some of these changes have contravened the Freedom of Association and Protection of the Right to Organise Convention, 1948 (No. 87).

At the same time, however, there has been progress in various countries in achieving rights to freedom of association. Governments have lifted some of the legal restrictions on trade union activity. This is the case in Algeria, Belarus, Bulgaria, Colombia, Finland, Hungary, Iceland, Madagascar, Mali, Peru, Ro-

mania, Ukraine, the former USSR and Venezuela. A recent case is that of Pakistan where a government requirement that it have the final selection of union delegates for international conferences was lifted in March 1991. And in Nigeria a decree denying trade union organisations the right to join international federations was lifted at the end of 1991.

Export processing zones

Even if unions are free to operate in most sectors of the economy some governments in developing countries make an exception of export processing zones (EPZs). Bangladesh, for example, exempts EPZs from its Labour Code and does not permit trade unions to operate in them. The Government points out that wages in such zones are above the national average and does not consider it expedient to allow the formation of trade unions for the time being. ILO Conventions, however, apply equally throughout the country, including export processing zones. Similar restrictions apply in a number of other countries. Pakistan, for example, has also exempted EPZs from the scope of its Industrial Relations Ordinance and denies workers there the right to strike – though the Government has indicated that it is now committed to allowing trade unions to organise.

Alternatives to trade unions

New types of organisations emerged with the formation of *solidarist* associations in Central America, particularly in Costa Rica. Solidarist associations are financed by both workers and employers according to the principles of mutual benefit societies. They aim to provide such things as savings, credit, housing and educational programmes and operate in a spirit of unity and cooperation between employers and workers.

Trade unionists in Costa Rica have complained to the ILO that workers are often obliged to join solidarist associations if they wish to keep their jobs and that the Act which governs such associations violates trade union rights. Such groups have certainly become much more significant: between 1986 and 1990 their membership grew from 32,000 to 113,000. Trade union membership increased during the same period from 139,000 to 154,000. Wage and other agreements made by solidarist groups tend to be by "direct settlement" rather than free collective bargaining. In Costa Rica, from the beginning of

1990 to February 1991, there were 32 collective agreements but 40 direct settlements.

The ILO's Governing Body requested in 1990 that a Direct Contacts Mission be sent to Costa Rica. Based on the report of this mission (in April 1991) the ILO's Committee on Freedom of Association has concluded that such associations do raise problems for freedom of association. Since solidarist associations are often started up by employers, are partly financed by them, and comprise not just workers but also senior staff and personnel who have the employers' confidence, they cannot be considered as independent organisations for collective bargaining purposes. The Committee also stressed that direct settlements between non-unionised workers and employers (even when a union existed in the undertaking) did not promote collective bargaining.

In addition, the Committee concluded that legislation in Costa Rica grants solidarist associations major advantages over trade unions – including such areas as the minimum number of workers required for their formation, and access to compensation in cases of justified dismissal. The legislation also provides inadequate protection against acts of anti-union discrimination.

The Government, for its part, received the Committee's conclusions in a positive spirit and has requested the technical assistance of the ILO. It has now decided to introduce legislation to ban interference by solidarist associations in collective bargaining and to introduce statutory protection against anti-union discrimination.

Replacement of workers during strikes

One thing which can discourage workers from striking is the threat that their jobs will be taken permanently by replacement labour. This is an issue in the United States, for example, where the use of permanent replacement labour during disputes has resulted in complaints to the Committee on Freedom of Association. In strikes involving unfair labour practices strikers do have a legal right to be reinstated after the dispute. But for economic strikes the United States courts have interpreted the labour legislation so as to allow employers to hire replacement labour for an indeterminate period both during and after the strike.

The Committee on Freedom of Association has concluded, however, that this practice entails a risk of derogation from the right to strike – one of the essential means through which workers can defend their economic and social interests. This basic right is not really guaranteed when workers who exercise it legally risk losing their jobs permanently to other workers. The United States legislative authorities are currently examining a Bill aimed at abolishing this practice.

The elimination of child labour

The exploitation of child labour is one of the most disturbing aspects of the international labour scene. No one knows for sure how many children are working. Statistics are difficult to come by; most of these children are unpaid family workers, or are in the informal sector, or are working illegally – invisible to the collectors of labour force statistics. But the total number is certainly in the hundreds of millions. And although the condition of child workers has worsened dramatically in recent years, and their number has certainly increased in many countries, few have yet developed comprehensive plans to deal with this serious and difficult problem.

Asia has some of the highest numbers of child labourers – accounting for up to 11 per cent of the total labour force in some Asian countries. India probably has the largest number – an estimated 44 million. And in Indonesia, for example, there are 2.7 million working children aged between ten and 14.

African countries are reported to have up to 20 per cent of their children working, making up to 17 per cent of the total workforce. In Nigeria, for example, an estimated 12 million children participate in various categories of work.

Latin America is the most urbanised region of the developing world, so children here are more likely to be working in cities. Up to 26 per cent of children in some countries may well be working. Brazil has the greatest number of working children – seven million, according to a government household survey which indicates that around 18 per cent of Brazilian children between ten and 14 are economically active. And a similar proportion of Mexican children between 12 and 14 years old are also working.

Child labour may be concentrated in developing countries, but it is certainly not confined to them. Italy has some of the highest numbers in Western Europe. There have been reports of tens of thousands in the Naples region alone, with the leather industry a particular cause for concern. Spain, too, has signifi-

---

1.2   **From work to exploitation: Some characteristics of child labour**

- *Working too young* – children in developing countries often start factory work at the age of six or seven.
- *Working long hours* – in some case 12 to 16 hours a day.
- *Working under strain* – physical, social or psychological, in mines, for example, or sweatshops.
- *Working on the streets* – in unhealthy and dangerous conditions.
- *For very little pay* – as little as $3 for a 60-hour week.

- *With little stimulation* – dull repetitive tasks, which stunt the child's social and psychological development.
- *Taking too much responsibility* – children often have charge of siblings only a year or two younger than themselves.
- *Subject to intimidation* – which inhibits self-confidence and self-esteem, as with slave labour and sexual exploitation.

---

cant numbers – some sources suggest more than 100,000 – with most of the children working in agriculture, generally on family farms. In the United Kingdom a survey in 1985 discovered 40 per cent of the children questioned were working, the majority doing so illegally, either in terms of the hours they worked or the jobs they were doing.

In the United States the majority of child workers are employed in agriculture and a high proportion of these are from immigrant families. The United Farmworkers Union reported in 1985 that hundreds of thousands of children work on farms and plantations throughout the country. And many children are also employed in everything from fast-food stores to garment factories. A 1990 study by the General Accounting Office showed a 250 per cent increase in child labour law violations from 1983 to 1990. And a "sting" operation carried out by the United States Department of Labor during three days in 1990 found more than 11,000 children working illegally.

Child work and child labour

Most children work. After the age of six or seven they may help around the home, running errands, or spending time helping their parents on the family farm. This can make a healthy contribution to their development; in rural areas in particular such work can prepare children for the tasks of adulthood and help pass traditionally acquired skills from one generation to the next. Children learn to take responsibility and pride in their own activities. Even in the wealthiest countries, children are encouraged to work for a few hours a week.

"Child labour" implies something different – that young people are being exploited, or overworked, or deprived of their rights to health or education or just to childhood. Some of the characteristics which might indicate exploitation are indicated in box 1.2.

More children are at risk of such exploitation nowadays because more families (particularly those in cities) are now working for wages – so their children too are more likely to be working outside the home, away from parental protection.

Why children work

Most children work because their families are poor. And if family survival is at stake everyone has to lend a hand. In the developing countries rural working children will often help parents maximise the meagre output from their family farms. But they can also work alongside their parents in commercial agriculture. In Zimbabwe, for example, workers on tobacco and cotton plantations are paid according to each task they complete – and children from the age of seven can be drawn in to help parents complete the task more quickly.

In urban areas children are more likely to work for wages outside the home – generally having been sent there by their parents. A study for the ILO of child workers in leather tanneries in Cairo asked parents why the children were at work rather than school (the average age of the children was 12 years). Over 90 per cent of the parents replied that the family needed the children's income.

Interestingly though, when the children were questioned, only 50 per cent of them gave "the family needs the money" as the first reason. The children tended to play down the fact that they had been obliged to work. Under these circumstances, if a child has to work she or he often thinks it is their choice.

Those children with the least choice about working are those trapped in debt bondage. This is the most shocking way in which poverty can drive children into hard labour. According to a report noted by the ILO's Committee of Experts, there are several million child bonded labourers in South Asia. Such servitude can arise in a number of ways. Often it is the result of the parents being given a loan to meet some urgent need. The debtor has then to repay this by working. In practice the debt does not decrease; it climbs ever upwards – a combination of usurious interest rates and outright fraud. The whole family becomes permanently enslaved and the moneylender even claims repayment from succeeding generations.

Children can also be enslaved on their own. Parents may send them to work in the house of a landlord or moneylender. These children may stay for many years, not knowing how long they must work, or even the size of the debt they are paying off.

Such practices may be illegal but they remain widespread in certain countries – sustained by ignorance, fear and intimidation. An estimated one million children in India work in bonded labour in brick kilns, stone quarrying and construction and thousands more in carpet-weaving. Similar practices are found in Pakistan – though thousands of people here have recently been released from bonded labour in the brick kiln industry by a court order, and the Government has pledged to release them all.

Work and school

Poverty may be the most significant cause of child labour, but it is not the only one. Many children work because there is little else to do: schools are unavailable, inadequate or too expensive. Indeed, one way to estimate the number of working children is to start from school enrolment ratios. Most poor children in developing countries, when not at school, can be presumed to be working. And with primary school enrolment rates as low as 27 per cent in Burkina Faso and Niger, for example, the chances are that many children are spending their days herding cattle or goats.

But even if all children out of school are counted as workers this would underestimate their numbers. Many working children, probably the majority of those in the cities, *also* go to school. In Asunción, the capital of Paraguay, for example, 77 per cent of working street children attend school. As one commentator put it: "One cannot help but admire the initiative demonstrated by working children who manage to keep up in their studies. Trying to keep up the demands of both work and study must place them under considerable stress. The wonder is not that some drop out, but that so many persist."

The relationship between school and work can be complex. Children may not necessarily be kept away from school by the need to work. In Lima, for example, only a quarter of working children not attending school said that their work prevented them. Another 23 per cent said they just didn't like school, 18 per cent said they lacked the necessary funds, and 12 per cent said they did not have the legal documents.

Then again, many children actually work *in order* to go to school. In Kenya, for example, the cost of uniforms, books, stationery and other items can be 2,000 Kenyan shillings (US$70) per year. And they may need to work in the streets to earn the necessary money. In Cochabamba, Bolivia, it is the children *not* working who have the lowest levels of educational achievement.

The work children do

Most child work is agricultural. Children in developing countries (and in some developed ones too) join in the activities of the family farm from a very early age. Starting with light tasks, such as looking after animals, collecting firewood and fodder and drawing water, they will later learn to sow and reap. In commercial agriculture, on plantations for example, they often work as part of the family team: weeding, spreading fertiliser, tending plants; though they often share in the heavier tasks.

Nowadays rural peasant families also provide labour for other activities. Many parents have to send their children to work in mines, or in small factories – making matches or carpets, perhaps. Others migrate as a family in search of work. In Peru, for example, families migrate seasonally from the highlands to the tropical lowlands for gold-panning. An ILO study in the Department of Madre de Dios has shown that 20 per cent of the workers in gold production are aged between 11 and 18. And in July 1991 local labour inspectors discovered 71 secret cemeteries containing the bodies of dozens of children.

Children who live in cities tend to be involved in a much broader range of activities – from factory work to domestic service, to small handicraft enterprises, to selling newspapers, to prostitution.

Employers often claim that there are types of work for which children are particularly suited. The carpet weaving industry in India employs around 300,000 people, of whom about one-third are children. Employers say that children have nimble fingers and

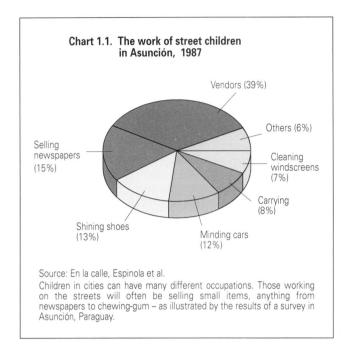

Chart 1.1. The work of street children in Asunción, 1987

Vendors (39%)

Others (6%)

Cleaning windscreens (7%)

Carrying (8%)

Minding cars (12%)

Shining shoes (13%)

Selling newspapers (15%)

Source: En la calle, Espinola et al.
Children in cities can have many different occupations. Those working on the streets will often be selling small items, anything from newspapers to chewing-gum – as illustrated by the results of a survey in Asunción, Paraguay.

keen eyesight, and will sit in the same posture for hours at a time. Small size is also an advantage for the 28,000 Indian children who work in the mines at Meghalaya. They have to crawl through tunnels 90 centimetres wide. Indeed, as they become older they no longer fit and lose their jobs. But most child work could also be done by adults. The real attraction of children is that they will work long hours for low pay and make very little trouble. Inexperienced and lacking adult confidence, they are easily intimidated by adults and, when working illegally, they are understandably unwilling to protest against their conditions.

Domestic work, particularly for young girls, is one of the largest (and least visible) users of child labour in urban areas. This will often be in the child's own home; a young girl takes on responsibilities and frees her mother for work elsewhere. But girls are also likely to work as domestic servants to richer families in the city. This is a feature of most developing countries. A study in urban areas of Colombia, for example, found that 40 per cent of 11 and 12 year-old child workers were domestic servants.

City children have a range of other options. Aside from domestic service, they may be employed in small factories, or work at home or on the streets. The streets of Mexico City, for example, are full of children selling lottery tickets, selling chewing gum,

washing windscreens, unloading trucks, shining shoes or a multitude of other tasks. The range of occupations of street child workers in Asunción, Paraguay, is shown in chart 1.1.

There may be a diverse choice of occupations in the city, but children do not, as is commonly supposed, flit frequently from one to another. In Lima only 14 per cent of girls, and 43 per cent of boys, had ever had a different occupation. Children often have much more invested in their work than meets the casual eye, either in terms of the skill they have acquired, or the network of contacts and agreements among those with whom they share the streets.

All child labourers, wherever they work, sell some of their childhood – but none sell as much as those driven to prostitution. Children in the largest cities are at greatest risk. And it is a problem for rich countries as well as poor. Studies in Europe and North America show how runaway children are the most likely to sell their bodies.

But developing countries have the greatest numbers of poor children and so have the most severe problems. A study of 4,000 child prostitutes in the city of Concepción in Chile in 1990, for example, suggested a correlation between the number of marginalised families and the incidence of child prostitution. The children involved were girls between 9 and 14 years old; they were ostensibly in the city centre selling sweets but took on adult poses and wore exaggerated make-up. The study reported, however, that the girls took to prostitution not just to earn money but also as a form of "aggression" against the society around them.

Children in most countries have always been used as prostitutes, but the situation in some Asian countries, like Thailand, has been aggravated by the expansion of mass tourism. Prostitution is illegal in Thailand, though there are very few prosecutions. A new Brothel Elimination Act came into force in October 1991.

Prostitution is a job for both boys and girls. Indeed in Sri Lanka, for example, the majority of child prostitutes are boys. Here there is a very protective attitude towards girls just before and after puberty, while boys have a greater freedom of movement, particularly at night.

What children earn

Most child workers "earn" nothing at all, since their work consists of helping their parents. Bonded labourers, too, see no financial reward for their efforts. Other child workers may only receive payment in kind. This is often the case for those who work in restaurants or in domestic service. But even those employed as wage labourers can receive pitifully small amounts for many hours of work. Children in electric light bulb factories in Indonesia, for example, work from 7 a.m. to 3 p.m. six days a week for US$3 per week. Child coffee pickers in Zimbabwe earn roughly the same for a ten-hour day six-day week. In Nepal children in carpet factories earn US$1 per day or less.

Children are employed in such tasks because they will work for less than adults. And some employers say they would have to close down if they could not employ children. Some 15 per cent of workers in the match and firewood industries in Siwakasi in India are under 15. To replace them with adult workers would cost around 32 million rupees (US$1.5 m) a year and the employers have threatened to resort to subcontracting the work should child labour be banned from their factories.

Though they may be paid relatively little, children can make a substantial contribution to family income. Working children in Brazil, for example, earn on average only one-third of the minimum salary. But 20 per cent of working children aged between 15 and 17 contribute around one-third of family income.

Children tend to be better paid on the streets. Child street hawkers in Nigeria, for example, often earn more than adults. In Recife, Brazil, the municipal Government found that children could make up to three times the minimum wage by begging or selling fruit at the busier intersections; many of these children would certainly be earning more than their parents. Prostitution can be one of the most highly-paid "jobs" for children. Though many sell themselves for pitifully small sums, others can earn relatively large amounts. In the Philippines, for example, they can earn US$15 a night though the median is around US$5.

The costs of child labour

Putting children to work may seem a rational approach to poverty with financial benefits for everyone concerned. But there are heavy costs too.

Some of these are clear enough. Children crushed by cars in busy streets, or infected with HIV through numerous sexual contacts, or victimised (or even killed) by police as an expendable inconvenience.

But there are also subtler and more insidious effects. Poor children are generally malnourished already, but their work then increases their energy requirements and their calorie deficit. And if they suffer from anaemia, fatigue and inadequate sleep they become much more susceptible to infectious diseases and tuberculosis. Reports on the carpet factories in Pakistan in 1991 estimated that half the 50,000 bonded children in the industry never reach the age of 12 – victims of malnutrition and disease. A WHO report on child workers cites other physical health hazards including bony lesions and postural deformity attributable to such work as carpet-weaving, embroidery and lifting heavy weights. Young, growing bodies suffer from strain when over-loaded, since the bone structure (especially the spine) is still soft. The eyesight of young girls working for 12-14 hours a day in microcomputer factories or embroidery is reported to be damaged within a period of five to eight years.

Children are also more susceptible to accidents. Long hours and fatigue can often prove fatal in sweatshops using poorly maintained and dangerous machinery.

There are social and psychological costs too. Working children can be separated from their families. Children whose social interactions are restricted because of their long working hours suffer in their social and emotional development. And street children faced day after day with adult hostility can have a serious problem in maintaining a healthy self-esteem.

Heavy though the price paid by individual children may be, one must also add the cost to society as a whole: a diminished contribution in the future from adults whose health, education and energy have been sacrificed during their childhood.

Agenda for action

Although almost everyone agrees that child labour is regrettable, not everyone agrees that something can, or should, be done about it. The doubters fall into two camps:

• *Radicals* argue that child labour is yet another symptom of economic and social injustice, and that no improvement can be expected in the absence of more radical social change.

1.3   **Basic minimum age for employment in various countries**

12 years: Bangladesh, Belize, Costa Rica, Ecuador, Egypt, Fiji, Haiti, Jamaica, Morocco, Nigeria, Qatar, St Lucia, Sierra Leone, Singapore, Solomon Islands, Sudan, Syrian Arab Republic, Thailand, Trinidad and Tobago, United Republic of Tanzania, Uganda, Yemen.

13 years: Cyprus, Jordan, Lebanon, Myanmar, Saudi Arabia, Swaziland, Tunisia, United Kingdom.

14 years: Angola, Argentina, Bahamas, Bahrain, Belgium, Benin, Bolivia, Brazil, Burkina Faso, Cameroon, Cape Verde, Central African Republic, Chad, Colombia, Côte d'Ivoire, Djibouti, Dominican Republic, El Salvador, Equatorial Guinea, Ethiopia, Guatemala, Guinea-Bissau, Guyana, Honduras, Indonesia, Italy, Kuwait, Liberia, Madagascar, Malaysia, Mali, Malawi, Mauritania, Mexico, Namibia, Nepal, Nicaragua, Niger, Pakistan, Panama, Papua New Guinea, Peru, Portugal, Rwanda, Sao Tome and Principe, Senegal, Sri Lanka, Suriname, Togo, Venezuela, Zambia.

15 years: Afghanistan, Albania, Austria, Barbados, Botswana, Chile, Comoros, Cuba, Denmark, Dominica, Finland, Ghana, Greece, Hungary, Iceland, India, Islamic Republic of Iran, Iraq, Ireland, Israel, Japan, Lao People's Democratic Republic, Lesotho, Libyan Arab Jamahiriya, Luxembourg, Malta, Mauritius, Mozambique, Netherlands, New Zealand, Norway, Paraguay, Philippines, Poland, Seychelles, Somalia, Switzerland, Turkey, United Arab Emirates, Uruguay, Yugoslavia.

16 years: Algeria, Antigua and Barbuda, Bulgaria, Burundi, China, Congo, Czechoslovakia, France, Gabon, Guinea, Kenya, Mongolia, Romania, Spain, Sweden, United States, former USSR, Zaire.

Note: This table is intended only to give a general picture. In many countries the basic minimum varies according to sector of production. The lowest figure is used here. "Child labour: Law and practice", *Conditions of Work Digest* (Geneva, ILO) Vol. 10, 1/1991, provides specific information on each country.

- *Conservatives* agree that child labour is the inevitable result of poverty, but conclude that the way forward is to tackle poverty.

Either approach risks postponing change into the indefinite future. Action can be taken now on a broad front, social, economic and political – with governments, employers, trade unions, non-governmental organisations (NGOs) working alongside each other. And within governments this will involve coordination between many departments, not just ministries of labour but also of health, for example, and education and welfare.

Many children who, for the present, *have* to work need as much support and protection as they can be given. This might mean health services, or feeding programmes, or non-formal education schemes which can fit in around their work. They can also be given vocational training which could allow them to get better, less exploitative jobs, both now and in the future.

But the longer term aim must be to reduce and eventually eliminate child labour. And experience shows that there are many practical steps which can help achieve this. These include:

- *Improving and enforcing legislation*
- *Promoting school enrolment*
- *Raising public awareness*
- *Supporting community action*
- *Targeting hazardous environments*

Improving and enforcing legislation

The basis for any approach to child labour is effective legislation. Since 1919 the ILO has adopted a number of Conventions, of which the Minimum Age Convention, 1973 (No. 138), is the most significant. This requires member States to specify a minimum age for employment – not less than the age of completion of compulsory schooling and, in any case, not less than 15 years.

Countries with less developed economies and education systems may, however, specify 14 years as the minimum. And the age can also be varied according to the type of work – lower (13 to 15, or 12 to 14) for lighter work, higher (18) for work likely to jeopardise a child's safety, health or morals. There have been more than 100 ratifications of the earlier minimum age Conventions and 40 governments have now ratified Convention No. 138.

In practice, most governments have set 14 or more as a basic minimum age (box 1.3), with variations: for light work the minimums are generally about 12 and for hazardous work between 16 and 18.

Governments thus diverge somewhat from the age standards set in the Convention. And national legislation often falls short in other respects too. It can apply only to people working under a contract of employment and thus exclude those working in the informal sector or in family enterprises, where the majority of child labourers are actually found. Then again, the laws may only cover certain industries such as factory work or mining. Agriculture (the major employer in many countries) is a common exclusion.

1.4   The challenge from Brazil's children

Brazil has around seven million child labourers, many of them working on the streets. For years they were treated merely as delinquents; and only NGOs and charitable organisations tried to help them.

Then in 1985 the Government decided to step in and take a fresh approach. It established, in conjunction with UNICEF, the Alternative Services for Street Children Project – a scheme which differed radically from previous approaches. First, it was to serve as a "dissonant" voice in Government, challenging the bureaucracy and acting as the spearhead for policy and programme change. But just as important, it would avoid becoming bureaucratised by moving away from the Government professionals and opening it up to broad public participation.

The Government recognised that community programmes tended to be more creative, more practical and much less expensive than those of the Government. These included protected employment for children so they could earn money without being exploited. They worked as messengers, for example, and many businesses were happy to pay for this new and reliable service. Other projects provided small "restaurants" for the children that offered nutritious food and places for the children to meet each other, as well as make contact with project volunteers.

This programme turned up a host of new ideas. But it also discovered familiar problems. The number of programmes helping children did double. But they still covered only a fraction, perhaps 10 per cent, of those in need. The project had certainly challenged the Government system, but it exposed the limitations of the load which community groups can be expected to shoulder.

In 1990 the Government took two major steps towards taking a greater share of that responsibility. It enacted a Statute of the Child and the Adolescent and it created a new Ministry for Children. There will also be a National Council on Children and Adolescents (made up of both government and NGO representatives) to supervise all projects and programmes concerning children.

The children themselves are demanding action. A group of poor children in São Paulo, for example, took to the streets in 1991 with street theatre to dramatise their plight. Said 12-year old Claudette Nunes: "We want to see the changes which will allow parents to look after their children – to see law become reality"

But enforcement can also be a problem. Many countries find it difficult to follow through on their own legislation. In one region of Egypt, for example, there are only four inspectors covering 20,000 establishments and they have to examine all aspects of working conditions. Indeed, a problem for inspectors in many countries is the diversity of issues which they have to address. In several countries in Europe, Africa and Latin America they are required to intervene in labour disputes, leaving relatively little time to actually inspect premises and supervise the application of the law. Though many countries, including Colombia, Peru and India, have special bureaux for child labour these do not have an enforcement mechanism of their own.

Hong Kong is one of the most striking examples of what can be achieved with strong legislation, a well staffed inspectorate and rigorous enforcement. The fine for illegal employment of children is 10,000 Hong Kong dollars (US$1,300). Inspections are regular and persistent and carried out by 244 inspectors of the Women and Young Persons Division of the Labour Department. In 1986, for example, 250,167 inspections were carried out in 19,274 establishments. Such a strict approach evidently works. In 1986 only 123 cases were discovered and most of these were mere technical offences rather than serious exploitation.

Promoting school enrolment

Education is the single most important means of drawing children away from the labour market. Millions of children never complete even a basic education; primary school drop-out rates are high in many parts of the developing world, as in Mexico (31 per cent), Togo (48 per cent), Bangladesh (80 per cent). In other countries the drop-out rate is very low, as in Singapore and the Republic of Korea where the incidence of child labour is also very low.

The first step is to ensure that primary education is free and universal. Parents are certainly dissuaded from sending children to school by school fees. In Nigeria, for example, primary school enrolment dropped from 92 per cent in 1981/82 to 75 per cent in 1985/86, partly because some states introduced fees.

For poor children to be able to afford to go to school it is not enough that it be free, however. Enrolment rates can be increased (as well as child nutrition) by providing food supplements at school. But parents must also be convinced that the education offered is of a sufficient quality and relevance that it also justifies the loss of their children's earnings. A good starting point may well be non-formal education for working children. In India, for example, a scheme run by the Indian Institute of Education has been operated for 4,000 working chil-

---

1.5   **The children of Smokey Mountain**

A thousand children clamber over a 200 metre pile of rotting, smouldering garbage. Each with a sack in one hand and a metal spike in the other, they dodge around dump trucks, diving onto the latest cascade of rubbish to see what treasures it might offer.

Smokey Mountain, on the outskirts of Manila in the Philippines, is so visually shocking that it has become an international symbol of child exploitation. Less visible, though just as striking, are the efforts which many organisations – from government agencies to churches, to local community groups – are making to offer the children of Smokey Mountain new hope and a new direction.

The ILO, in conjunction with the Philippines Department of Labour and Employment, and with finance from the Government of the Netherlands, launched in 1989 a pilot project to take advantage of all this commitment and effort.

The project's immediate aim is to offer protection to the working children. A "drop-in" centre has been opened in the heart of the dump site. Here the children can find drinking water, a free lunch, and a safe place to play and rest, as well as first-aid attention and informal counselling.

The next aim is to help children leave the dump. In a rented apartment, the "Sabana", at the foot of the mountain, children can get informal schooling and some vocational training and even start income-generating activities like painting and selling T-shirts. The idea, however, is not to create new institutions but rather to capitalize on what is already available. The local community has been involved in planning the programme from the outset. And the

project also draws its staff from the community – people who understand the problems and are prepared to work for long periods in these difficult conditions. Then there are the local NGOs, which are such an effective force in the Philippines – some specialise in urban poor programmes, others in community development, others in legal issues. All have the experience to provide back-up and support to the community workers.

The pilot project has been so successful that in March 1991 it was decided to extend it for a further three years. This will continue not just the practical benefits of the project but will also work on some of the broader aims of the scheme. These include extending this model of operation to other garbage sites and to other types of hazardous employment. The partnership between the Government and the NGOs has been demonstrated to be particularly effective. But the project will also explore just how such activities should fit into government policy. Since legislation in most countries bars children from such dangerous activities, this leaves unclear what help governments can offer to those children who are working. The experience here, it is hoped, will help show how this policy vacuum can be filled.

The project also aims to create awareness of the dangers of child labour in general – and of how it can be tackled. So it will also be used as the basis of public information campaigns, both national and international. Smokey Mountain may in the end be a symbol not of despair but of hope.

---

dren in a group of villages in Maharashtra. Teaching of subjects like languages and mathematics was closely linked to the children's daily needs. Only about 25 per cent of the children dropped out (often because of domestic responsibilities); most of the parents have been very enthusiastic.

It should also be noted, however, that there can be gaps in legislative provisions – with a gap of one or more years between the age to which education is compulsory and the age at which children may start work. In these cases it may be helpful to amend the laws on education.

Raising public awareness

Child labour is accepted as a way of life in many countries. Much needs to be done to alert public attention both nationally and internationally to the problem. There have been innovative approaches in several countries. In Kenya, for example, community drama has been used in schools to illustrate to both parents and children the exploitative nature of much child labour.

But the mass media can also play an important role. A striking success story is the campaign against child prostitution in the tourist resort of Pagsanjan in the Philippines. By 1983 there were an estimated 3,000 boys aged between nine and 14 working as prostitutes for male homosexual tourists. A local pastor alerted Australian newspapers and television to what was going on. In 1985 the *Melbourne Age* carried a feature article: "Monsters in shorts and thongs", which was followed up by other TV and newspaper coverage.

This produced a strong response in Australia and elsewhere. The press in the Philippines ran a series of articles on the problem, on what local people were trying to do and on the Government response. The campaign grew in strength, working with the families concerned and through the schools. The number of children now involved has dropped to around 300.

"In Pagsanjan," says one local citizen, "we swallowed our pride, and endured the humiliation of having our town tarnished because of its association with child prostitution. But we expose this evil so that other towns can learn from our experience."

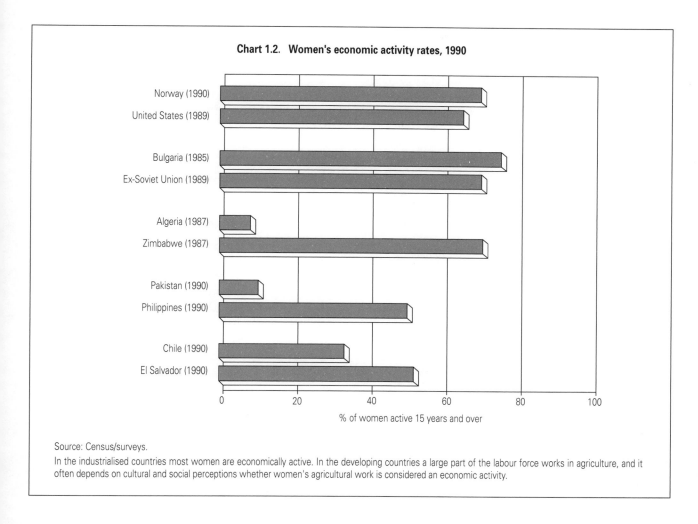

Chart 1.2. Women's economic activity rates, 1990

Norway (1990)
United States (1989)

Bulgaria (1985)
Ex-Soviet Union (1989)

Algeria (1987)
Zimbabwe (1987)

Pakistan (1990)
Philippines (1990)

Chile (1990)
El Salvador (1990)

% of women active 15 years and over

Source: Census/surveys.
In the industrialised countries most women are economically active. In the developing countries a large part of the labour force works in agriculture, and it often depends on cultural and social perceptions whether women's agricultural work is considered an economic activity.

Supporting community action

All successful community development prog-rammes are based on the involvement and initia-tives of the communities themselves. For child labour the logical place to start is with the children.

Brazil, with some of the most serious child labour problems in the world, also has some of the most imaginative ways of tackling them – but much of the energy and many of the ideas come from non-governmental and community-based groups. The National Movement of the Boys and Girls of the Streets, for example, has been formed from spon-taneous popular groups which arose in the early 1980s. Their primary aims include the defence of children's rights and training – both for children and for "street educators" for children. When the Government was debating its new Statute of the Child and the Adolescent, for example, the children themselves went to the legislature to argue their case. The background to the Brazilian approach is outlined in box 1.4.

Similarly in Ecuador the Premature Workers Programme, run by the National Institute of the Child and the Family, gives support to non-govern-mental organisations working with child workers – as well as giving direct support in terms of health and nutrition and contacting children through its own network of street educators.

Targeting hazardous environments

The long-term aim must be to eliminate all child labour. But there are some urgent immediate priorities. Children can be removed from the most dangerous environments – from the glass factories, from the construction sites, from the coal mines – places for which they have neither the experience nor the physical development to cope.

Among the worst of these working environments are the garbage dumps. Children all over the world spend their days rooting around for scraps of material they can salvage and sell. The most notorious perhaps is Smokey Mountain in the Philippines. But Smokey Mountain is now also an encouraging example of just how to tackle child labour in dangerous environments – some of the measures currently being taken are outlined in box 1.5.

An international challenge

Child labour is deeply rooted in poverty and social deprivation. Removing it will be a long and complex task – legal, social, economic and political. But progress *is* possible. More information will always be needed, more investigations, more analysis. In the end what counts is action, from communities, from employers, from trade unions, from governments, and from international organisations. A number of governments, including Brazil and India, now have national plans of action on child labour. The increasing number of ratifications for the ILO's Minimum Age Convention, 1973 (about 138), is another encouraging indication of the priority now accorded to this issue – as is the large number of countries which have ratified the United Nations Convention on the Rights of the Child.

The global community now has the opportunity to live up to such commitments: to enact the legislation and to enforce it; to make schooling a real and practical alternative for working children; and to allow poor families to give their children a happy childhood and prepare them for a healthy and productive working life.

Equal opportunities for women

Equality of opportunity is a principle to which almost every country subscribes. Discrimination on the grounds of gender, physical attributes, race or ethnic extraction, religion, or political opinion is prohibited in most countries.

Yet if you are disabled you are *four times* more likely to be unemployed in the European Community than an able-bodied person. If you are a woman in Japan you will earn on average *half* as much as a

man. If you are a Hispanic child in the United States you are *three times* more likely to drop out of high school than a white child.

The *World Labour Report* will concentrate each year on the employment situation of a different group. This year the focus is on the world's largest disadvantaged group, women – on the numbers of women who work, the jobs they do, the discrimination they face, and the legal and other changes needed to improve their position.

More women workers

More women are working outside the home than ever before. Many want to work – and now exercise a freedom denied to previous generations. Others are forced to work to survive. But the proportion of women who work – who are "economically active" – can vary greatly from one region and one country to another (chart 1.2).

Industrial market economies

Sweden now has the highest women's activity rate among the industrialised countries: 50.1 per cent of females are now working (or looking for work) compared with 55.5 per cent of males. And about 75 per cent of women workers in industrialised countries are in services, 15 to 20 per cent in industry and around 5 per cent in agriculture.

In manufacturing women are concentrated in the same "women's industries" in most countries: clothing, footwear, textiles, leather and (in some countries) tobacco. And they are usually on the lower rungs of the employment ladder.

But the status of women's jobs is slowly changing. In most economies the share of women among managerial and administrative workers has been rising faster than their share in total employment – particularly in the United States, Canada and Sweden. Table 1.1 shows, for the United States, the changes for certain occupations between 1975 and 1988. Women now have a slightly smaller share of traditionally female jobs, like elementary school-teacher – and are correspondingly better represented amongst the ranks of professional occupations such as architects and dentists, as well as in craft and technical jobs such as telephone repairers.

Legislative changes have played a part here. Certain professions such as the armed forces or the

Table 1.1 Women in different occupations: United States, 1975 and 1988 (percentages)

Occupation	1975	1988
Airline pilot/navigator	—	3.1
Architect	4.3	14.6
Auto mechanic	0.5	0.7
Bartender	35.2	49.6
Bus driver	37.7	45.8
Cab driver/chauffeur	8.7	12.5
Carpenter	0.6	1.5
Child-care worker	93.8	97.3
Computer programmer	25.6	32.2
Data entry keyer	92.2	88.2
Dentist	1.8	9.3
Economist	13.1	35.3
Editor/reporter	44.6	51.1
Elementary schoolteacher	85.4	84.8
College/University teacher	31.1	38.5
Fire-fighter	—	2.1
Lawyer/judge	7.1	19.5
Mail carrier	8.7	22.0
Office equipment repairer	1.7	6.4
Physician	13.0	20.0
Police officer	2.7	13.4
Secretary	99.1	99.1
Telephone installer/repairer	4.8	12.1
Waitress/Waiter	91.1	82.6
Welder	4.4	4.9

Source: S.E. Rix (ed.): *The American woman 1990-91: A status report* (New York, Norton, 1990).

police have previously been barred to women in certain countries, or been subject to physical requirements that effectively excluded them. But in Belgium since 1987, for example, and Spain since 1988, women are no longer prohibited by law from entering the armed forces. In Italy women were allowed to enter the police in 1981 and by 1987 made up 2.3 per cent of the force.

More women are also starting their own companies. Women are starting two-thirds of the new businesses in Canada and own 25 per cent of businesses in the United States. Around 30 per cent of all entrepreneurs in Finland are women, 25 per cent in Sweden, and 21 per cent in France.

But women do not usually make it to the top of large corporations. The number of women holding top jobs is substantially lower than their education or experience would warrant. In the United States in 1990 a survey of the 1,000 largest companies showed that of the 4,012 people listed as the highest paid officers and directors of their companies only 19 were

women (less than half of one per cent). And in Japan a major company such as Toshiba had only ten women among its 7,000 managers.

Eastern Europe and the former Soviet Union

Eastern Europe has had high rates of female participation for some decades. And while the numbers stagnated, or in some countries even declined, in the 1980s, the levels still remain relatively high. The wide availability of publicly supported child-care facilities has greatly contributed to the high rates of participation.

About half of these women are employed in services, one-third in industry and one-fifth in agriculture.

As elsewhere women are often concentrated in particular kinds of job – though not necessarily the same ones as in Western countries. Some professions, such as doctor, are less highly regarded in Eastern Europe, and tend to be female dominated. And finance and insurance services have also had a lower status, with a predominantly female workforce – though this could well change in the future.

On the whole though, the "women's jobs" syndrome has been somewhat less marked in the planned economies. This is partly because the State has controlled the jobs which people can take. And such rigid channelling has also brought a certain amount of discontent. In Czechoslovakia's metal and engineering industries in 1988, for example, a survey found that only 20 per cent of women working there had chosen that profession deliberately.

The status of women workers in Eastern Europe and the former Soviet Union, however, still does not reflect their potential. In the former Soviet Union women hold only 5.6 per cent of high-level managerial posts. And in Poland they occupy only around 10 per cent of higher posts, even in branches where they predominate such as health services and social welfare.

Developing countries

In developing countries women make up a smaller proportion of the official labour force (31 per cent) than they do in the industrial countries (40 per cent).

But many women actually work in the informal sector unseen by many collectors of statistics. Indeed, during periods of recession and structural adjustment their numbers are believed to have gone up. As men have lost their jobs in the formal sector, women have been forced to seek informal sector employment to maintain the family's living standards – what UNICEF has called "invisible adjustment". Some of the highest women's participation rates are in Africa – 87 per cent in Malawi, for example, and 71 per cent in Zimbabwe – where many women work as farmers. Indeed women make up 80 per cent of the food producers in some African countries.

But there have also been significant increases in waged employment, notably in South-East Asia. Female labour has provided up to 80 per cent of the workforce of the export processing zones; indeed the industrialisation process of countries like the Republic of Korea and Thailand has been as much female-led as export-led – though women have usually been confined to repetitive assembly-line jobs in industries like electronics, food-processing, textiles and footwear.

Some of the Asian countries which have been centrally planned also have high participation rates (77 per cent in China) – though here agriculture is much more significant.

In Latin America women's participation rates tend to be lower – around 35 per cent in Chile, Costa Rica and Ecuador, for example. The services sector is particularly important here – employing around 70 per cent of all economically active women, of which the highest proportion are in domestic service.

The lowest official rates anywhere in the world are to be found in the Arab countries (8 per cent in Algeria, 10 per cent in Egypt) where there are considerable social, cultural and sometimes legal barriers to women working outside the home. However, this does not mean that women do not work. A high percentage work on family farms, but for traditional reasons they do not receive wages and are not considered part of the labour force.

Part-time, temporary or unemployed

Women workers may be increasing in numbers but the jobs they do are more likely to be part time, precarious and low paid.

For women in the industrial market economies (excluding the United States) part-time employment grew at a faster rate than full-time employment in the 1980s. Often this was because full-time work was not available to them. Women thus confined to part-time work often miss out on benefits such as maternity leave, as well as on opportunities for promotion.

Temporary work provides another kind of flexibility. But the gender gap is somewhat narrower here. In a group of six European countries it accounts for 8.6 per cent of female employment compared with 6.3 per cent for males.

Women in the industrial market economies are also more likely to be unemployed than men – more than twice as likely in Italy, Belgium, Spain and the Netherlands, for example.

In Central and Eastern Europe women have always been able to work part time – in theory. In practice, employers and governments have been reluctant to permit this. In Czechoslovakia, for example, in 1989 only 11.6 per cent of women worked part time, though up to 27 per cent wished to do so. Since 1989, however, when the regulations were changed, about 40 per cent of all women workers (mostly mothers with young children) have been working part time.

Women in developing countries, whether in agriculture or in the cities have generally fitted any work around family responsibilities. Activities like market trading and street vending have offered this kind of flexibility. In West Africa women dominate this type of work: they make up 93 per cent of market traders in Accra, for example, 87 per cent in Lagos and 60 per cent in Dakar.

Table 1.2 Women's pay outside agriculture, 1980, 1984 and 1988 (men's pay=100)

Country	1980	1984	1988
Australia[1]	86.0	85.8	87.9
Belgium[2]	69.4	74.4	75.1
Cyprus	54.3	57.9	59.1
Czechoslovakia	68.4	68.4	70.1
Denmark	84.5	84.4	82.1
France	79.2	80.7	81.8
Germany, Fed. Rep. of	72.4	72.3	73.6
Iceland	85.5	94.1	90.6
Japan	53.8	51.8	50.7
Luxembourg[2]	64.7	64.9	63.1
Netherlands[2]	77.9	77.0	76.7
New Zealand	77.2	78.4	80.4
Switzerland	67.6	67.2	67.4
United Kingdom	69.7	69.5	—

[1] Non-managerial employees. [2] Wage earners.

Source: ILO: Tripartite Symposium on Equality of Opportunity and Treatment for Men and Women Workers in Industrial Countries, Technical Background Paper (Geneva, 1990).

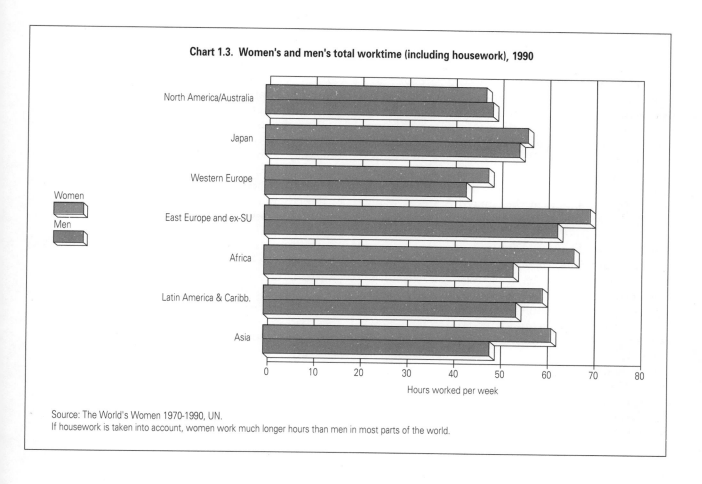

Chart 1.3. Women's and men's total worktime (including housework), 1990

Source: The World's Women 1970-1990, UN.
If housework is taken into account, women work much longer hours than men in most parts of the world.

What women earn

In the industrialised countries the gap between women's and men's pay did not narrow substantially in the 1980s. Indeed it actually widened in some countries: women still earn typically between 50 and 80 per cent of men's wages. Table 1.2 shows women's salaries as a percentage of men's in selected countries.

This is based upon the ILO's *Year Book of Labour Statistics*, but individual country studies tell a similar story.

- *United Kingdom* – women's gross weekly earnings as a percentage of men's increased slightly between 1987 and 1990, from 73.4 per cent to 76.6 per cent.

- *United States* – between 1979 and 1988 the earnings of women working full time rose, as a percentage of male earnings, from 60 per cent to 65 per cent.

- *Japan* – women's monthly wages were 58.9 per cent of men's in 1975, fell to 55.3 per cent in 1980, and climbed again in 1987 to 57.6 per cent.

- *Canada* – for full-time workers there has been a steady progression from 59.7 per cent of men's earnings in 1971 to 65.9 per cent in 1987.

Such gaps are partly due to job differences. Women may be working shorter hours and be employed in low-level or part-time jobs. Even so there is a residual difference in earnings which it is reasonable to attribute to wage discrimination.

In Eastern Europe there are similar gaps. Surveys in Czechoslovakia, for example, show that women's earnings are lower throughout their lives. In 1984 the average female wage was 68.9 per cent of the male wage; by 1988 it was 70.9 per cent.

In developing countries women also earn less than men, though they tend to do better in the public than the private sector. In the informal sector they may also earn much less. A study of the informal services sector in Bangkok, for example, showed that women earned less than half as much as men.

The roots of discrimination

Many justifications are offered for the inferior position of women workers. Physical strength is a common basis of segregation – an unconvincing explanation to anyone who has seen construction or road workers in Asia or Eastern Europe, and likely to become even more so as manual work is increasingly mechanised. A difference in psychological make-up is another argument: women are said to be insufficiently ruthless. But this stereotype, too, may be going out of fashion: in the United States it is now thought that women may be even more suited to running the corporations of the 1990s since these are likely to be less hierarchically organised.

The real issue, however, is women's "reproductive" role. This does not refer merely to the biological process of reproduction (which need affects women only for a couple of months for each child) but the social reproduction of the family. Housework, food preparation and responsibility for bringing up the children, all cut into a woman's opportunity for outside work, or more often add to it to produce a "double burden".

Men and women could share the social reproduction role more equally. Men are not physically disqualified from such tasks yet they do seem to disqualify themselves culturally. A study in the Nordic countries, for example, indicated that when men's hours of work were reduced they chose to increase their leisure time rather than devote more time to child care or housework. In Poland men, even in young married couples, do not help with the most elementary housework. And in Japan it is reported that men spend only 15 minutes a day on household activities.

If housework is taken into account, women work much longer hours than men in most parts of the world. Chart 1.3 collects the results of a number of studies within each region. However, women in industrialised countries are, it seems, spending less time on housework than they used to – probably because they are having smaller families and have more labour-saving devices.

Women in many developing countries do not have these advantages and here the "double burden" is especially heavy. Women farmers in Africa regularly have to put in a 16-hour day. And even in Cuba, where men are legally supposed to assist women with housework, 82 per cent of women in Havana (and 96 per cent of those in the countryside) have sole responsibility for domestic chores. In India a sample of working mothers indicated that while around 40 per cent of their husbands would help with child care or shopping they were highly unlikely to do household chores; dishwashing was the least popular (95 per cent of the men did it rarely or never).

Women who have to look after children are understandably reluctant to look for employment. But they also have to cope with employers who assume that women will not be committed to the job and are thus "bad investments". They may be subtly or directly placed in a "mommy track" which carries less status and fewer opportunities or have to renounce childbearing to make progress.

Another form of discrimination at work (and increasingly recognised as such) is sexual harassment – a widespread problem, as revealed by a series of recent studies. In the United States 42 per cent of women employed by the federal Government said they had experienced some kind of uninvited sexual attention at work. In Belgium one study revealed that over 30 per cent of women had experienced such embarrassment and unease. And in the Netherlands 58 per cent of women surveyed said they had been sexually harassed at their workplace. Workers in the agricultural sector seem to be more vulnerable to such advances, as do those in clerical positions. And though it does occur at all levels of employment, those with lower status jobs are more likely to be victims.

In developing countries the situation can be even worse. Here a woman who steps out of her accepted family role can be seen as "loose". And women who desperately need the work may find themselves unable to refuse demands for sexual favours.

Tackling sex discrimination

The exclusion of women from certain jobs. A bias towards men for promotion. Unequal pay for work of equal value. Sexual harassment. All are forms of discrimination very firmly established in most countries. Uprooting them has proved a slow and difficult task.

Women themselves have taken some of the most important steps, demanding their rights, and achieving higher levels of education and training despite the odds stacked against them. Legislation has also played an important part particularly in the field of equal pay for equal work. But it will require a

1.6   **Pay equity in Canada**

Canada's attempts to ensure pay equality for women have relied until recent years on "equal pay for equal work" legislation dating back to the 1950s. This has the weakness that men and women rarely do precisely the same job.

To remedy this, three jurisdictions (Canada is a federal State) introduced "equal pay for work of equal value" provisions in human rights legislation in the 1970s. This used the four standard factors: skill, effort, responsibility and working conditions; and added up scores on each to give a total for each job to serve as the basis of comparison. This ability to compare "apples and oranges" was a significant improvement but it has done relatively little to narrow the wage gap. The main problem is that it is "complaints-based" and the Canadian Human Rights Commission has handled only a dozen or so equal value cases for federal employees since the federal provisions came into force in 1978.

A new concept is now appearing which could change all this "pay equity" legislation. The key element is that it is "pro-active". Employees do not have to complain about their own specific problems. The onus is now on employers. Legislation obliges employers to examine their pay practices and remedy any inequities within a set period. The first Canadian jurisdiction to pass a pro-active Pay Equity Act was Manitoba (1984), followed by Ontario (1987), Prince Edward Island (1988) and Nova Scotia (1988).

Ontario's Act has the greatest coverage. Not only does it cover the public sector, it is also the first pro-active statute in the world to require a mandatory pay equity process for all private sector employers with ten or more employees. The others are limited to the public sector, and even then need not include the "broad" public sector workers like those in hospitals and schools. All four provinces have set up new administrative agencies to deal with pay equity matters.

The Acts aim to tackle, among other things, the inequity which arises from the segregation into male and female jobs. So all female job classes in an establishment are compared with the male ones and scored on the four factors mentioned earlier to ensure that they are being paid using the same measure of value. If not, the female's wages have to be altered. It may well be difficult, however, for the evaluators to work in a "gender-neutral" fashion — a concept mentioned in the legislation, but not defined.

There are a number of exclusions which reduce the power of the legislation. The most important is probably that there has to be at least one comparable male job class in the establishment. This excludes all-female workplaces such as child-care centres or nursing homes.

Another weakness is that the legislation applies only to discrimination based on gender. Race, ethnicity or age are not taken into account. This creates a problem, since women's jobs may then be compared with those of males whose wages are depressed because they are done by people from particular ethnic groups, for example.

Despite such weakness, however, these moves represent a considerable step forward towards equal pay for women.

sustained implementation of such measures, combined with a steady process of affirmative action and public education, if women are to achieve an equal role.

Equal pay legislation

Most industrial countries have constitutional or legislative provisions stipulating equal pay for equal work. But they may be limited in scope. They often exclude certain categories of workers: those in domestic work, for example, in agriculture, family businesses, or those working at home. Part-time and casual workers may also be excluded and since, for example, 70 per cent of jobs created in the EC between 1983 and 1987 were part time, and a high proportion of these were for women, this has become a matter of concern. The Irish Employment Equality Agency, for one, has announced that part-time work will be one of its priorities. There are similar concerns in Japan where the Japanese Trade Union Confederation has called for a Part-Time Employment Law to protect such workers.

Many women lose out, however, not so much on basic pay (which is relatively easy to monitor) but on additional payments, based on seniority or marital status, say, or on travelling allowances. In the United Kingdom, for example, the Equal Opportunities Commission has pointed out the widespread use of criteria such as length of service, or hours worked per day, which debar many women (particularly part-time workers) from such benefits as preferential mortgages and share participation.

Women doing jobs different from those of men, but requiring similar levels of education or skill, can also be discriminated against. This is particularly true for the jobs which have become associated with women. Here it is the principle of "equal pay for work of equal value" which has to be applied and which has been embodied in the ILO's Equal Remuneration Convention, 1951 (No. 100). The principle has been increasingly accepted, particularly in the industrialised countries. The EC laws do include it (and member governments have to bring their legislation into line). And a number of states in the United States have also adopted such laws though federal legislation does not include such a principle. Determining the value of women's jobs can, however, be difficult. It is tricky enough within one enterprise but even more so between different enterprises, perhaps across sectors. Where it has taken place, however, significant numbers of women workers have had their wages raised. In March 1990, for example, one of the largest retailers in the United Kingdom, Sainsbury, announced increases of between 8.5 and 21 per cent to 60,000 mostly female retail staff, following a job evaluation exercise.

In some countries legislation lays down requirements for such job evaluation or at least lists the criteria by which the value is to be measured. In Canada, for example, it is measured by skill, effort, responsibility and working conditions (box 1.6). Elsewhere the criteria for equal treatment may be listed but there may be no reference to job evaluation schemes.

Conflicts between work and family

Family responsibilities are at the heart of much discrimination against women. Women are expected to stay at home to look after children and are then treated as second-class workers because of this. Addressing this difficult issue will require considerable cooperation at all levels: between central and local government, employers and trade unions, workers and community groups.

There are, however, clear differences of approach between governments. Those in Eastern Europe and Scandinavia often make extensive provision for working mothers. But while Central and Eastern European governments follow the traditional division of labour between parents, those in Scandinavia propose changes in the roles of both sexes. Men *and* women, they argue, should be able to combine work and family responsibilities, so they offer comprehensive systems of parental leave, insurance and child care. The Scandinavian system (which inspired ILO Convention No. 156 and Recommendation No. 165) has since served as a model for legislation in Greece, New Zealand, Portugal and Spain.

Other countries take a different line. The Netherlands, the United Kingdom and the United States, for example, take the view that child care is primarily the responsibility of parents and should be left to local or private initiative. Even here, though, there is considerable consultation on the subject. The United States Department of Labor has established a "work and family clearing house" to provide information to

employers on how they can respond to employees' needs to care for children and the elderly.

Demographic changes, including increasing numbers of female-headed households are likely to impel further action on this subject. With an increasing number of women needing to work, more and more employers are having to look more closely at the need for child care.

Legislation on sexual harassment

The United States has thus far been ahead of European countries on this issue. In 1991, however, the EC Commission proposed a new code of conduct on this issue and France became only the second EC country after Spain to introduce legislation. In France it is now a criminal offence to solicit sexual favours from a subordinate – punishable by up to a year's imprisonment and/or a fine of 100,000 French francs (i.e. US$17,000).

Affirmative action

Maternity leave, paternity leave, child-care facilities, legislative provisions on discrimination, and a more equal sharing of the domestic workload all are important parts of the process of change. But many industrialised countries have realised that they are not enough, that a more active stance is needed to redress a persistent bias against women workers and other groups which suffer discrimination in the workplace.

Such "affirmative action" (also called "positive action") need not rely on quotas, which often antagonise other groups. Other options might include adapting working conditions to meet special needs or ensuring that recruiters are particularly aware of likely causes of discrimination.

Such measures go beyond an "equal opportunities" policy; affirmative action implies a systematic attempt to give special treatment to a particular group on a transitional basis until imbalances have been corrected. Some of the measures which can be taken are listed in box 1.7.

This might in itself be thought discriminatory. But the United Nations incorporated the principle in its Convention on the Elimination of All Forms of Discrimination against Women in 1979. This called for "temporary measures aimed at accelerating *de facto* equality between men and women". The

---

1.7 Affirmative action

Affirmative action can take many different forms according to local circumstances and the disadvantaged groups being helped. Some typical measures which employers take are:

- *Training* – ensuring that minority groups are adequately represented on training courses.
- *Quotas* – setting targets which encourage employers to include minorities in the proportions they represent in the local population as a whole.
- *Skilled personnel* – ensuring that recruitment, guidance and counselling services are familiar with the special problems of minorities.
- *Adapting working conditions* – providing more flexible working hours for women, for example, or allowing for use of minority languages.
- *Education programmes* – counteracting prejudice in other employees through information schemes or gender or racial awareness programmes.
- *Providing special services* – crèches for working mothers, for example, or language courses for linguistic minorities.

Council of the European Communities took a similar stance in 1984.

Legislation protecting governments and employers against claims of "reverse discrimination" (i.e. discrimination against members of a majority group) has been adopted in many countries, including Australia, Denmark, France, Greece, Iceland, Ireland, Luxembourg and Norway. Similar legislation is currently under discussion in Italy and the Netherlands. Thus far there are few similar measures being taken in developing countries.

Policies of affirmative action are under way in many countries. These generally have four important elements:

1. *Reporting*. In France, for example, employers with over 50 employees are required to submit detailed information on the status of all employees from designated groups.

2. *Goals and timetables*. In Canada, for example, the Employment Equity Act requires employers to prepare an annual equity plan, with numerical targets and dates. While such targets were out of favour in the 1970s, in the 1980s the trend seems to have been reversed.

3. *Monitoring*. Many countries have established agencies to monitor their affirmative action programmes. These often have powers of enforcement

as with the Australian Affirmative Action Commission, and the Equality Commissioner in Sweden.

4. *Training*. This is a priority area in most national policies. In Portugal, for example, every vocational training course has to have at least three female participants.

Affirmative action programmes are voluntary in many countries. They rely on encouragement and help from the government, rather than on coercion. Thus, in Belgium the Ministry of Employment and Labour has set up a training section to assist employers and trade unions to include affirmative action in collective agreements.

Financial incentives can also offer significant encouragement – bordering on coercion perhaps. In the United States and Canada, most government contracts are awarded only if companies comply with affirmative action programmes. In the United States 40 per cent of all civilian employees work in companies subject to this programme's requirements. And it clearly works: a Department of Labor study showed that women's employment had increased by 15.2 per cent in companies subject to affirmative action goals and targeted for women, compared with only 2.2 per cent in other establishments.

Affirmative action remains a controversial area though and there has been considerable litigation from individuals (usually white males) who claim their equal opportunities rights have been infringed.

Claiming rights

The injustices that women suffer, and human rights abuses in general, are committed against groups with neither the full power nor the knowledge to protect themselves. So how can people claim their rights?

Theoretically everyone has a legal remedy. In practice this is a difficult option: physically intimidating if the forces of law and order are themselves the oppressors, financially crippling if the legal process is complex and expensive, and emotionally draining for people unused to facing up to officialdom. Most people are, in any case, unaware of their rights and would not know how to start claiming them.

Workers have to rely on organisations, generally trade unions, taking up their case. The majority of abuses which the ILO considers have been referred by trade unions or international confederations.

Non-unionised labour can be very isolated. Those in agriculture (the majority of workers in developing countries) are generally beyond direct protection. And workers in the informal sector (the majority of urban workers in almost all developing countries) normally have only themselves to rely on.

Child and women workers are in an especially weak position. Since child labour is frequently illegal, it is unlikely to be organised. So defence of rights is left to sympathetic local organisations on an ad hoc basis. And women too are often without union protection, particularly if they are working part time. Even in developed countries women are under-represented within the unions. And in many developing countries young women are often recruited because they are thought to be docile and unlikely to make trouble.

Information is the first step in solving human rights problems. Local organisations and local press can help ensure that the legal system protects workers. And on a worldwide stage the activities of trade union federations and human rights NGOs can turn the spotlight on abuses which national governments are unaware of or would prefer to ignore.

But information has to be followed by action. One way is through the ILO's supervision of international Conventions. A distinguished judge referred to the insistent questioning by the ILO's committees as "like a dog tugging away at a bone". As old problems are resolved, others appear. New technologies, new forms of work, new political systems, all offer fresh challenges, and demand patience and persistence from those attempting to protect the rights of workers.

Chapter 2

Employment

The employment picture in 1992 is hardly encouraging. A recession which seems likely to continue in many of the industrial market economies, a radical shake-out of the underemployed in Eastern Europe and the former Soviet Union, and a continuing economic crisis in Africa. But there are a few bright spots. In Latin America several countries which have been restructuring their economies (at considerable social cost) may now have turned the corner. And in Asia the newly industrialised countries, in particular, continue to prosper. These are some of the issues which are covered in the regional summaries which make up the first part of this chapter.

On a global scale the world economy continues its steady process of integration. Capital, so far, has done most of the travelling, but the early 1990s see increasing numbers of workers searching out opportunities overseas. The second half of this chapter, therefore, looks at two of the more significant migration trails: from the poorer to the richer countries of the Pacific Rim; and from Eastern to Western Europe.

Industrial market economies

Unemployment is rising again in many of the industrialised countries. For the 24 member countries of the OECD the unemployment rate for 1991 is 7.1 per cent – 28 million people. A rate of 7.4 per cent is expected for 1992 (table 2.1).

The sharpest rises are in Australia, Canada, Finland, Ireland, New Zealand, Sweden, the United Kingdom and the United States. But unemployment is also expected to rise in most industrial market economies – the exceptions being Belgium, Germany, the Netherlands, Norway, Portugal and Spain. The estimated rates for 1991 and 1992 are also shown in table 2.1.

Table 2.1. Unemployment in OECD countries, 1990, 1991 and 1992 (percentages)

Country	1990	1991	1992
North America			
Canada	8.1	10.3	10.2
United States	5.5	6.7	6.7
Japan	2.1	2.2	2.3
Central and Western Europe			
Austria	3.3	3.4	3.8
Belgium	8.8	9.4	9.7
France	8.9	9.4	10.1
Germany	5.1	4.6	5.0
Ireland	13.7	15.8	16.5
Luxembourg	1.3	1.4	1.4
Netherlands	6.5	6.1	6.4
Switzerland	0.6	1.2	1.6
United Kingdom	5.9	8.7	9.9
Southern Europe			
Greece	7.2	8.6	9.6
Italy	11.2	10.9	10.8
Portugal	4.6	3.9	4.5
Spain	16.3	15.9	15.2
Nordic countries			
Denmark	9.5	10.3	10.2
Finland	3.5	7.7	9.8
Iceland	1.7	1.6	2.0
Norway	5.2	5.3	5.1
Sweden	1.5	2.7	4.1
Oceania			
Australia	6.9	9.5	10.1
New Zealand	7.8	10.4	11.5
Total OECD	6.3	7.1	7.4

Source: OECD.

Industry and construction have borne the brunt of the job losses. In the United States, for example,

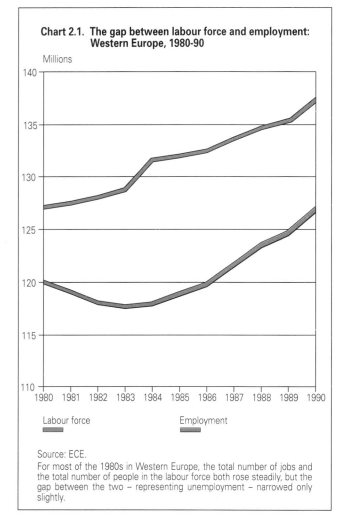

Chart 2.1. The gap between labour force and employment: Western Europe, 1980-90

Millions

Labour force   Employment

Source: ECE.
For most of the 1980s in Western Europe, the total number of jobs and the total number of people in the labour force both rose steadily, but the gap between the two – representing unemployment – narrowed only slightly.

This is illustrated for Western Europe in chart 2.1. While the total number of jobs and the total number in the labour force both rose steadily, the gap between the two narrowed only slightly, even during the growth years from 1984 to 1990.

And this does not take into account that many of those employed are working part time. In Sweden, for example, part-time work now accounts for 20 per cent of employment. Many workers take part-time or temporary jobs because they cannot find permanent ones. In Canada a study in 1988 found that 24 per cent of part-time work was involuntary. This means that real unemployment is certainly higher than the normal statistics suggest (typically around 20 per cent higher) since those in part-time work always count as "employed" even if they would prefer to work full time.

The changing nature of employment

Part-time work is just one aspect of a more general trend towards more "precarious" employment. In the United Kingdom, for example, 30 per cent of jobs in 1980 did not involve regular, full-time waged employment; by the end of 1991 the figure is likely to have risen to 40 per cent. And similar trends are evident elsewhere. Aside from part-time employment, workers are also likely to face:

- *Temporary or fixed-term contracts* – half or more of all new employment created in France, Germany, the Netherlands, Luxembourg and Spain in the 1980s was for workers on temporary contracts.

- *Working through agencies* – in Germany the number of temporary work agencies more than doubled between 1982 and 1987 (such agencies are, however, outlawed in Greece, Italy and Spain).

- *Self-employment* – in Portugal, for example, self-employment rose from 12 per cent of total employment in 1979 to 17 per cent in 1989. Such employment is probably, however, more prevalent in the poorer countries.

- *Working at home* – in Italy, for example, home workers account for about 4 per cent of the labour force.

The most obvious explanation for these changes is the rise in unemployment. Jobseekers are in a weaker position so employers can offer less attractive jobs. But many employers may have no choice about the jobs they can provide. Privatisation, for example, has put many European enterprises in different and more

employment in construction was down 9.7 per cent and in industry down 4.0 per cent in the year to March 1991, while employment in services actually rose 0.6 per cent. Indeed the services sector in general has done relatively well over the last decade and now accounts for 60 per cent of employment in the OECD region.

Over the longer term one of the most disturbing aspects of employment in the industrialised countries is that unemployment has been persistently high even during periods of sustained economic growth. This is a severe reversal. In the era after the Second World War Western European governments felt threatened if unemployment rose above 2 per cent; nowadays it seems impossible for many countries to bring unemployment below 6 per cent.

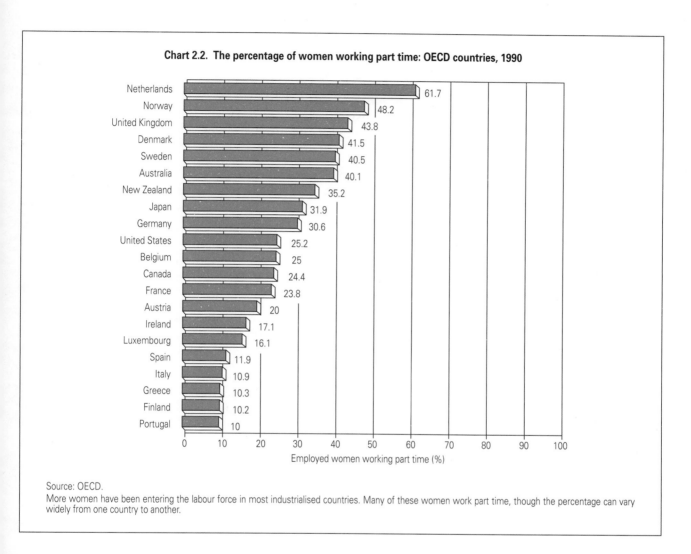

Chart 2.2. The percentage of women working part time: OECD countries, 1990

Country	Value
Netherlands	61.7
Norway	48.2
United Kingdom	43.8
Denmark	41.5
Sweden	40.5
Australia	40.1
New Zealand	35.2
Japan	31.9
Germany	30.6
United States	25.2
Belgium	25
Canada	24.4
France	23.8
Austria	20
Ireland	17.1
Luxembourg	16.1
Spain	11.9
Italy	10.9
Greece	10.3
Finland	10.2
Portugal	10

Employed women working part time (%)

Source: OECD.

More women have been entering the labour force in most industrialised countries. Many of these women work part time, though the percentage can vary widely from one country to another.

cost-conscious hands. And as international competitive pressures increase, many employers may need to avoid the costs associated with full-time staff.

In addition, there have been significant changes in the nature of the enterprises themselves. Many large manufacturing plants have closed and numerous small enterprises have appeared – particularly in services, which are more likely to use part-time staff. And even manufacturing companies have changed their working methods. Many now model themselves on the idea of the "flexible firm": they employ a secure group of core workers surrounded by a precarious periphery of temporary wage workers, outworkers or subcontractors. This allows them to adjust to production peaks and troughs without having to bear the costs of a permanent labour force.

The changing labour force

The composition of the labour force has been changing – partly as a response to these new working patterns, but partly, too, for demographic and social reasons.

The labour force for all OECD countries grew 1.3 per cent per year between 1980 and 1989. Three-quarters of this was due to the growth in the population of working age. But added to this were increasing numbers of people who wanted to (or had to) work.

More women, for example, started to work, and especially mothers. Thus in Canada the participation rates for mothers with young children rose from 41 per cent in 1976 to 62 per cent in 1986. And in the

United Kingdom women may well form the majority of the workforce by the year 2000. A significant proportion of these women, however, work part time, and particularly in services (see chart 2.2).

At the same time the participation rate for older men (aged 55-64) dropped substantially in many countries. In Australia, for example, it fell from 85 per cent to around 65 per cent in 1989. Fewer men are working, partly because of the decline of older industries but also because many governments tried to cut unemployment by reducing the age of retirement.

Wages and inequality

Real wages in manufacturing for the OECD countries as a whole fell by 0.3 per cent in 1990 (compared with a 0.1 per cent drop in 1989). However this average covers a variety of experiences. In Australia, Germany, Japan and Spain, for example, real hourly earnings in manufacturing grew by more than 2 per cent, while in Australia, the United States and New Zealand they dropped by more than 1 per cent. In almost all countries the growth rates for 1992 are expected to remain basically similar.

Despite moderate real wage increases, many people became much poorer in the 1980s. According to the European Commission, about 44 million people were receiving less than half the average income of their country in 1989. The European poor represented about 12 per cent of the population in 1975; by 1989 they were 18 per cent. Similarly, in the United States in the same year 32 million people were living in poverty – 13 per cent of the population.

The unemployed account for a higher proportion of poor people nowadays. In the European Community the fastest growing category of the poor is the unemployed.

If both average incomes *and* poverty are increasing, then inequality must also be on the rise. In the United Kingdom, for example, the top 10 per cent of male wage earners earned 57 per cent more than the median earnings in 1979, but by 1989 the top 10 per cent were earning 80 per cent more. Indeed, in many countries wage differentials between industries, occupation groups and the sexes seem to have widened, or at least stopped narrowing, in the 1980s.

Some of this inequality has been caused by industrial restructuring. In the United States one-third of workers displaced by plant closures or "down-sizing" are believed to have suffered permanently lower incomes. And the spread of casualisation has also contributed. Again in the United States, research suggests that 40 per cent of the increased wage inequality in the early 1980s is because more people are working part time and earning proportionately less than full-time workers.

Eastern Europe and the former Soviet Union

The traumatic political and economic changes in Eastern Europe and the former Soviet Union have already cost millions of jobs. But the worst is yet to come. Industrial production fell dramatically in 1990 (by 23 per cent in Poland and 20 per cent in Romania, for example) but unemployment increased surprisingly slowly. Indeed, apart from Poland where the rate is now around 10 per cent, unemployment levels are still generally below those of Western Europe. In the long term though, rates of 15 to 20 per cent are possible; massive unemployment in this region is a disaster waiting to happen.

Current developments are best considered by looking at three different classifications of countries.

- *The early starters* – Poland, Hungary and Czechoslovakia, where reforms have now been underway for some time.

- *The late starters* – Bulgaria and Romania, where many elements of reform, such as privatisation, have yet to be implemented, and the political situation is still very fluid.

- *The former Soviet Union* – which has also yet to make much headway in privatisation and which has distinct regional and ethnic problems.

The early starters

Of these Poland took the "big bang" approach to reform at the end of 1989 – aiming to balance the budget, fight inflation and privatise at a rapid rate. The country now has inflation more under control certainly, but by June 1991 1.6 million of its workers were unemployed and by the end of 1991 the number is expected to have risen to 2 million – 11 per cent of the labour force (see chart 2.3). And Poland still has some way to go with privatisation: the state sector still accounted for 66 per cent of employment in 1990.

In Hungary the process started earlier, and has been much more gradual. Hungarian workers started

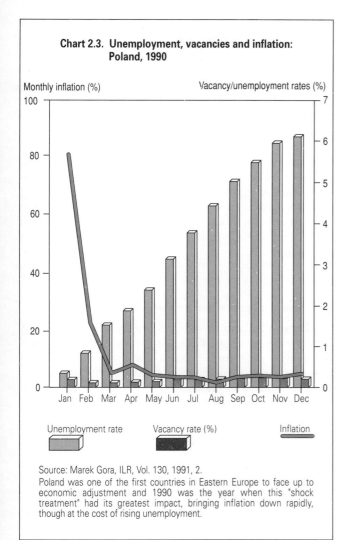

Chart 2.3. Unemployment, vacancies and inflation: Poland, 1990

Monthly inflation (%)

Vacancy/unemployment rates (%)

Unemployment rate

Vacancy rate (%)

Inflation

Source: Marek Gora, ILR, Vol. 130, 1991, 2.
Poland was one of the first countries in Eastern Europe to face up to economic adjustment and 1990 was the year when this "shock treatment" had its greatest impact, bringing inflation down rapidly, though at the cost of rising unemployment.

4.7 per cent. But many more people will lose their jobs as reforms expose the previously "hidden unemployment" in state enterprises. Exactly how many have been unemployed in this way is a matter of speculation. Some estimates suggest around 6 per cent, though for certain enterprises the figure may be as high as 25 per cent.

Workers also had to face a sharp rise in inflation in 1990 as a result of cuts in subsidies for food and other products. In the first quarter of 1991 retail prices rose by 41 per cent.

The late starters

Bulgaria liberalised prices dramatically in February 1991, with prices rising 150 per cent in one month alone. And although the Government has yet to carry out many elements of the reform, such as privatisation, many more people are already out of work. Official unemployment rose from 0.8 per cent in July 1990 (when registration formally began) to 5.4 per cent by May 1991 – though the real figure was probably higher, and is accelerating rapidly.

In Romania many of the laws affecting industry and employment started to take effect by the beginning of 1991. Relatively few workers have been laid off, however, as enterprises have preferred to adopt other measures such as reductions in working hours subsidised by the State. By June 1991 there were only 169,900 registered unemployed – about 1.5 per cent of the workforce.

The former Soviet Union

The experience of *perestroika* has not been reassuring in economic terms. National income fell sharply in the first quarters of 1991 – dropping by between 8 and 12 per cent compared with corresponding periods in 1990. Inflation was officially 10 per cent in 1990 (but probably much more in reality) and the number of unemployed rose to between 3 and 6 million (there are few reliable data on unemployment).

Substantial numbers of workers are also underemployed. The Government estimated that in 1990 the labour surplus in the state sector was about 15 to 20 per cent of total employment – up to 23 million people.

Only 16 per cent of employment was outside the state sector by mid-1990, but the proportion is rising

to face unemployment first in 1986. By July of 1991, 4.6 per cent of the workforce were officially employed. The majority – about 85 per cent – still work in the state sector, though it is intended that the proportion should be reduced to 50 per cent in three years.

Czechoslovakia's approach to reform falls somewhere in between those of Poland and Hungary. Here 1990 was a year of transition when open unemployment emerged for the first time. In the first half of the year, political and administrative changes eliminated 96,000 positions (1.3 per cent of all persons employed). Then, in January 1991, the full reform programme started and by July unemployment was rapidly. In July 1991 the Supreme Soviet passed a law which said that half of all state property would be privatised by the end of 1992 and as much as 75 per cent by the end of 1995.

The unemployed

For most countries, whatever stage of reform they have reached, unemployment levels can show considerable regional variations – ranging from 3 per cent to 14 per cent in different *voivodships* (counties) of Poland, for example, and from 1 to 10 per cent in different regions of Hungary.

Unemployment is highest where the old heavy industry dominated the local economy. In the Slovak Republic of Czechoslovakia, for example, where there have been substantial cuts in steel, in weapons production and in heavy engineering, unemployment is twice as high as in the Czech Republic.

The fate of heavy industry also affects the distribution of unemployment between men and women. In Hungary heavy industry was cut back most, so men have been the hardest hit; according to the census of January 1990, the unemployment rate was 2.9 per cent for men and 1.7 per cent for women. In other countries, such as Bulgaria and Poland, a broader range of enterprises have been affected and women have come off worst: two-thirds of the unemployed in Bulgaria, for example, are women.

Women are more likely to lose their jobs in the future. Many have been doing low-level clerical jobs for which the demand is likely to fall – partly because the break-up of large enterprises should remove the need for several layers of bureaucracy, but also because companies trying to reduce costs and increase efficiency will increasingly turn to more sophisticated information technology.

The decline of heavy industry in the former Soviet Union could also increase ethnic tension in some of the republics. In Estonia and Latvia, for example, the Russian speakers are concentrated in industry, while native Estonian and Latvian speakers work in agriculture, services and in the newer enterprises. If unemployment rises unevenly, social tensions could build up between the different groups.

Wages and incomes

Workers now find that the size of their wage packet has a more significant impact on their standard of living. This is partly because they have to pay for many social services which used to be free. But more money is also needed for consumer goods as well as for holidays and housing. Acquiring these in the past required not just money but also influence and good connections, while in a less politicised environment hard cash speaks louder.

Unfortunately for many people, their wages are worth less. While wages in the private sector are relatively high, workers in the state sector have had their incomes frozen and have to watch their purchasing power dwindle. In Bulgaria in 1990, for example, real wages dropped by 10 per cent. And in Poland by mid-1991 about 40 per cent of the population were estimated to be living at bare subsistence level. All of this has significantly altered the patterns of inequality.

Employment prospects and policies

Many of the most qualified people have moved out of the state sector, taking their clients, contacts and knowledge with them and starting up thousands of new enterprises: there are now around 400,000 registered companies (including the self-employed) in Czechoslovakia. And in Hungary, where in 1987 there were no limited companies, by 1990 there were 18,317.

Here, as elsewhere, there has also been a substantial change in the average size of enterprise. The break up of the larger state operations has produced many medium-sized enterprises (though they may still be controlled by a central unit). And private initiative is also creating many small enterprises. Around 60 per cent of companies employ 20 people or less, although these are as yet responsible for only around 10 per cent of production.

Only a small fraction of jobseekers will get work in private enterprises. Those with skill and initiative will find it easiest. But millions of others will lose their jobs as privatisation proceeds – and they will probably stay unemployed for quite some time, with neither the skills nor the knowledge to set up in business for themselves. In Hungary, in February 1991, the unemployment rate for non-manual workers was 1.5 per cent. For manual workers it was 10 per cent.

Most governments have only started to consider employment issues at a time when unemployment is rising, so they have naturally been preoccupied with "passive" employment measures such as unemployment benefits (see Chapter 4).

Governments have yet to take many active, employment-promotion steps. Some have organised public works programmes (such as street cleaning or reafforestation) for jobless workers who are hard to place or not entitled to unemployment benefit. But such programmes have negligible training content and will therefore bring few long-term benefits to the workers concerned.

Employment services, too, are generally very underdeveloped. Czechoslovakia only started to establish a system of employment offices in November 1990. And while in Poland there are 390 such offices, and in Hungary 160, they are understaffed and unable to cope with the demands placed on them. In the former Soviet Union in July 1991 the Russian Federation became the first of the republics to open employment agencies. Unemployment in Russia is estimated at 8 per cent and in Moscow alone the agencies expect to register about half a million people.

Africa

The average urban unemployment rate in sub-Saharan Africa is about 18 per cent – up from 10 per cent in the mid-1970s (see table 2.2 which collects the most recently available figures). Nine million people are unemployed in Africa's towns and cities. In the rural areas, however, unemployment is much lower – 0.3 per cent in rural Kenya in 1988/89, for example.

The employment outlook for the 1990s is gloomy. The number of productive jobs, according to ILO estimates, will increase only 2.4 per cent per year while the regional labour force is projected to expand by 3.3 per cent. As a result, the number of urban unemployed is expected to triple over the next decade from 9 to 28 million people, raising the urban unemployment rate to 31 per cent. The unemployed in Africa tend to be young and educated. Typically the youth represent between 60 and 75 per cent of the region's unemployed, though they account for only one-third of the labour force. And while education and training might be thought of as the keys to future employment, in fact in Africa the more educated you are, the less likely you are to find suitable work. Secondary school leavers are at present the most likely to be unemployed (see chart 2.4). But graduates too are finding things increasingly difficult.

Most unemployment will be converted to underemployment through jobsharing, particularly in the informal sector. Indeed the informal sector will provide the majority of new jobs – an estimated 71 per cent. The rural sector will provide 23 per cent and the modern industrial and service sector no more than 6 per cent.

Economic performance

Africa's problems are legion and have been extensively documented elsewhere. They include:

- *The debt burden* – the debt/GNP ratio reached 97 per cent in 1989 for sub-Saharan Africa, by far the highest in the world. The debt service ratio was 22 per cent.
- *Commodity price collapses* – the real world prices for cocoa, coffee, cotton and tea fell by 50 per cent between 1980 and 1990.
- *Low capital investment* – falling by 53 per cent in real per capita terms between 1980 and 1989.
- *Less investment in people* – in the United Republic of Tanzania, for example, expenditure on education and health fell by 52 per cent between the periods 1979/81 and 1985/87.

The economic decline in sub-Saharan Africa has been such that per capita GNP fell by one-fifth between 1980 and 1989, wiping out most of the gains made since independence. Around 50 per cent of the region's people now live in poverty and the number of poor people is expected to have increased by 50 per cent between 1985 and the year 2000.

About two-thirds of the countries in the region are implementing programmes of economic stabilisation

Table 2.2. Urban unemployment rates in sub-Saharan Africa, mid-1980s (percentages)

Country	Year	Rate
Botswana	1984/85	31.2
Côte d'Ivoire	1985	20.0
Ethiopia	1981	23.0
Kenya	1986	16.2
Nigeria	1985	9.7
Senegal	1986	17.3
Sierra Leone	1988	14.8
Somalia	1982	22.3
Tanzania, United Republic of	1984	21.6
Zambia	1986	19.0
Zimbabwe	1986/87	18.3

Source: National labour force surveys.

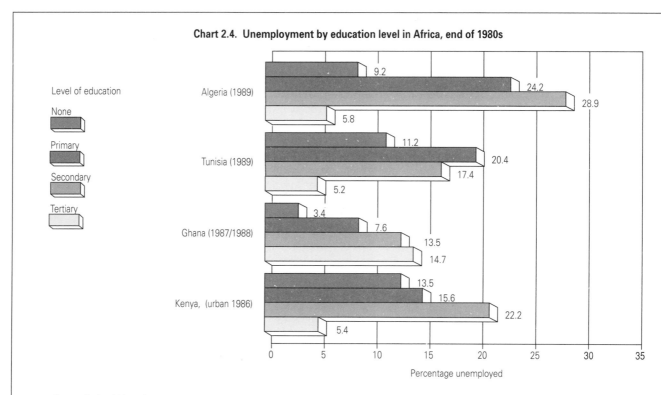

Chart 2.4. Unemployment by education level in Africa, end of 1980s

Level of education

None

Primary

Secondary

Tertiary

Algeria (1989)
9.2
24.2
28.9
5.8

Tunisia (1989)
11.2
20.4
17.4
5.2

Ghana (1987/1988)
3.4
7.6
13.5
14.7

Kenya, (urban 1986)
13.5
15.6
22.2
5.4

Percentage unemployed

Source: National labour force surveys/censuses.
The unemployed in Africa tend to be young and educated. Unemployment is often highest for those who have completed secondary education, but graduates too can have problems finding suitable employment.

and structural adjustment. Except where their resolve to restructure has attracted external finance, however, few countries can point to significant progress – inflation rates persisted at around 20 per cent throughout the 1980s, and budget deficits have often remained high. In Ghana, for example, which for some years has been considered as a test case for adjustment programmes, real GDP growth was only 2.7 per cent in 1990. No one doubts that adjustment is necessary in Africa, though there is a greater awareness that a wider variety of policies will be needed if adjustment is to bring lasting benefits (box 2.1).

Employment and wages in the modern sector

The modern sector accounts for only around 10 per cent of the labour force in sub-Saharan Africa, and in several countries it has been falling even lower in absolute terms – down 33.6 per cent in the Central African Republic between 1980 and 1986, for

example, and down 27 per cent in the Gambia between 1979 and 1986.

The public sector, too, has seen a slow-down in wage employment. According to recent ILO data, employment growth in the public services of a group of eight sub-Saharan African countries fell from 7.3 per cent per year in the period 1975-80 to 2.4 per cent in 1980-85. Thousands of public sector workers were retrenched in the 1980s – 45,000 in Ghana, for example, 40,000 in Guinea, 27,000 in the United Republic of Tanzania and 16,000 in Cameroon. However, not all retrenchment programmes have reached their target. The political ramifications are such that governments are tempted to seek out less disruptive options.

Some governments, on the other hand, have sustained high levels of public sector growth. Public sector employment in Kenya grew annually at a rate of 4.2 per cent between 1980 and 1989 – with the fastest growth among those in basic social services like education.

2.1   Three generations of adjustment

Many developing countries have re-orientated their economies since the beginning of the 1980s. They had little choice. Declining prices for raw material exports, recession in the industrial countries, high interest rates on foreign debt and the drying up of new private loans and capital – all had helped produce steep balance-of-payments deficits.

The response of many developing countries has been "structural adjustment" – to keep their economies in line with the new realities of the international market place. "Adjustment" has been the word applied to the process throughout. But in reality there have been distinct generations of adjustment policy.

1. Stabilisation

The first generation of policies was deflationary, trying to cut balance-of-payments deficits quickly – by reducing both fiscal deficits and credit limits, for example, and devaluing the currency.

The result was recession. Despite loans from the IMF and international banks, both industry and the public sector contracted. And the poorest people (particularly in the urban areas) suffered most as they lost their jobs and saw public services deteriorate.

2. Promoting production

The damaging impact on public welfare drew protests from many quarters and most people recognised that there would have to be changes. The second generation of policies put less emphasis on deflation, therefore, and more on the stimulation of the economies through deregulation and privatisation. Excessive market regulation, it was argued, as well as state ownership of enterprises, tended to reduce efficiency.

However, such changes often failed to produce the expected response from the private sector. For one thing, the recession was just too deep for many industries to revive. But there was also insufficient external finance to support the restructuring. And overall, the implementation of policies was weak.

3. Growth and human development

The debate which followed the failure of the second generation of policies (from around 1987) produced a broad international consensus on the principles which might underpin the third generation.

First, it was clear that there could be no quick solutions. Neither deflationary policies, nor deregulation and privatisation would solve the balance-of-payments problems of developing countries rapidly. Some emergency measures might be appropriate, but the real task is to restructure economies fundamentally so as to put them on a sound basis of economic growth.

Second, there was a greater awareness that social concerns had to be an integral part of the process. Not just because increased poverty and social dislocation are in themselves unacceptable, but also because future growth depends critically on a healthy, well-nourished and educated population. And this "human development" must include a high level of participation: there should be a broad social consensus on the nature of the problems and the solutions acceptable to society as a whole.

The third generation of adjustment policies is therefore much broader. It includes everything from employment creation to education and health care, to the promotion of human rights – less narrowly defined objectives certainly, but probably more realistic.

Along with a general faltering in the growth of employment, there has been a sharp fall in real wages, which for all modern sector workers dropped 30 per cent on average between 1980 and 1986. And there has been a corresponding fall in minimum wages: in a sample of 29 countries the real minimum wage fell by about 20 per cent over the period (see chart 2.5).

The decline has been most pronounced in the public sector. A recent survey of civil service pay in Africa showed that in the decade up to 1985 the real salary for the lowest grades fell by 36 per cent, and that for the highest grades by 58 per cent.

Wages have fallen much more steeply than overall per capita income, suggesting that wage earners have shouldered the bulk of the crisis. And, in response, civil servants have had to look for other sources of income – spending more time on family plots growing food, or looking for an opportunity to moonlight. In Uganda, for example, many civil servants work less than half a normal day in their primary job. And the greater the income, the greater the likelihood of moonlighting – since those with better education and contacts are in a better position to find a second job.

The informal sector

This has become the "survival sector" in urban Africa, the employer of last resort. It currently employs an estimated 61 per cent of the urban labour force. And it will be required to take up even more – generating some 93 per cent of all additional jobs in urban Africa in the 1990s.

Most informal sector enterprises are trade-related. A 1988/89 survey in Dakar, for example, showed that 72 per cent of enterprises were in commerce – with the rest in production, building trades, transport and services.

This does not mean that most of the urban labour force is self-employed. Recent studies have shown that most of the urban labour force works for wages rather than for profit. In Abidjan, for example, over two-

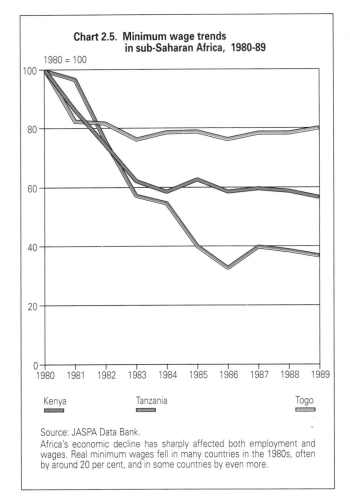

Chart 2.5. Minimum wage trends in sub-Saharan Africa, 1980-89

1980 = 100

Kenya   Tanzania   Togo

Source: JASPA Data Bank.
Africa's economic decline has sharply affected both employment and wages. Real minimum wages fell in many countries in the 1980s, often by around 20 per cent, and in some countries by even more.

is a "missing middle" between the informal and the formal. The lack of an entrepreneurial culture in Africa is sometimes blamed for this failure to progress. But there are certainly institutional obstacles:

- *A disabling environment* – many countries operate with high official standards, for workshop buildings for example, and are reluctant to relax them.
- *No fiscal incentives* – formal sector enterprises often have advantages denied to the informal, such as access to foreign exchange or permission to import goods.
- *Lack of credit* – the financial system is generally biased against informal enterprise.

Some countries, such as Kenya and the United Republic of Tanzania, have tried to promote the informal sector but have ultimately succeeded only in helping micro-enterprises (the small end of the formal sector).

Rural employment

Between two-thirds and three-quarters of people in sub-Saharan Africa make their living from agriculture. And very few of them are unemployed, or even underemployed. Indeed most people work long hours to eke out a meagre living – mostly producing for their own consumption.

Agricultural producers' prices for food have increased more rapidly than general wages and prices, so many farmers are now relatively better off and the urban-rural income gap has narrowed somewhat. But those relying on primary commodities like cocoa or cotton have seen their incomes fall. The prices which commodity producers received dropped by 54 per cent in Côte d'Ivoire in 1989, for example, and by 45 per cent in Cameroon.

A significant and growing proportion of the rural population now get income from sources other than farming – as in Kenya where the percentage contribution of non-farm income nearly doubled between the mid-1970s and the early 1980s. Most of this income comes from jobs similar to those of the urban informal sector.

Asia

Asia outperformed every other region of the world economy in the 1980s, and in 1990 the developing economies of the region achieved an average growth

thirds of households get their income solely from wages.

One effect of the increasing informalisation of the urban economy is that more women are now working. In Kenya between 1977/78 and 1986, for example, women's participation in the urban labour force rose from 39 per cent to 56 per cent. Many such women are working just to help their families survive after their male partner has lost his job or his income has dropped. Women find it easier than men to get jobs in the informal sector.

While the informal sector might be thought to be the first step on the ladder to business prosperity, in fact it is very difficult for informal entrepreneurs to build their enterprises into formal ones. Unlike in Latin America, where entrepreneurs can operate businesses all along the size spectrum, in Africa there

Table 2.3. Restructuring policies by employers in some ASEAN countries (%)

Policy	Extensive	Limited	None
Management changes	16.7	0.0	83.3
Retrenchments	45.8	12.5	41.7
In-firm training	62.5	20.8	16.7
Mechanisation/computerisation	66.7	25.0	8.5

Source: Asian Employment Programme.

rate of 5.4 per cent. Thailand had the highest figure (9.5 per cent), followed by Malaysia (9.2 per cent), the Republic of Korea (8.8 per cent) and Singapore (8.3 per cent). The lowest included the Philippines (2.7 per cent) and Hong Kong (2.5 per cent). Other countries making something of a recovery in 1990 were Bangladesh and Sri Lanka, although they did so from a very low base – moving from around 2.5 per cent in 1989 to around 5 per cent in 1990.

The Asian economies also had to adjust to the hostile economic climate of the 1980s, but they did so more successfully than most – creating jobs and improving real incomes to a much greater extent than other developing regions.

In terms of macroeconomic policy some were, of course, more successful than others. Thus both Thailand and the Philippines, for example, responded to the 1979/80 oil shock and falling primary commodity prices by stepping up public investment. But they financed this in different ways. In Thailand the resources came from domestic borrowing and direct foreign investment and this injection helped produce a sustainable revival after about 1983. The Philippines, however, financed its counter-cyclical investment through external borrowing and when interest rates started rising the economy sank under the burden of increased debt-servicing obligations.

But the actions of individual enterprises have been just as significant as those of governments. Faced with falling demand and increased energy costs, employers responded with a variety of measures, including shedding outmoded technology, reorganising production, retrenching some labour and increasing training. A study in Indonesia, the Philippines, Malaysia and Singapore asked employers the kind of measures they were taking. Their responses are summarised in table 2.3, which indicates the priority which employers gave to technological development.

A significant proportion of employers also altered their patterns of labour use. Some of the areas of change included:

- *Core workers* – reducing their numbers and replacing with temporary or casual employees. And making greater use of women, apprentices and migrants.

2.2   Subcontracting in Asia

Subcontracting has been growing steadily in Asia over the past two decades – most frequently in industries such as garments, footwear, and woodworking. With "component subcontracting", whole components are contracted out by larger firms to smaller ones and homeworkers. Then there is "labour contracting" within the enterprise, where workers are engaged, not on indefinite, but on fixed-term contracts – a feature now even of state enterprises in China.

Employers often argue that they have to move to subcontracting because overstringent employment and wage regulations impose excessive burdens on formal sector enterprises. But it seems doubtful that this can be the most important reason, since subcontracting is a feature not just of countries with relatively strict labour legislation, like India and Pakistan, but also of countries like Malaysia and the Philippines where the legislation is more liberal. Indeed, taking the example of the garments industry, a higher proportion of output is produced by subcontracted or casual labour in the liberal Philippines than in stricter Pakistan. For large-scale enterprises the reason is probably more fundamental.

Exposed to a rapidly changing competitive environment, they can become vulnerable dinosaurs if they cannot adjust rapidly to competitive pressures. The experience of industrialised countries like Japan and Italy has shown that component subcontracting has increased not only flexibility but also employment.

Other enterprises, however, are certainly trying to evade the law. This is particularly true for labour contracting. In the Philippines, for example, contract workers may work alongside regular employees and do the same job – yet earn less and have none of the fringe benefits of permanent employment. There have even been cases in Malaysia where regular workers have been sacked and re-hired as casual workers at much lower wage rates.

Unions in Asia have responded to such trends by requesting stricter legal curbs on subcontracting. But it is doubtful that this will achieve a great deal since many firms may be breaking existing laws. A more productive approach for unions may be to organise the non-permanent employees. Unions in certain cases in India and the Philippines have succeeded in making the employment of casual workers permanent after a certain period (usually one year).

- *Shifts* – increasing the numbers per day and using more overtime.
- *Pay systems* – moving from those based on working time and length of service to systems based on the performances of individuals and enterprises.
- *Training* – introducing internal schemes to aid redeployment within the enterprise.
- *Trade unions* – either reducing their influence, or establishing company unions which are easier to control.
- *Subcontracting* – to external manufacturers or to service companies (such as transport or maintenance) to work on factory premises. Some of the forms which subcontracting has taken in Asia are indicated in box 2.2.

Newly industrialised economies (NIEs)

Since this is such a diverse region, both in types of economy and in their recent experience, it is probably better to consider other recent trends through groups of countries.

- *Newly industrialised economies (NIEs)* – Hong Kong, the Republic of Korea, Singapore, and Taiwan (China). By the end of the 1980s these four economies accounted for half the manufactured exports of developing countries. They all have low unemployment rates: Hong Kong, 1.1 per cent; Republic of Korea, 2.6 per cent; Singapore, 2.2 per cent; Taiwan (China), 1.6 per cent. Much of their success to date has been based on low labour costs, combined with an effective policy framework. But as wages rise and competition from elsewhere gets fiercer, the NIEs are attempting to base their economies on higher levels of skill.

- *The prospective NIEs* – Indonesia, Thailand and Malaysia are also on their way to joining the club of newly industrialised economies, and they have had high growth rates which have helped reduce unemployment and increase wages. In Indonesia, however, population growth demands the creation of 2.5 million new jobs each year. And in Indonesia, as in other countries, there is a serious mismatch between skills and employment: around 80 per cent of high-school graduates would prefer to go into government service, and if they cannot do so will carry on studying in the hope of becoming better qualified for future openings.

Thailand still has serious problems of poverty and underemployment in parts of the country – overall 7.5 per cent of men and 4.3 per cent of women were unemployed in 1988.

Malaysia has become the second most industrialised ASEAN country after Singapore. Industry rose from 17.9 per cent of GDP in 1960 to 35.6 per cent in 1986. But it still has relatively high unemployment at 7.9 per cent.

- *Countries with respectable growth, but employment obstacles* – India and Pakistan. The economies here have performed well enough, but have relatively controlled and rigid economic systems which have hampered growth.

Both, however, have been taking steps towards deregulation. Pakistan has an economic restructuring programme which includes extensive plans for privatisation. It is also aiming to deregulate the economy and has, for example, reduced import restrictions on industrial raw materials and announced extensive exchange and payments reforms.

India, too, has announced a drastic shake-up of industrial policy designed to improve the performance of the formal sector; this employs around 11 per cent of the workforce, but it has been highly protected and productivity has been low – public enterprises have been inefficient and private industry has been tangled in a web of controls.

Most of the onus of providing new jobs has fallen, therefore, on the informal sector. During the 1980s, while the organised sector had an annual growth rate of around 2 per cent, the urban informal sector managed around 4 per cent and even 8 per cent in certain sectors such as construction. Many informal enterprises are in fact suppliers to the formal sector and have grown up around its fringes.

In 1991 India's new Government declared its intention to release controls on enterprises. Licences will no longer be needed to set up new businesses, for example, or expand old ones – which will, it is hoped, make the economy more dynamic and increase employment. Foreign investment, too, could provide more employment in the formal sector. And in order to attract investors, the rules on foreign investment have been changed to allow foreign majority holdings.

- *Countries with serious employment problems* – Bangladesh, Myanmar, Nepal, Philippines, Papua New Guinea, Sri Lanka. Here there has been low growth in output, compounded by political problems and in some cases natural disaster.

- *Economies in transition* – China, Viet Nam and Mongolia. All three are moving towards more market-based economies and discovering new employment problems on the way.

China took rapid steps in this direction up to 1989, shedding significant quantities of surplus labour and relying on market forces rather than official placement to decide where and how people should work. This exposed some problems, however, and many young and educated people found themselves without work.

The Government response was to encourage rural industries – which expanded at a phenomenal rate between 1982 and 1988. The number of private enterprises and of self-employed workers grew rapidly, many of these in the service sector.

However, in 1988, in an effort to overcome inflation, the Government introduced austerity measures. These did indeed bring down inflation, from around 20 per cent to under 5 per cent today. But growth also suffered: from 11.2 per cent in 1988 it fell to 3.6 per cent in 1989, recovering somewhat to an estimated 5.0 per cent in 1990. This had a serious impact on employment, especially in construction and in rural industries.

Viet Nam has undertaken a programme of *doi moi*, or "renovation", since 1986. It has been establishing private property rights, privatising state assets and placing a greater reliance on markets. The programme has had some success. Viet Nam increased rice production dramatically; it used to import rice but in 1989 became the world's third largest exporter.

Many Vietnamese have now become unemployed, however. About one-fifth of state enterprises have had to close because they failed to show a profit, and in 1989 nearly half a million state employees lost their jobs. The Government estimated the total number of unemployed to be 1.6 million in 1990 – though unofficial sources suggest figures several times greater. Urban unemployment is around 20 per cent.

Mongolia is also restructuring, with new laws on state enterprises and cooperatives passed in 1989 and 1990.

Poverty in the rural areas

The employment attention in this region is often concentrated on the urban areas. But in countries like India and China the mass of the population lives in the rural areas – where poverty is likely to be greatest. Indeed, while this region has in some respects been more successful than most, it also has more poor people than anywhere else in the world.

Here too, however, the story seems to be relatively optimistic. A series of studies for Asian countries in the 1980s indicates that the incidence of poverty has fallen almost everywhere. Nepal and Sri Lanka are exceptions and the position in the Philippines is unclear, but Bangladesh, China, India, Indonesia, Malaysia, Pakistan and Thailand all seem to have made progress.

The reasons, however, seem to vary from country to country. In Indonesia, for example, the poor seem to have benefited from the high growth of agriculture and rural non-farm activities, while in Pakistan remittances from overseas workers made an important contribution to the reduction of poverty. In India, special programmes targeting the rural poor, such as the Integrated Rural Development Programme which offered credit and subsidies to start up rural enterprises, have also made a contribution.

Latin America and the Caribbean

Latin America has become so much poorer in the 1990s than the 1980s that the last ten years are frequently referred to as the "lost decade". One economic indicator after another registers the decline.

- *GDP per capita* – is 9.6 per cent lower in 1990 than in 1980.
- *Consumption* – has fallen by 6 per cent.
- *The rate of investment* – fell from 21.2 per cent of GDP in the period 1975-80 to 17.8 per cent in the 1980s.
- *Inflation* – reached an average of 1,500 per cent in 1990 (though much of this is accounted for by hyperinflation in Argentina, Brazil and Peru).
- *Capital transfer* – switched direction, with Latin America and the Caribbean becoming net exporters of capital to the industrialised countries.

None of these problems is new in the continent's economic history. What is new is that they have all arisen simultaneously. And they have often been associated with a painful, but necessary, process of economic adjustment.

Economic adjustment was inevitable for many countries for a number of reasons: the drop in the

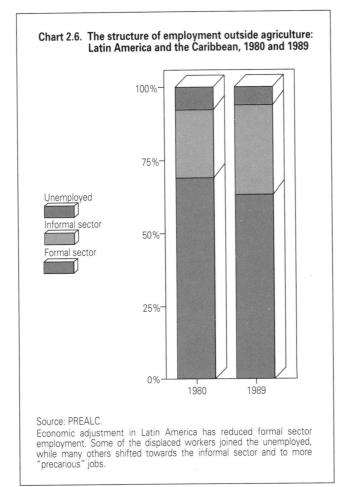

Chart 2.6. The structure of employment outside agriculture: Latin America and the Caribbean, 1980 and 1989

Unemployed

Informal sector

Formal sector

Source: PREALC.
Economic adjustment in Latin America has reduced formal sector employment. Some of the displaced workers joined the unemployed, while many others shifted towards the informal sector and to more "precarious" jobs.

Workers also found their jobs had become much less secure. The proportion working in more "precarious" ways, part time, perhaps, or on fixed-term contracts increased substantially. And more and more enterprises turned to subcontracting. The percentage of workers employed for fewer than 24 hours a week rose during the decade from 3 to 8 per cent in Panama, from 5 to 8 per cent in Argentina, and from 6 to 10 per cent in Colombia. In Greater Buenos Aires the proportion of casual workers in enterprises which employed casuals increased from 18 to 28 per cent between 1983 and 1988.

Real wages also fell at the same time. In the modern sector they fell by around 7 per cent during the period 1980-89. For certain groups of workers however, the drop was even larger – 30 per cent for those in small enterprises, 30 per cent also for public sector workers, and 42 per cent for those in the informal sector. Minimum wages in agriculture fell by 20 per cent.

Poverty has, therefore, been increasing for the region as a whole. The poverty rate has risen since 1980 from 35 per cent of the population to 44 per cent today. Currently, 183 million people have incomes which place them below the poverty line. This increase has been largely confined, though, to the urban areas where the percentage of poor households increased from 25 per cent in 1980 to 31 per cent in 1989. Poverty rates were more stable in the rural areas.

The picture is not very bright at present. But there are at least some grounds for optimism. The first half of the decade was responsible for much of the deterioration indicated above, while the second half showed some signs of recovery – particularly for certain countries. Thus, in Colombia, Chile, Uruguay and Venezuela, the rate of urban unemployment fell by between 3 and 10 percentage points after 1985. A similar pattern was noted in informal sector employment, whose share dropped after 1985 in countries like Brazil, Colombia and Chile, though it stayed relatively constant elsewhere, as in Costa Rica and Venezuela.

The trend in wages was also reversed in some countries during the second half of the decade – as in Brazil, Colombia, Chile and Uruguay though wages continued to fall in Argentina, Costa Rica, Mexico and Peru.

On the whole the experiences of individual countries have diverged more during the second half of the decade. Countries which were further along, either in

price of raw material exports; the external debt crisis; and the internal fiscal imbalances as the public sector has become increasingly indebted to the central banks and to the financial sector.

All this has had a serious impact on employment. Many workers have had to move from the formal to the informal sector (see chart 2.6). Thus, though a smaller proportion of workers were unemployed at the end of the decade than at the beginning, the proportion of those in non-agricultural work who were in the informal sector rose from 25 per cent to 31 per cent.

The shift to less productive activities also means that more of the workforce is underemployed. The total underutilisation of the workforce (underemployment plus unemployment) increased during the decade from 40 to 42 per cent.

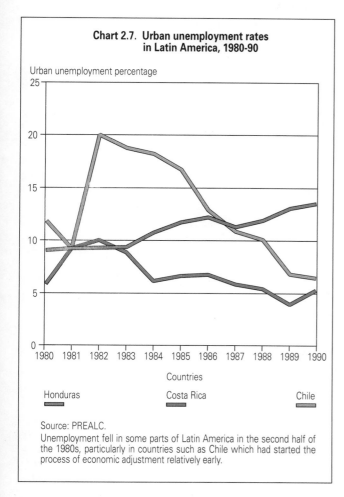

Chart 2.7. Urban unemployment rates in Latin America, 1980-90

Urban unemployment percentage

Countries

Honduras   Costa Rica   Chile

Source: PREALC.
Unemployment fell in some parts of Latin America in the second half of the 1980s, particularly in countries such as Chile which had started the process of economic adjustment relatively early.

Mexico. Marseilles, for Arab workers from the Maghreb, hoping for a job in France. Tokyo, for the Thais or Filipinos, freshly landed in Japan.

The political, economic and social transformations of recent years are causing striking new patterns and concentrations of migration. There are now 8.2 million legal immigrants in the European Community – and probably another 2 million more illegal. Some 12 million Mexicans already live in the United States and an estimated 135,000 join them illegally each year. And around 750,000 Asians have, until recently, moved each year to the Gulf. About two million Arab and Asian migrants to Iraq, Kuwait and Saudi Arabia and other Gulf states left for home prior to the Gulf war – often in distressing conditions. And thus far (August 1991) relatively few workers seem to have gone back to the Gulf. Migration itself is hardly new. Indeed, most countries are built up of layer upon layer of different ethnic groups over dozens of generations. Famine, political oppression, poverty, or just a sense of adventure, have shaped and reshaped the global community. What *is* new, however, is the speed with which people can move. Rapid communications and transport, along with accelerated population growth, have combined to allow people to respond to new opportunities quickly – and in great numbers.

This year's *World Labour Report* reviews two currently significant areas:

- *Eastern Europe and the former Soviet Union* – and the potential flows from East to West as borders open up.

- *Asia and the Pacific* – where workers are converging on Japan, the Republic of Korea, Singapore and Taiwan (China).

the process of structural adjustment, or in terms of macroeconomic balances, such as Costa Rica and Chile, seem to have had better growth and employment results than countries like Honduras which had taken fewer such measures (see chart 2.7).

Migrant workers

Families from all points east converged on Budapest's Keleti station in 1991. From the former Soviet Union, Poland, Bulgaria, Romania, they crowded into its waiting hall, just hoping for a visa maybe, or a ticket, or a train that would take them to Austria and the West.

Budapest is one of dozens of gateway cities through which the world's migrants pass. El Paso, Texas, for the "wetbacks" who crossed the Rio Grande from

Eastern Europe and the former Soviet Union

The dramatic changes in Eastern Europe and the former Soviet Union have raised the prospect of a stream of migrants across Europe on a scale not seen since the end of the Second World War.

The majority of those who have migrated so far have come from distinct ethnic groups. Romania, for example, had around 200,000 *Aussiedler*. These are ethnic Germans who have the right to return to Germany and to work. Many of these left during the upheaval following the Romanian revolution. And it looks as though most of those in Romania will have gone by the end of 1992.

Table 2.4. Ethnic migrants from Central and Eastern Europe to Western Europe, 1989 and 1990

Ethnic group	1989	1990
Germans from Poland, former USSR, Romania, etc.	377 000	400 000
Germans from former DDR	344 000	60 000*
Greeks from former USSR	11 000	17 000
Greeks from Albania	—	20 000
Turks from Bulgaria	325 000	70 000

* Before reunification
Source: ILO estimates.

But the largest numbers of *Aussiedler* – 2.5 million – are in the former Soviet Union, many of them descendants of people whom Stalin forcibly relocated to Kazakhstan. Around 150,000 of these left in 1990, taking advantage of exit visas which the former Soviet Union used to grant for the reunification of families. In an attempt to persuade the others to stay, Germany has secured the right to set up German schools and libraries, as well as radio and television stations, within the former Soviet Union.

However, the majority of those leaving the former Soviet Union in 1990 – about 300,000 – went to Israel. The Jews are still one of the largest ethnic groups in the former Soviet Union (1.5 million), though their numbers are falling rapidly both because of migration and because of an ageing population.

Table 2.4 shows the flows for ethnic groups to Western Europe in recent years.

Temporary migrants

But many people also move from East to West on a seasonal basis. Cars bulging with Polish migrant workers head down the *Autobahns* through Germany, France and elsewhere – for fruit picking, for example, or for temporary jobs in hotels, catering and construction. At the peak of the agricultural season around 600,000 Poles work illegally in Germany.

The financial incentive is clear enough, with a considerable gap in earning power between Eastern and Western Europe. Polish workers in 1988 would have had to work eight times longer than their counterparts in the Federal Republic of Germany to earn the money for a car. Hungarians would have had to work eight times longer for a kilo of butter; and

Bulgarians five times longer to buy a colour TV. Even a modest salary paid to an emigrant or seasonal worker in the European Community has in recent years been convertible (on the black market) to around six to eight times the salary which they would get at home.

To soak up such earnings, a flourishing series of parallel markets offer land, houses, and goods and services for which only Western currencies are accepted. Housing has been one of the most important items on sale as there is a severe shortage in Eastern and Central Europe.

The situation is most critical in Poland, which in 1988 was short of 1.2 million dwellings. Around 28 per cent of families shared an apartment with another family, while the waiting list for a cooperative apartment was ten years. Houses are available on the free market but at prices beyond the reach of most working people so the option of working two or three years abroad to pay for this is certainly attractive.

Future migration possibilities

Many more people may now consider leaving for much longer periods, perhaps permanently. As governments loosen travel restrictions and economic conditions worsen, the pull of healthier Western economies could prove irresistible. Estimates of the numbers likely to move can only be speculative. One survey carried out in Czechoslovakia, Hungary, Poland and around Moscow in mid-1991 suggested that nearly two million people are definitely intending to leave – and most of these would bring their families. Another 7 to 20 million are thinking about it. The main incentive is "to get a better standard of living". This was the reason given by 57 per cent of Czechs, 51 per cent of Hungarians, 49 per cent of Poles and 47 per cent of Russians.

The former Soviet Union has the greatest potential for migration. A new law allowing anyone with a passport to leave was approved "in principle" in May 1991 but does not come fully into effect until January 1993. One of the authors of the statute believes that the emigration is likely to continue at roughly the present level – about 500,000 per year – though accepts that temporary migration will increase substantially. The Minister of Labour of the former USSR suggested in 1991 that up to two million would leave if they could, and that 6 million would seriously consider emigrating. The All-Union Centre for the Study of Public Opinion in the former USSR

2.3　　　　　**Employment opportunities for migrants in Western Europe**

There are numerous employment opportunities in Western Europe for which Central and Eastern Europeans are qualified, in which they would be interested, and which could be exploited for mutual benefit.

Normal work – there are shortages in a variety of industries and services. These include openings for skilled factory workers, construction workers, nurses, and auxiliary personnel in cleaning enterprises.

Project-tied work – through which a Central or Eastern European employer brings workers from his or her country of origin to work on a specific project in Western Europe. In Germany this is known as *Werkvertrag* and it has offered work to 30,000 Central and East Europeans each year. Employers and workers frequently pick up new skills in the process.

Seasonal work – France and Switzerland have long-established migration programmes for work which depends on seasonal

conditions. This normally includes agriculture, hotel and catering and (in some countries) construction. Many Central and Eastern Europeans already work illegally in this way. Their presence could be put on a legal footing and their number increased.

Frontier work – where migrants work in a neighbouring country but return home at least once a week. This already happens to a minor extent. Since December 1990, for example, workers who return to Czechoslovakia each night (or who stay over at their workplace for a maximum of two nights a week) can obtain work permits for Austria. And Western European employers might consider locating plants and services close to borders to help promote such schemes.

Training – could be either a primary or ancillary purpose of such employment. Bilateral agreements could define how this might be organized.

---

conducted a poll in June 1990 which suggested similar figures.

Whether the citizens of the former USSR will manage to leave in practice is another matter, for they will find political obstacles replaced by bureaucratic and financial ones. The first problem will be to get a passport; the waiting list is currently two years long. It could also be difficult for migrants to get transport, certainly by air. Migrants will need a fair amount of cash, too. The passport alone costs 1,000 roubles (about three month's average salary). And on top of that there will be the difficulty of acquiring sufficient hard currency to make the trip. Those who leave at present on overseas visits are only allowed to take US$200 in foreign currency, and that exchanged at the official rate (which comes to about a year-and-a-half's salary).

Receiving countries

The choice of destinations is quite varied. When asked where they would like to go, Russians and Poles make the United States and Canada their first choice, while Hungarians would choose Germany. In practice, most migrants are likely to head for Germany, which is easier to reach and offers some prospect of work.

People may be free to leave their home countries, but it is unclear at present how they will be received in Western Europe. At present the Poles have the greatest freedom of movement. Following the Schengen agreement in 1991, they do not require

visas to enter Germany, France, the Benelux countries, Italy, Spain or Portugal. They would still, however, need a work permit to get a job. A similar agreement is likely to be concluded for people from Hungary and Czechoslovakia.

The European Community as a whole is currently deciding who will be offered visa-free entry to the single market. From Eastern Europe it looks as though the EC will accept non-visa arrivals only from Hungary and Czechoslovakia – the two potentially richer countries of Central and Eastern Europe whose citizens (unlike those of Poland) have not in the past shown any great propensity to migrate. Poland is at present excluded from this arrangement.

Citizens of the former USSR will have more limited options and may be tempted to migrate illegally. Quite a few have already done so. Around 80,000 now live illegally in Poland and another 60,000 in Hungary. Indeed, there is a risk for Poland that many more citizens of the former USSR might get that far and no further.

Benefits and costs of migration

Migration brings potential benefits to both sides. Germany, for example, despite the unemployment in the East following unification, could well make productive use of migrants as labour shortages increase, as the workers now entering the labour market come from the low birth-rate years. On the other hand, an uncontrolled flow of migrants could cause considerable disruption.

Workers who migrate will, if only temporarily, relieve unemployment pressures in their home countries, as well as gaining experience of work in a competitive environment and sending valuable remittances. But if they are obliged to work illegally, with the risk of low wages and exploitative working conditions, they will derive little benefit.

A "brain drain" is another concern. A study carried out in the former USSR found that those most likely to move were young people living in urban areas. And of those wanting to go abroad, 27 per cent had higher education and 34 per cent some vocational or technical training.

A cooperative migration policy

An uncontrolled movement of workers could damage both sending and receiving countries. But there is at present no international body in Europe able to regulate the employment of migrant workers. So if the process is to take place on a cooperative basis, individual countries will have to make a series of bilateral agreements. Such agreements could cover a wide number of issues, including the number of workers permitted, the jobs they would do, how they would travel and where they would live (see box 2.3).

There have, however, been few such negotiations as yet – though Germany has an agreement with the former Soviet Union for 15,000 workers, mostly tied to particular projects, and Belgium has agreed with the former Soviet Union and Poland to take 500 workers from each country.

In 1991 Ministers of Labour from many of the sending and receiving countries held some of their first meetings – and placed particular emphasis on the potential for training Central and Eastern European workers, especially during the transition period.

Asia and the Pacific

Other regions of the world struggle with pacts, and federations, and economic integration, but the Pacific Rim seems to be achieving much the same result on a more informal basis. Capital and labour are swirling around the region in currents of ever increasing complexity.

The more dynamic economies like Japan, the Republic of Korea, Singapore and Taiwan (China), export their capital to build factories in countries where labour is cheaper – like China, Malaysia, the Philippines and Thailand. But labour is also streaming towards capital. Annual flows of workers to the more developed economies have increased from about 30,000 per year in 1980 to around 150,000 today. And these are just the official figures. Taking illegal migrants into account the numbers of workers on the move each year is probably at least 300,000.

Investment flows

Investment was stepped up in earnest in the 1960s. Japan, seeing labour costs rising, started to move the more labour-intensive processes overseas. Initially the destinations were often the Republic of Korea and Taiwan (China). Then, when costs began to rise there too, some production migrated to yet cheaper areas like Indonesia, Malaysia, the Philippines and Thailand.

Location decisions nowadays are very finely tuned to labour costs. High technology, with its research and development, often takes place in Japan. Processes with intermediate requirements tend to go to the NIEs like the Republic of Korea and Taiwan (China), and the most labour-intensive assembly work tends to take place in ASEAN countries like Indonesia or Malaysia. Thus, Sony now makes videorecorders by taking parts from Singapore and Taiwan (China), and assembling them in Malaysia (see box 2.4).

The Republic of Korea, Singapore and Taiwan (China), have in turn become significant overseas investors. Facing rising labour costs at home, they too are relocating some of their own production to the less developed countries of the region. Employers in Singapore, for example, would have to pay the equivalent of US$400 a month for skilled labour, but just 12 miles away, on the Indonesian island of Batam, they need only pay US$100 a month for a factory hand, so production can be conveniently split between the two countries.

Labour migration

Some managers usually migrate along with capital and many ASEAN countries have large and growing Japanese, Taiwanese and Korean communities. About 30,000 Japanese live and work in Thailand, for example, and 5,000 live in Malaysia where there are nearly 250 Japanese manufacturing operations.

2.4   Japan's distinctive multinationals

Multinational enterprises (MNEs) now employ around 65 million workers around the world. Of the top 343 companies, the largest number come from the United States (153) followed by Germany and Japan (37 each), the United Kingdom (31) and France (17).

Most overseas employment by MNEs is in other industrialised countries. Thus US multinationals have 69 per cent of their employees in industrialised countries and 31 per cent in developing countries. The figures for Germany and Italy are similar, but for Sweden and Switzerland the proportion in industrialised countries is much more – 81 per cent.

Japan is the exception here. The expansion of Japanese companies into other parts of Asia means that the majority of their employees (62 per cent) are in developing countries.

MNE employment actually declined in the early 1980s due to the general fall in international economic activity. At this point many took the opportunity to rationalise their production, divesting certain enterprises, concentrating on core activities and attempting to cut costs through world-wide economies of scale.

In the second half of the 1980s, however, they started to expand again, though this time mostly through mergers and acquisitions – shuffling ownership to take advantage of more liberal international trade regimes. Japan is again the exception here. Japanese companies have expanded by establishing their own subsidiaries in Europe and North America, because of trade friction and fears of protectionist measures against imports from Japan.

But the expansion has not been limited to large companies. Many specialised small and medium-sized enterprises have attempted to establish niche positions in overseas markets by acquisitions and alliances – as with Canadian and Italian enterprises which have acquired US companies. And many smaller companies from Japan as well as Hong Kong, the Republic of Korea, Singapore and Taiwan (China) have been investing overseas. According to a recent survey, foreign subsidiaries or affiliates of Hong Kong companies employed over 100,000 people in 1989 and produced 13 per cent of the companies' manufacturing output.

The greatest area of expansion into developing countries has been in export processing zones – which, world-wide, now employ about two million people. Indeed, the majority of new multinational investment in developing countries may well be in such zones – primarily in textiles and clothing, electronics, automobile parts (in Mexico) and more recently in data processing – as in Jamaica and Barbados.

Such managerial and technical staff do need work permits, but these are not difficult to get.

For unskilled workers the situation is rather different. If they want to move from the Philippines to Malaysia, or from Indonesia to Japan for example, they will not find it so easy. Most countries prefer to balance labour and capital by exporting capital rather than by importing labour. There can be a number of reasons for this:

- *Fear of social disruption* – some countries regard the European experience with trepidation. They know they cannot offer jobs to everyone who wants to come, so they want to control migration, or prevent it. Japan, for example, is concerned about the social effects that extensive migration could have on a relatively homogeneous society.

- *The desire to speed up structural change* – the availability of cheap labour can remove the incentive to increase productivity. The Government in Taiwan (China), for example, is keen to move away from labour-intensive production.

- *Trade union resistance* – trade unions, such as those in Hong Kong, fear that incoming foreigners may keep wages low.

Japan

Japan is the only developed country not to have relied on legal foreign workers to overcome labour shortages. It has instead exported many of its labour-intensive processes and increased the productivity of those industries it kept at home.

But the shortages now seem much more acute. The annual rate of growth in the labour force will dip to 0.8 per cent in 1989-95 and 0.4 per cent in 1995-2000. And the absolute size of the labour force will decline in the twenty-first century. Currently there are 1.46 vacancies for every jobseeker – the highest rate for 17 years.

The causes are partly demographic. The birth rate is dropping and the number of children in Japan is now the least since records began in 1920.

The structure of production has also been changing – less manufacturing, more construction and services. And while manufacturing (for large companies at least) can be relocated overseas, this can hardly be done with construction and services.

Finally, young people are rejecting some of the jobs on offer. They are more educated and more choosy about the work they will do, tending to avoid what in Japanese are the three "K's" – *kitanai, kiken* and *kitsui*; (and in English three "Ds" – dirty, dangerous and difficult). Construction is a three-K industry and in the midst of a building boom Japanese construction is facing a 39 per cent labour shortage. But services are suffering too. The number of taxi-drivers in Tokyo dropped by 7,000 between 1983 and 1988.

The Government has resisted filling the gaps with unskilled foreign labour – concerned about the impact that this might have on Japanese society and on demands that immigrants might place on housing and other services. Indeed, the position became even firmer with the revised immigration law of June 1990, which further refined the classifications of permitted workers.

The new law did make some concessions, particularly for foreign nationals of Japanese descent. Hundreds of thousand of Japanese emigrated to Latin America, for example, earlier this century. Japan would be happy to reabsorb them or their children as immigrants and 50,000 are thought to have entered the country in the last six months of 1990, mostly from Brazil and Peru.

But the policy of not permitting other unskilled workers was reiterated. And now employers hiring such illegal workers, or brokers supplying them, can be imprisoned for up to three years and fined up to 2 million yen (US$6,000). Workers too can be imprisoned and fined.

The Japanese Trade Union Federation (RENGO) has also opposed the import of foreign workers, arguing like the Government that many of the gaps could be filled by employing greater numbers of women and older people – and by decentralizing more production away from the Tokyo area. They also point out the dangers of exploitative conditions for foreign workers.

No one knows exactly how many illegal workers there are. The Government, says 100,000, though industrialists have claimed up to 500,000. Mostly they enter Japan as tourists. Some are happy to stay just the three months that the visitors visa allows, working 12-14 hours a day, seven days a week to make as much money as they can. Others overstay their visa. Generally they use job brokers to find work for them for a fee – up to 100,000 yen (US$600) per job. And employers, for all the risks they run, feel obliged to take them on, since very few local people apply for factory jobs paying around 250,000 yen (US$1,500) a month. The work that illegal immigrants tend to do is indicated in charts 2.8a and 2.8b.

People can also work by bending the employment rules. Around 30,000 students, for example, entered

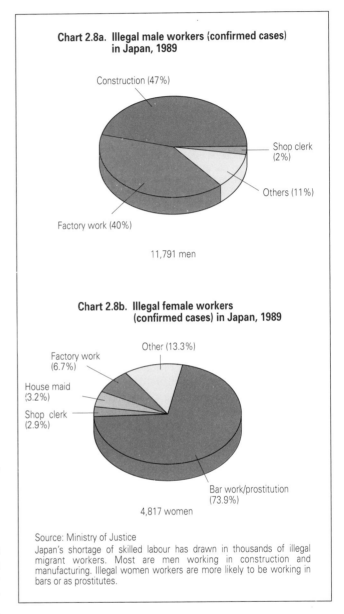

Chart 2.8a. Illegal male workers (confirmed cases) in Japan, 1989

Construction (47%)
Shop clerk (2%)
Others (11%)
Factory work (40%)

11,791 men

Chart 2.8b. Illegal female workers (confirmed cases) in Japan, 1989

Other (13.3%)
Factory work (6.7%)
House maid (3.2%)
Shop clerk (2.9%)
Bar work/prostitution (73.9%)

4,817 women

Source: Ministry of Justice
Japan's shortage of skilled labour has drawn in thousands of illegal migrant workers. Most are men working in construction and manufacturing. Illegal women workers are more likely to be working in bars or as prostitutes.

in 1990. They are allowed to work up to four hours daily. In reality, many students supposedly learning the Japanese language are actually putting in ten hours or more work a day and rarely showing up for their classes. Then there are those who come in as "trainees" (37,000 in 1990). These are supposed to be learning skills at the workplace, but in practice many employers use trainees to offset labour shortages.

The Japanese Government says that the new law is having the desired effect – and that employers in particular are anxious to avoid imprisonment. The Government is also deporting an increasing number of foreign workers each year. In 1990 a record 29,884 were sent home – 46 per cent more than the previous year. The greatest number of these were from Bangladesh (19.8 per cent), followed by the Republic of Korea (18.5 per cent) and then Malaysia (14.9 per cent).

Despite the new regulations, public opinion seems actually to be in favour of allowing more immigration. A government survey published in 1991 reported that 71 per cent of those questioned favoured allowing unskilled foreign workers to work in Japan, although 56 per cent would attach certain conditions, such as limits on their periods of stay.

The business community is also arguing for a different approach. Even the Bank of Japan describes the employment of foreign workers as "an urgent issue which requires review from every angle". And employers frequently ask the Government to reconsider their position. One suggestion from the Japan Food Service Association, representing 336 major Japanese restaurant operators, is that one per cent of the total labour requirement (about 600,000 jobs) should be opened up to foreign workers. Allowing immigration for unskilled labour on a more systematic basis would, they argue, help guarantee them the same working conditions and wages as Japanese.

The newly industrialised economies

The four newly industrialised economies (NIEs): Hong Kong, Republic of Korea, Singapore and Taiwan (China), are all facing problems similar to those of Japan, though they are responding in different ways.

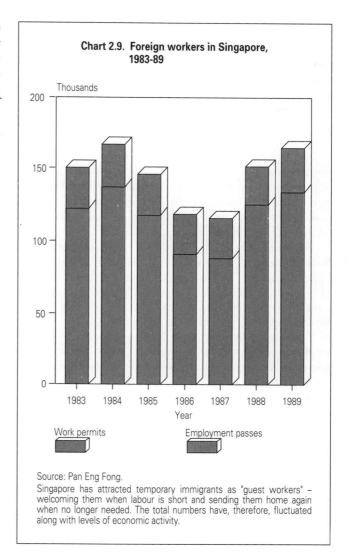

Chart 2.9. Foreign workers in Singapore, 1983-89

Source: Pan Eng Fong.

Singapore has attracted temporary immigrants as "guest workers" – welcoming them when labour is short and sending them home again when no longer needed. The total numbers have, therefore, fluctuated along with levels of economic activity.

Labour shortages

All four are short of labour. In Taiwan (China), for example, the labour force contracted slightly for the first time in 1990. Unemployment has stayed under 2 per cent for the last five years, and the Government's Council on Economic Planning and Development projects a shortage of roughly 120,000 unskilled and semi-skilled workers by 1996.

Similarly, in the Republic of Korea, a 1991 report from the Ministry of Labour estimated that the manufacturing sector was short of 190,000 workers. The unemployment rate has been falling steadily, and is now 2.9 per cent.

As in Japan, the shortages are caused by a slowing in population growth combined with increasing levels of education. In the Republic of Korea, for example, a survey by the Institute of Social Sciences shows that 95 per cent of high-school pupils want to go on to college and 18 per cent of pupils in vocational high schools hope to continue their studies rather than take a job.

Hong Kong faces similar problems of slowing population growth and higher aspirations but here these are compounded by emigration which each year carries away 45,000 of probably its most skilled and educated workers.

Previous immigration policies

Previous policies on the unskilled overseas migrants have varied from absolute prohibition, as in the Republic of Korea, to the relatively open approaches of Hong Kong and Taiwan (China). China has supplied most of the migrants in these cases and immigration has either been legally permitted or not too closely monitored.

Singapore has also taken in substantial numbers of immigrants – indeed, it has one of the highest dependencies on immigrant labour in Asia. There are more than 150,000 foreign workers (out of a total workforce of 1.3 million). Of these most are Malaysian and Filipinos.

But immigration to Singapore has been very carefully controlled. Immigrants here have always been "guest workers" – brought in when labour became very short, then expelled when no longer wanted. The way the numbers have fluctuated according to the business cycle is indicated in chart 2.9.

Employers in Singapore have been able to import workers (without their families) on two-year contracts but only up to a certain percentage of their workforce – currently 50 per cent for construction and 40 per cent for manufacturing. Each employer has to pay the Government a flat levy for each worker who is not a college graduate and earns less than the equivalent of US$900 a month. The levy can be up to US$200 a month.

Moving up the technology scale

However, all the NIEs are looking for a change of direction. They see the next phase of their development as a move to higher technology and higher productivity – and are nervous that allowing more migrants in would delay this.

High wage costs have to some extent already triggered the process. In Taiwan (China), for example, between 1985 and 1989 average real monthly wages increased 53.8 per cent while productivity only went up 37.2 per cent. Wage levels are now between three and seven times higher than in South-East Asian countries and ten to 15 times higher than in mainland China. As a result, more than 80 per cent of the shoe-making enterprises that Taiwan had five years ago have since left the island for mainland China.

But the Government is intent on accelerating the process. Its modernisation programme is based on a six-year plan which will involve spending US$143 billion on infrastructure projects. Unfortunately

though, the construction industry is the hardest hit by the labour shortage – needing around 45,000 more workers to complete even existing projects.

Singapore too has fairly successfully restructured the economy towards higher technology industries. But it also has problems meeting the demand for labour.

Current policies towards immigrants

All four NIEs are now taking a fairly tough line, both on the arrival of future unskilled workers and on those currently working illegally.

Taiwan (China) announced that from 1 March 1991 it would enforce its ban on foreign workers. At that point there were an estimated 90,000 illegal workers of whom 22,000 gave themselves up before the deadline. Those remaining now face fines equivalent to US$1,000 and have to leave at their own expense. The largest group volunteering to leave were Malaysians, followed by Filipinos, Indonesians and Thais. Companies can still apply to import a small number of foreign labourers, but only under very strict rules. Such foreign workers are paid 50 per cent less than the locals, are housed in company camps, are granted seven day's annual leave and are provided with a return ticket home.

The Republic of Korea maintains its ban. It does have a small number working illegally – unofficial estimates suggest about 10,000. About 1,000 were caught and deported in 1990.

Korean employers have been pressing for a relaxation of the current restrictions – perhaps issuing permits for foreign workers for specific projects, for a limited period. But the Government seems set against such an option and, in an attempt to fill the gap, it announced in 1991 that 10,000 conscripts would be allowed to swap their military service for a five-year period in industry. Hong Kong is also much more restrictive nowadays in its issue of work permits. In 1990 it issued permits for 12,000 semi-skilled workers, for example. But the trade unions protested vigorously even at this level, arguing that the economy was growing weaker and that the country should instead accelerate the introduction of technologically more advanced production. Singapore takes a harder line than most on illegal employment of immigrants. Both employers and workers can now be caned if caught. But it does not propose to ban such workers altogether, merely to continue to control their numbers.

One innovative proposal in Singapore is an auction for immigrant workers. In March 1991 the Government suggested that employers wanting to take on unskilled foreign workers beyond their current allowances should tender for the necessary certificates. Such certificates would not be linked with named workers, who would be free to change jobs as usual, and the certificates could also be sold subsequently if employers no longer needed them.

Employers are unsympathetic to the idea, believing that the uncertain outcome of an auction would make it difficult for them to plan ahead. Trade unions are in favour, though they argue that in the long term the country's dependence on foreign labour should not exceed 15 per cent of the workforce.

Chapter **3**

Labour relations

The 1980s and early 1990s have seen some radical shifts in labour relations. In the industrial market economies employers have become more assertive. Technical innovation and high unemployment have helped them transform both their production methods and their relationship with the workforce. And trade unions have been more on the defensive.

In Eastern Europe and the former Soviet Union, however, the trade unions have been the main actors – working with new governments to develop new forms of political and economic democracy and facing up to the idea that there *is* such a thing as labour relations. Employers here have yet to emerge as a significant autonomous group.

In most developing countries it is governments that tend to dominate formal labour relations. The trend here, though, may be for government control to slacken – at least in Africa, where multi-party democracy is appearing on the horizon, and in Latin America where electoral democratisation is close to complete.

Industrial market economies

Persistently high unemployment rates. The switch from manufacturing to services. The rise of part-time and other "new" forms of work. Working life in industrial market economies has become much more diverse in recent years. And there has been a corresponding tendency to individualise labour relations and to decentralise collective bargaining.

But labour relations systems vary greatly between one country and another – even among countries with relatively similar economies.

Trade unions

Trade union influence certainly differs widely from one country to another – as can be seen in chart 3.1.

Membership tends to be higher in Europe (with the notable exceptions of France and Spain) than in the United States, and higher in smaller countries than larger ones.

In most countries the trend over recent decades was downwards until the end of the 1980s. Although unions made substantial gains in the 1970s, they lost around 5 million members in the OECD countries in the subsequent decade. The sharpest falls were in the United States, the United Kingdom and France, but membership in most countries either fell, or grew at a slower rate. For the OECD countries as a whole, the average proportion of workers in unions – the "density rate" – dropped from 37 per cent in 1975 to 28 per cent in 1988. Even this will underestimate the real falls, since in some countries like Italy an increasing proportion of union membership has consisted of retired workers. Declining unionisation has been attributed to a number of factors, including:

- *High unemployment* – not just because there are fewer people employed but also because employers find it easier to resist unions and discourage membership.

- *New kinds of job* – flexible production systems and the rapidly expanding services sector make it much more difficult for unions to organise.

- *New kinds of worker* – temporary, part-time or contract workers are less likely to join unions.

- *Government action* – trade union legislation in some countries has been tightened, making recognition harder, de-recognition easier and limiting the right to strike.

- *Union weakness* – many unions have been forced to concede crucial representation rights.

There are signs, though, that in recent years union density levels have now stabilised in most countries with even slight increases in some countries – as in the

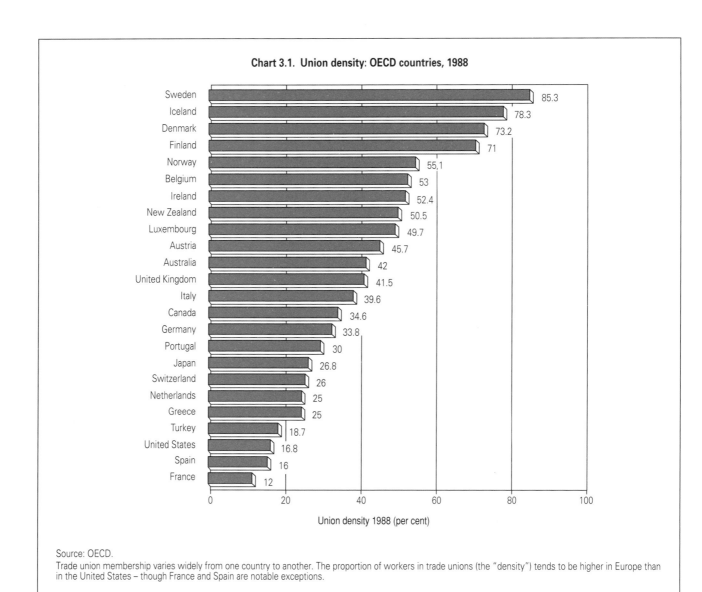

Chart 3.1. Union density: OECD countries, 1988

Country	Union density 1988 (per cent)
Sweden	85.3
Iceland	78.3
Denmark	73.2
Finland	71
Norway	55.1
Belgium	53
Ireland	52.4
New Zealand	50.5
Luxembourg	49.7
Austria	45.7
Australia	42
United Kingdom	41.5
Italy	39.6
Canada	34.6
Germany	33.8
Portugal	30
Japan	26.8
Switzerland	26
Netherlands	25
Greece	25
Turkey	18.7
United States	16.8
Spain	16
France	12

Union density 1988 (per cent)

Source: OECD.
Trade union membership varies widely from one country to another. The proportion of workers in trade unions (the "density") tends to be higher in Europe than in the United States – though France and Spain are notable exceptions.

Netherlands and the former Federal Republic of Germany.

Collective bargaining

The three main levels of bargaining are all used in the industrial market economies.

- *Central* – for the whole country – as in Finland for example, .where employers, workers and the Government conclude central agreements on macroeconomic and wage policies (the current

one runs from 1990 to 1992). And in Portugal a central accord was signed in 1990, covering many issues from salaries to vocational training.

- *Sectoral* – for one industry. This is the dominant form in Germany, where the agreement signed for the engineering industry tends to set the pattern for other sectors. A similar system applies in Austria.

- *Enterprise* – for individual companies – the normal form in the United States, Japan and the United

---

3.1   Multinational consultation in Europe

1992 offers multinational companies new opportunities in Europe for cross-national production and trade. But does it offer anything to their workforces? A series of agreements in recent years suggests that changes are on the way.

- *Thomson-Grand Public* – with the European Metalworkers Federation established in 1985 what has been called the "first European works council", with a Liaison Committee which includes workers from France, Germany, Italy, Spain and the United Kingdom.

- *BSN-Gervais Danone* – with the International Union of Food Workers (IUF) set up in 1986 a permanent mechanism for international consultation covering plants in seven countries: Austria, Belgium, France, Germany, Italy, the Netherlands and Spain.

- *Bull* established in 1988 a European information committee with trade union representatives from 12 European countries.

- *Nestlé* – met in 1990 with IUF, ECF-IUF and national trade union officials in the first of what are expected to be a series of annual meetings.

- *Volkswagen* since 1990 has had a European-level works council with representatives from VW, Audi and Seat (Spain) which will soon include joint ventures from Eastern Europe such as VW-Skoda (CSFR).

- *Elf Aquitaine* in July 1991 established a European Information and Consultation Committee.

These are some of the successes. There have also been attempts with other companies, though these failed in the end to produce an agreement – as with Unilever, Gillette, Digital and Opel.

International meetings between unions and management are, of course, nothing new. Even in the early 1970s companies like Nestlé, BSN and Thomson arranged similar meetings, though most were ad hoc and did not lead to any permanent machinery. Why the renewal of interest? There may be a number of factors.

1. *International instruments* have appeared which recognise trade unions' need for information on multinational enterprises (MNEs) – including the OECD guidelines (1976) and the ILO Tripartite Declaration (1977).

2. *International proposals* have also been made, within the EEC and from the UN, which although not formally adopted have focused attention on information requirements.

3. *The internal market* – from 1993 this will allow companies to relocate more easily across national borders and require more sharing of information.

None of the agreements above envisages international bargaining (which was considered a possibility in the 1970s). They are limited to information and consultation. And a further contrast with earlier agreements is that the parties entered into them voluntarily, rather than reacting to dramatic events like plant closures.

Thus far the meetings are limited to Europe, although not confined to the EC. Nestlé, for example, has declined to extend the practice to North America (though agreed to keep the matter under consideration). Such meetings are also common within Scandinavia though no more than two or three Nordic countries are usually involved.

It is too soon to say if such meetings do represent a genuine trend. However, a couple of recent events may sustain them. First, a proposed EC draft directive requires companies with over 1,000 workers operating in at least two member States (with at least 100 workers in each) to have "Euro works councils". And the Nordic Council has voted to consider a similar approach.

The momentum could be sustained by a greater use of the trade union "World Councils" for the workers of individual multinationals. These are organised by the international trade secretariats who invite managements to participate. SKF, the Swedish engineering company, for example, attends the SKF World Council meeting. And increasing such contacts could help demonstrate what can be achieved through greater cross-national cooperation.

Kingdom. However, even enterprise agreements may in practice be linked to each other. In the United Kingdom, for example, the agreement signed by workers for the Ford Motor Company often sets the going rate for other agreements. And in Japan individual trade unions agree amongst themselves in the annual "spring offensive" – the *shunto* – what their range of demands should be before they each negotiate with individual enterprises. However, all three levels can operate in the same country – as in Australia, Belgium, Finland, France, Ireland, Italy and Portugal. Here the sectoral form dominates but central negotiations and enterprise bargaining also play a part.

If there is a trend in Europe, however, it is towards more decentralised bargaining. Sectoral bargaining remains important in most countries, but central bargaining is becoming relatively less significant while enterprise bargaining is gaining ground. But some unions doubt the advisability of taking the enterprise bargaining route. Even in the United Kingdom the Trades Union Congress has now suggested that a system of coordinated bargaining, more centralised and over a shorter time period, might be a better way to fight inflation.

One other possibility for labour-management relations is consultation at an international level – between multinational enterprises and international trade unions. This is considered in box 3.1.

The scope of collective agreements

Trade unions may have fewer members but their influence goes far beyond their own membership because the agreements they reach are often extended to cover the whole of the relevant workforce, unionised or not. Thus in Spain only 16 per cent of employees are unionised but collective agreements cover 82 per cent of the workforce. Similarly, in Australia, 53 per cent of the workforce is organised in unions, while almost 80 per cent are covered by national awards or collective agreements. And in France 12 per cent of the workforce is unionised, but 80 per cent of workers benefit from the agreements – leading to suggestions that France is moving towards "unionism without members".

The situation is somewhat different in the United States, however. Here trade unions have only slightly more impact than their memberships might warrant since management is not obliged to bargain with unions if they do not represent at least 50 per cent of the relevant workforce.

Some employers extend agreements voluntarily, but others are forced to do so by law. In Germany, for example, in sectors such as construction, textiles and retailing, where rates of unionisation are low, the Minister of Labour uses "legal extension" to bring union-negotiated benefits to non-unionised labour.

Subjects for agreement

The nature of negotiations has changed somewhat in recent years. Unions previously tended to bargain for "more of the same" (for wages, or holidays) or "less of the same" (for working hours). But from the mid-1980s unions have become more interested in qualitative improvements, such as employment security, training and job satisfaction.

Employers too, have been changing their perspective. Searching for ways of improving their competitive position, they have been looking for more flexibility from the workforce. They have, for example, tended to resist wage indexation and have tried instead to link pay to business success. They are also looking for more flexibility in working hours, a subject covered in more detail in Chapter 4.

Unions argue that flexible employment can finish up as "precarious" employment (see Chapter 2). So they have often strongly opposed the recruitment of casual or temporary workers (who have sometimes had to seek protection through the law rather than

through trade unions). In some cases, however, unions have included such workers in collective agreements. In France, for example, they signed an "interoccupational agreement" which gave better protection to such workers. Elsewhere they have been included in agreements only for the purpose of limiting their numbers – as in the Netherlands in 1990, where an agreement in the dairy industry is based on the proportion of such workers being reduced from 17 per cent to 10 per cent.

Human resource management

Human resource management is a rather diffuse concept, though substituting "people" for "human resources" may make things clearer. Many employers would prefer to deal with individual workers on issues like job security, or income or other benefits. They want to make the best use of the people at their disposal – through training, consultation, the organisation of work, or indeed anything which can help their operation run more smoothly.

But how do unions respond if employers have a closer relationship with the workforce? This could after all squeeze them out of the picture. In practice many unions have virtually stood by and watched – either because they were technically ill-equipped to deal with such developments or have had ideological reservations about involvement in issues like worker motivation or the efficiency of the enterprise. Some unions, however, have entered into consultation agreements with employers on human resource management (as in France, with Thompson CSF in 1989 and Renault in 1990) and, while it might be premature to call this a "trend", it does indicate an intention on the part of the unions to be concerned not just about security of employment but also about the competitiveness of the enterprise.

Government participation

Governments have taken a smaller part in collective bargaining during the latter part of the 1980s. Even in Belgium, Denmark and the Netherlands, where government influence has previously been strong, they have allowed full freedom of negotiation to be re-established. This is partly because governments are less nervous about inflation (which has been brought under greater control) but also because such intervention has sometimes created political problems, and the longer it lasted, the less effective it became.

In Sweden, for example, the Government proposed a freeze on rents, prices and salaries as well as a ban on strikes for wage increases. It was forced out of office as a result. The new Government, however, still exerts an indirect influence on wage negotiations.

Many governments do keep a very close watch over collective negotiations – and would probably be ready to step in again should they sense a danger of inflation or a loss of international competitiveness. In Norway, for example, the Government was prepared to intervene in the 1990-91 agreements if they had not been concluded within "reasonable" limits. Similarly in Australia, Finland and Ireland the governments continue to play a significant role in the bargaining system.

Eastern Europe and the former Soviet Union

"Labour relations" is a relatively new concept for most countries in the region – indeed many of the languages do not have an expression for it. Under the previous system everyone was supposedly united in the construction of socialism. Theoretically there could be no conflicts between workers, employers and the State.

That there really *were* conflicts was first accepted openly in Hungary, then in Poland, and later in the rest of the region.

Trade unions

New trade unions appeared all over the region in 1989-90 – both to represent workers and, often, to exert political pressure. And alongside them the "traditional" unions declared their independence of the State and usually changed their name.

The situation is still extremely volatile so the summary which follows should be taken as no more than an indication of recent developments. The numbers in brackets are estimates of membership.

- *Poland* – Solidarity (2.5 million), the original independent union in Eastern Europe, has now seen its ex-leader elected as State President. Membership is dramatically down, however, from around 10 million a decade ago.

  OPZZ (5 million) is the traditional union federation in Poland. This has declared itself independent of the Government and now operates as a much looser federation. Workers tend to belong to Solidarity as a political gesture but to OPZZ because it provides a wide range of social benefits (controlling, among other things, access to holiday homes).

- *Czechoslovakia* – Here the workers carried the revolution through in the workplace as well as the streets. They voted out the old union leaders and (unlike in other countries) democratised the union movement from top to bottom without splitting or creating rival unions. However, this new Czechoslovak Confederation of Trade Unions, KOS (5 million), formally established in March 1990, now seems in danger of dividing on ethnic lines with Czech and Slovak unions becoming more independent from the centre.

- *Hungary* – MSZOSZ (2.7 million) is the largest trade union federation. This is the successor to the official federation. It streamlined its operation by sacking 1,000 bureaucrats and now offers stiff opposition to the new Government.

  Of the other federations, two of the most significant are the National Federation of Workers' Councils (105,000) and the Democratic League of Independent Trade Unions (130,000), both of whom are closely allied with the Government.

- *Bulgaria* – The official trade union was dissolved in February 1990 to be replaced by the Confederation of Independent Trade Unions (2 million). Podkrepa (400,000) is one of the most significant of the new organisations – it means "support" in Bulgarian. It was created in 1989 by a group of intellectuals and is linked to the political opposition.

- *Romania* – The official union changed its name in December 1989 to the National Confederation of Free Trade Unions, CNSLR (3 million), and after this reorganisation lost 5 million members.

  Fratia (600,000), meaning "fraternity", also founded in December 1989, is the main opposition federation. Fratia has announced its support for the Government's economic restructuring programme but frequently opposes government policy. There are also several other trade union federations, including Alianta which claims 1.8 million members.

- *The former Soviet Union* – The trade union movement has been in a state of rapid flux since the coalminers' strike of 1989 which launched the new "workers' movement" with a considerable political, social and economic impact. The previous union federation, the VTSSPS, dissolved itself in October 1990 and re-emerged as the General Confederation of Trade Unions – though there are doubts that it has really changed very much. Many new trade unions have also appeared, notably the Independent Miners' Trade Union. And there are also some intersectoral associations which combine both workers and the intelligentsia – such as the Association of Socialist Trade Unions (SOTSPROF) which was established in 1990. Independent unions have also been established within individual republics – the largest federation of these is the Russian Federation of Independent Trade Unions. To these should be added yet another group of organisations which combine trade union activity with more overt political activity. The United Workers Front, for example, was set up by party workers and intellectuals who wanted to increase their influence among ordinary workers. Then there is the Confederation of Labour, which is based on the coalminers' strike committees. And finally there is the Union of Labour Collectives, which brings together collectives from a group of state enterprises, such as the Volzshki Automobile Factory.

Trade union assets

A contentious question in several countries is: who should inherit the property and assets of the old official trade unions? If it is merely the direct successor organisations this will give them a substantial, and possibly unfair, advantage. In Czechoslovakia this was dealt with relatively smoothly – assets were transferred to a body set up by the new trade union federation in 1989. Elsewhere things are more difficult. In Romania the Government froze the assets of the CNSLR in 1990 until it decides what to do – though it may be that some of the funds escaped and in any case the CNSLR retains a highly profitable chain of hotels and restaurants. In Hungary the Government froze the assets of MSZOSZ in July 1991 and set up a committee representing dozens of workers' organisations to decide how the assets should be shared out.

In Poland the situation is rather different but equally controversial. The assets of Solidarity were seized in 1980 when martial law was declared and many of proceeds were passed to the OPZZ. Parlia-

ment decided in 1991, however, that these should be returned. This will certainly right a wrong, but the OPZZ argues that this is being done for purely political motives.

Employers' organisations

Employers' organisations were previously of three kinds:

1. *Chambers of commerce* – (or of "industry" or "economy") which brought together large state enterprises to promote contacts between each other as well as foreign trade.
2. *Associations of cooperatives* – these united industrial, agricultural, or consumer cooperatives, effectively acting as "cooperative ministries".
3. *Organisations of small craftsmen* – and retail traders.

None of these were involved in the conduct of labour relations. But the situation has now changed considerably, starting in the 1980s in Hungary and Poland and from 1989-90 in the other countries.

First, the chambers of commerce were separated from the State. They became autonomous bodies which were supposed to represent the interests of the enterprise and were reorganised into more decentralised and democratic structures. However, they remain dominated by the big state enterprises. One of the most significant of these is Hungary's Chamber of Economy, which grew from 700 member enterprises in 1984 to 1,500 in 1988 and has formulated the enterprises' policy position on the Government's economic policy.

Private entrepreneurs have also been getting together – as with the National Association of Entrepreneurs in Hungary, and the Union of Citizens for Economic Initiatives in Bulgaria. And some of these organisation have united as federations. A confederation of Polish Employers was established in 1989, for example, covering 90 per cent of state employers and 60 per cent of private employers; it advises the Government on labour legislation and the status of employers.

Many of the employers' organisations are involved in collective bargaining and national tripartite negotiations. However, the situation is still rather confused. The surviving cooperative organisations, for example, as well as small craft organisations and retail traders, are still registered as employers' organisations – though it is debatable if they really qualify.

Collective bargaining

Collective agreements used to be limited to the implementation of centrally-issued instructions. But governments throughout the 1980s did make efforts to loosen the state's decisive influence. These resulted, for example, in the Bulgarian Labour Code (1986), the former Soviet Law on State Enterprises (1987) and Hungary's amended Labour Code (1989). But on the whole, progress was slow.

The past couple of years, however, have seen some remarkable developments – as in the former Soviet Law on Enterprises (1990), the Czech and Slovak Labour Code (1990) and the Hungarian Labour Code, currently being prepared. These are a radical break with the past – an attempt to create the legal framework for genuinely "free bargaining".

These efforts include:

- *Eliminating previous restrictions* – on what collective bargaining and agreements should cover.

- *Decentralising the bargaining procedure* – and establishing a sound balance between sectoral, branch and enterprise levels. In most countries, as in the former Soviet Union, the emphasis is on the enterprise, though others, such as Hungary, envisage sectoral agreements.

- *Guaranteeing the best representation* – on the workers' side at least (the employers' side remains somewhat vague).

- *Linking collective bargaining with national coordination* – on wages, incomes, employment and social policies.

As for the representation of workers, two alternative (and much debated) proposals have been made as to who should be involved in bargaining.

1. *Trade unions* – which would engage in collective bargaining and conclude an agreement on behalf of the workforce.
2. *Works councils* – or some other permanent body or special representative of the workforce within the enterprise which would take responsibility for bargaining and any agreements.

Goskomtrud (the Ministry of Labour in the former USSR) has put forward the second alternative. And in Hungary, too, the draft Labour Code opens up the possibility of bargaining by works councils. Trade unions are understandably sensitive about this – since it might seem to limit the scope of their activities.

Tripartite negotiations

National level tripartite bodies have been established in many countries in recent years. In Hungary the Council for the Reconciliation of Interests was revitalised in 1990. In Czechoslovakia a Council of Economic and Social Consensus was initiated in 1990. And in Bulgaria a National Commission for the Coordination of Interests was established in 1990.

But despite such bodies, and the signing in several countries of industrial peace (Bulgaria, Czechoslovakia, Poland and Romania), the relations between trade unions and governments have been far from friendly.

In Hungary the levels of unemployment caused by the Government's austerity measures are such that the League of Democratic Trade Unions says that a social explosion "cannot be ruled out". In Poland Solidarity (the trade union) has effectively broken with Solidarity (the Government) and has organised strikes against the policies of its former leader. In Romania Fratia complains that the Government has gone back on agreements and in November 1990 the Fratia drivers' union demonstrated against price increases by driving 1,000 trucks around Bucharest for three hours.

It will be some years before new models of labour relations emerge in Eastern Europe and the former Soviet Union. They may in part be based on models from elsewhere but in the end will have to arrive at solutions appropriate both to the transition period and to the economic structures towards which these countries are moving.

Africa

Since most of Africa's population is dispersed in small farms and only urbanised workers are likely to be organised, formal labour relations issues generally touch only a small (and relatively privileged) section of Africa's population. Organised workers probably represent only a small percentage of the active workforce.

This group also tends to have been closely controlled. In order to hold multi-ethnic societies together, most African countries and areas have had, until recently, a strong central power – usually a one-party State – which has closely managed labour relations. Since the State is generally by far the largest employer – about 60 to 70 per cent of formal employment is in state or parastatal organisations –

such control has been relatively easy to exert. But even workers in the much smaller private sector have had their options restricted.

Trade unions

Trade unions from the outset have had a significant political role. Many were an important part of the struggle for independence. And a number of the early political figures came from the trade unions. After independence, however, when trade unions started to criticise the new governments – whether for bad planning, or nepotism or corruption – governments responded by dissolving the unions and imprisoning their leaders.

The unions continued to grow despite such obstacles. Initially, they proliferated as enterprise unions but these were later restructured into industrial unions and then linked in federations. Most African countries have a single national trade union centre – the exceptions are Burkina Faso, Chad, Gambia, Lesotho, Madagascar, Mauritius, Morocco, Reunion, Senegal and Sudan. In many cases these centres have been established by law and industrial unions are obliged to join them (contrary to the ILO's Convention No. 87 on freedom of association). This is the case in Cameroon, Egypt, Ghana, Nigeria and Zambia. Some countries have only *one* trade union, with branches and sections in districts and industries throughout the country – as with the UGTA in Algeria.

A restriction common to many countries is that civil servants are forbidden to organise; in Ghana, even teachers are not allowed to join unions.

Employers' organisations

Employers' organisations have more recent origins than trade unions. Nigeria, for example, has had a national trade union organisation since 1963 but an employers' organisation only since 1983. Some of the earlier ones were in Egypt, Gabon, Ghana, Kenya and Senegal – and many others appeared in the 1960s. But in other countries they hardly exist at all – as in Algeria, Angola, Ethiopia, Libya, Mozambique, and Somalia.

Employers' organisations are of three main types. The first is the chamber of commerce, which is usually either a government institution or a quasi-government one. A second is the federation of employers' associations, whose main functions are the promotion of good industrial relations. The third category is a blend of the two, providing a wide range of commercial and labour-related services.

Public enterprises are full members of employers' organisations in most countries.

Elsewhere public enterprises may only have associate membership – as in Cameroon, Ghana, Lesotho, Mauritius and Sudan. And in certain countries they are positively excluded – as in Congo and Madagascar.

Employers' organisations should have the same rights to freedom of association as trade unions. But in Africa, in the socialist countries in particular, employers have been reluctant to claim such rights because of a fear of being drawn into the ruling party. Hence in many countries, such as Ethiopia, Ghana and the United Republic of Tanzania, employers' organisations are governed by laws different from those for trade unions.

Governments

African countries have ratified many ILO Conventions and have established legal frameworks of labour relations that meet international standards. In practice, however, they have restricted the rights of trade unions and employers' organisations. Claiming an overriding imperative of national unity and labour peace, they often put down strikes and disturbances with repressive measures. And if the government is provisional or military, it may suspend laws and clamp down on union activity – as has happened in Benin, Nigeria, Seychelles and Uganda.

Even in normal circumstances unions can find it difficult to go about their business. In Swaziland, for example, workers have the legal right to organise but in practice they need police approval to call a meeting of their members.

Intervention seems to have increased in recent years. Ethiopia, Nigeria and Zambia, among others, have restructured the trade unions not just to rationalise (and possibly strengthen) them but also to make them easier for the State to control. Socialist governments have taken the most deliberate steps in this direction. In Algeria, Benin, Ethiopia and the United Republic of Tanzania, trade unions have been "mass organisations" closely linked with the government.

Governments have also weakened trade unions by establishing rival or parallel organisations – as in Benin, Libyan Arab Jamahiriya, Swaziland, the United Republic of Tanzania and Zambia. Works committees or political groups or youth organisations have often been created, or the same effect has been achieved by promoting traditional organisations, such as Ndbazabantu in Swaziland.

A further way in which governments have weakened unions and employers' organisations is by coopting their leaders. By drawing them into political activities (perhaps with a symbolic role) they have tried to attract the members' support. Using the unions for party information has also undermined their independence.

Collective bargaining

As understood in other parts of the world, collective bargaining is not very widespread in Africa. But it is much more evident if one expands the concept to include other forms of consultation and discussion.

African methods might incorporate traditional forms of organisation. In the ports, for example, loaders and unloaders usually come from one or two particular tribes. And there is a clear division of labour. The younger members will do the heavy work, the elders will do the negotiating, and the chief will take a commission.

Even where employers and unions are free to engage in collective bargaining the government may restrict their options on wages and salaries. Many governments want to enforce an incomes policy, for example. One way this can be achieved is by a statutory tripartite body making recommendations for the pay of the civil service and public sector employees. These recommendations then have to be followed by parastatals and the private sector. So employers and unions can find that the margin for bargaining is very small – restricted to the area between the minimum wage established by minimum wage boards and the maximum awards to public employees. In Algeria and Côte d'Ivoire wages are altogether excluded from collective negotiations: they are imposed by the State.

Democratisation

Although labour relations in Africa are still strongly shaped by a history of one-party and often autocratic government, the wave of democratisation sweeping across the continent is beginning to take effect. There is a trend now for governments to reduce their level of involvement in labour issues and to allow or invite unions and employers to participate more or to resolve issues themselves. So tripartite labour advisory boards are being established (or inactive ones revived) to consider issues such as minimum wages and health and safety. And ministries of labour, which have become overburdened with disputes and workers' complaints, are now looking for other ways to solve problems. A dispute in the mines in Swaziland, for example, was settled by engaging an outside arbitrator.

Both employers and workers now often prefer the government to stay out of negotiations – as in Botswana, Senegal and Zambia. Trade unions do not like the government to set a minimum wage since employers have often treated this as a maximum.

In this new environment trade unions have also become more active. They are frequently the only mass organisations which cut across tribal lines, so they can offer a political focus in countries where opposition parties have previously been outlawed. Indeed, they have often been key actors in the transition to democracy (see box 3.2).

Asia

Labour relations in the developing countries of this region depend first of all on levels of development. Union influence is growing in some of the poorer countries but declining in the more developed ones.

In Bangladesh, for example, union membership increased by 27 per cent between 1987 and 1989. But one of the largest increases has been in the Philippines (38 per cent) where the 2.9 million members represent 12 per cent of the labour force. Here, as in the other poorer countries, unions have to concentrate on some the more basic labour issues. One of the most serious problems they face is simply that of pay. Unfair labour practices – usually non-payment, either of the correct wages or of legislated benefits – accounted for 76 per cent of disputes in 1989. The Philippines Department of Labour and Employment reported that up to 60 per cent of establishments inspected from January to September 1990 were not implementing one or other of the labour standards laws embodied in the Labour Code.

In the more developed countries such as Singapore the situation is rather different. Trade union density may be high but unions are also becoming less influ-

---

3.2 **Unions spearhead democracy in Africa**

In the absence of political structures in Africa, trade unions have become an important focus of political change. The pressure that they have helped exert in many countries has speeded up democratisation.

Zambia – The single national trade union centre, the ZCTU, has been in the vanguard of the democracy campaign. After a long series of popular demonstrations the Government has accepted the principle of multi-party democracy. The chairman of the ZCTU was the main opposition candidate and won the Presidential election in October 1991.

Congo – CSC, the trade union confederation, announced a general strike in September 1990 which led the President to accept the principle of multi-party democracy. By the end of the year 50 parties had been registered. The CSC continued to exert pressure until the convening of a national conference in June 1991 which appointed a transitional Government to organise free elections.

Niger – The workers' union of Niger (USTN) has fought hard for the introduction of political pluralism – and seen its leaders arrested and strikers subject to harsh repression. But in 1991 the Government was finally forced to accept constitutional amendments leading to multi-party democracy.

Mali – In April 1991 the national workers' union of Mali (UNTM) declared its independence from the ruling party; and an indefinite strike, strongly supported by the country's youth, hastened the Government's departure. The UNTM kept up the pressure until the interim Government promised to organise multi-party elections before the end of the year.

Mauritania – The national trade union centre (UTM) published an open letter to the President in April 1991 saying it was ready to ''fight to the end'' for democracy. The President has now announced that a referendum on a new Constitution will be held before the end of the year.

---

ential. Workers are better educated and their demands are becoming more sophisticated; they look for better conditions and shorter working hours and may consider trade unions a less important way of achieving such goals. Singapore's National Trade Union Congress has 76 affiliated unions which represent 25 per cent of the workers who can engage in collective bargaining – one of the highest union densities in the region. However, the number of disputes here is negligible. There has not been a strike since 1986 – and that only for two days involving 61 workers.

In the Republic of Korea the unions have made significant progress since the process of democratisation started in 1987. The number of union members increased from one million in 1987 to 1.9 million in 1990.

Union strength – and weakness

Union membership in most parts of the region is still relatively low. Apart from Singapore and the Republic of Korea, it involves only around 10 per cent of the salaried workforce. Unions tend to confine themselves to the formal sector – whose contributions can offer a greater degree of financial security. Workers in the informal sector thus go largely unprotected.

A further weakness is union fragmentation. In Hong Kong, for example, there are 439 registered unions with 416,000 members – with "multi-unionism" in many workplaces and industries. In Nepal, too, where there used to be just one imposed trade union federation, now there are 20 to 30.

Indian unions too are very fragmented. In many workplaces several trade unions compete for the loyalty of the same body of workers and their rivalry is usually bitter and sometimes violent. It is difficult even to say how many trade unions operate at the national level since many do not affiliate to an all-India federation. The early splits in Indian trade unionism tended to be on ideological grounds – each linked to a particular political party. Much of the recent fragmentation, however, has centred on personalities and occasionally on caste or regional considerations.

Flexible pay systems

One of the most significant trends in the developing countries of the region is the move towards the kind of flexible pay systems which operate in Japan. At present workers often get annual increments – 5 per cent in Malaysia, for example. But employers are finding this too rigid and expensive a system and are looking for alternatives.

Employers in the Republic of Korea and elsewhere express similar doubts about a fairly rigid system of bonuses. This started out as a kind of profit sharing. But workers' wages are often so low that they now rely on the bonuses for a living wage. According to one survey, 37 per cent of companies now pay a productivity bonus on top of the regular bonus.

Singapore has the most advanced flexible pay scheme – dating back to 1985 when the country was becoming internationally less competitive. Although a wage freeze at the time helped turn the economy around, the Government realised that a more permanent solution was required.

A flexible wage system was decided upon with the following elements:

1. *A basic wage* – to reflect the value of the job and to provide a measure of security to the worker's income.
2. *An annual wage supplement (AWS)* – of one month's basic wage which may be adjusted under exceptional circumstances.
3. *A variable wage component* – based on company productivity and/or profitability, to be paid yearly or half yearly.
4. *A service increment* – in recognition of service, loyalty and experience. This can either be negotiated annually or fixed for the duration of the collective agreement.

In practice, up to 20 per cent of the wage may be variable. A survey of 551 companies in Singapore in 1990 found that 269 had adopted flexible wage schemes. Of these, 27 per cent had based the AWS on the company's productivity, 55 per cent on its profit – the others choosing a combination or a different model.

A similar principle is being discussed in Malaysia on the initiative of employers. The unions at first resisted the idea but are now more open to it – though calling it "wage reform" rather than flexible wages.

Economies in transition

China, Laos and Viet Nam are currently aiming at economic "renovation" and are now reviewing their labour relations systems and laws. China has drafted a new Labour Code and has asked the ILO to assist in a review of its labour laws.

In Viet Nam the previous system relied on workers also having subsidised housing, transport and medical care, so they would depend less on wages. They now want to move away from this system and have made some progress.

Export processing zones tend to be in the forefront of such changes. Viet Nam now allows workers in export processing zones to earn 50 per cent more than those elsewhere.

Latin America and the Caribbean

Democratisation has certainly improved labour relations systems in Latin America in recent years. Governments' routine response to labour disputes in many countries used to be simple repression, forcing trade unions to operate illegally. Now governments all over the region have been working on new labour codes and tripartite agreements, and there is talk of more *concertación social* (social pacts) as a way of maintaining industrial peace.

But some governments still respond firmly to labour unrest. Peru, for example, has a democratically elected President who in mid-1991 faced disputes with teachers, health workers and social security workers and sent in the police to deal with their protests on the streets of Lima.

Government and labour relations

With some exceptions (notably Uruguay) Latin American governments, democratic or dictatorial, always try to keep firm control over labour issues. Not content with setting the general legal framework, they also try to determine how trade unions should work, what salary levels should be, and how disputes should be resolved – a system known as *reglamentarismo*.

Labour legislation is certainly copious, covering virtually every aspect of working life. But it can be so complex that it is difficult to apply or to comply with. As a result, a gap has opened up between legislation and reality.

- The law may prohibit most strikes but this does not prevent them, so the majority are illegal.
- Governments may withhold official recognition from the most powerful union organisations yet still deal with them as representatives of the workers.
- The law may prohibit certain kinds of collective agreement (either in terms of subjects they cover or the level at which bargaining takes place) but such agreements are often made anyway.

Trade unions

Trade unions tend to be closely regulated. In many countries (Argentina, Brazil and Uruguay are the most prominent exceptions) the law insists that unions organise by enterprise – and even by different parts of the same enterprise. So the same company may have a number of unions and each country finishes up with thousands of mini-unions. The fragmentation reaches right to the top: only in Bolivia, Cuba and Uruguay are there single trade union federations.

Union membership is fairly low. Around 50 per cent of the labour force in Latin America is in the formal sector and around 30 per cent of this is unionised, though density rates do vary considerably from one country to another – highest in Argentina, Cuba, Nicaragua, Uruguay and Venezuela and lowest in Costa Rica, the Dominican Republic, Ecuador, El Salvador, Guatemala, Haiti, Honduras and Paraguay.

Still, the unions may well have influence beyond their membership. They can often, for example, mobilise many non-members to support union action. And union leaders may also hold important political positions: in Colombia, Mexico and Venezuela, for example, union leaders hold parliamentary seats and in Argentina and Brazil, in 1990, the Minister of Labour came from the trade union movement.

One reason for low membership is that the law may exclude certain categories of workers from union membership. In Peru and Venezuela, for example, the law says a union cannot operate unless it has at least 20 members. This excludes a significant proportion of the workforce (and has led to suggestions that a fairer way to express union density would be take union members as a proportion of unionisable workers rather than the whole workforce).

Colombia is another case of fragmented union organisation. Of the economically active population of 12 million, 6.7 million are in the informal sector (and therefore beyond union protection) and 2.3 million have temporary or fixed-term contracts (and by law are not allowed to unionise). Just 2.3 million Colombians are full-time employees – of whom one million are unionised. And even those in the public sector who are unionised may not be allowed to strike or engage in collective bargaining. In Colombia the weakness of the unions is compounded by the general climate of violence (see Chapter 1).

Unions elsewhere, however, may be in a better position. In Chile, for example, they gained strength from the need to work clandestinely, frequently with people now part of the new Government. And, largely as a result of agreements reached with the new Government in April 1990, the restoration of democracy was not accompanied by industrial unrest – as had happened elsewhere, in Argentina, Brazil and Uruguay. In Chile there has been a flow of much more favourable legislation, as well as a sizeable increase in real wages.

In Central America union membership has been affected by the growth of the "solidarist", organisations which recruit workers as members but are allied with, and often controlled by, employers (see Chapter 1). Union membership is also low in the export processing zones along the Mexican border. Although the rate for all Mexican workers is around 25 per cent, in the *maquilas*, the assembly plants, only about 10 per cent of the .400,000 workers are unionised.

In Nicaragua the unions are much stronger and now occupy a key political position. After the revolution in 1979 labour organisation grew from only 133 unions representing 5 per cent of the labour force to over 1,100 unions representing 55 per cent of the workforce by 1984. However, they did not achieve much material advance for their workers during the war years – indeed union leaders were constantly calling on their members to make more sacrifices. The Sandinista Government wanted to ensure that unions supported them and most did so freely (so that today 90 per cent of unions are affiliated with the six FSLN confederations). But there were also legal restrictions placed on opposition unions (and some illegal intimidation). Today there are three main non-Sandinista confederations of which the strongest is probably the Permanent Workers Congress (CPT), which is allied with the UNO Government.

The Sandinista unions, however, managed to organise two general strikes in the first two months of UNO rule. Clearly, the form which labour organisation takes in Nicaragua will profoundly affect the country's future.

Employers' organisations

Employers' organisations in Latin America have been increasingly coming together in central organisations – though such national federations do not yet exist in Argentina, Brazil, Colombia, Ecuador and Uruguay. However, one may question their representativeness since most do not include public enterprises (which are often the largest employers in the formal sector) and do not usually represent the interests of multinationals or, at the other end of the scale, the smallest companies.

The liberalisation of the economies of Latin America (see Chapter 2) has created new competitive challenges. And the democratic openings which have allowed the unions a greater voice may also make life more difficult for employers. In general there have not been too many changes here in recent years. Many employers are waiting to see how the new labour scene will develop.

Collective bargaining and concertación social

Bargaining at present takes place largely at the enterprise level though there are suggestions that it might be better to move to negotiations by sector or by branch of activity. In Argentina, Brazil and Uruguay collective bargaining is mainly industry based.

Various countries also have ways of determining salaries through tripartite organisations such as "wage boards". The degree of decentralisation varies greatly. There might be just one organisation (as in Argentina, Colombia and Panama) or a large number, one for each sector of the economy (as in Costa Rica, Ecuador and Uruguay). In Uruguay the wage board machinery played an important role in 1985-86 after the restoration of democracy, such boards being now less important than bilateral collective bargaining.

Another development in recent years has been attempts to arrive at *concertación social* – a more general process of bargaining on a package of social and economic issues. One of the most successful examples has been Mexico's Economic Solidarity Pact of 1987 which seems to have achieved many of its objectives, including reducing inflation and public expenditure and controlling salaries and prices.

Similar pacts were signed in Venezuela (1989) and Chile (1990). In Venezuela this emphasised the need to fight inflation and introduced a series of new tripartite consultative mechanisms. In Chile the pact included a 44 per cent rise in the minimum wage, as well as increases in pensions and family allowances.

However, such pacts often only work for a short time, if at all. One reason for their weakness has been that the social partners making the agreements may not be very representative and cannot really deliver their part of the bargain – this applies both to trade unions and employers' organisations.

In Brazil, however, some unions and employers have accused the Government of dragging its feet and have decided to "privatise" the social pact. The CUT (the most radical labour federation) and FIESP (the São Paulo Industrialists Association) have been talking about negotiating a new wage policy between them.

Privatisation

Wages and the running battle with inflation are the constant theme of labour disputes in the region. But in recent years union energy has also been directed against plans for privatisation.

Argentina has the most extensive programme, which started in 1990 with the telephone system and the national airline. And many of the strong public sector unions, despite their protests, will find themselves dealing with private employers. The Government has announced that all the railways will be privatised by the end of 1992 and has also presented plans for electricity, gas, water and sewerage, and says that state companies marked for privatisation will be closed down if the sell-offs are delayed. The Government has said that it will be shedding 127,000 public sector jobs during 1991/92. Several Argentine trade union leaders have broken their alliance with the Government, partly because of opposition to the sales of steel and oil enterprises, and say they plan to form a new political party.

In Brazil, Colombia, the Dominican Republic, Panama and Peru organised labour has been trying to stall privatisation moves, but without much success. Protests, strikes and go-slows by Colombian telephone workers, for example, over plans to sell a part of Colombian Telecom resulted in the three unions involved losing their licences.

In Uruguay the unions called a 24-hour general strike in July 1991 in protest both at wage levels and at the Government's privatisation plans – though the Government responded that this was not the union's concern since it had a mandate from the electorate which was still supported by public opinion.

Bolivian protests against privatisation seem to be on a stronger footing. Here it is not just the unions that are resisting the sale of mines and oilfields. Public opinion and the management of the enterprises are also opposed. The Government, though, is determined to press ahead – arguing that privatisation should also be extended to health, education and social security.

Chapter 4

Social protection and working conditions

Each year the *World Labour Report* will focus on topical issues in social protection and working conditions – on how workers are treated, in and out of work.

Social protection alone covers a wide range of issues, from social security to food subsidies to health services – indeed almost anything which affects a worker's income and welfare aside from wages and salaries. And working conditions, too, is a very broad umbrella – working hours, for example, or holidays, or health and safety at work.

This year the Report concentrates on just three issues:

- *Social protection in Eastern Europe and the former Soviet Union* – these are the countries undergoing the most rapid challenges to their systems of social protection as they move towards a market economy and have to cope with the fact that there *is* such a thing as unemployment. This section looks at the problems and opportunities they face.

- *Flexible working time* – millions of workers are now working in new and more flexible ways, often with patterns of shifts and hours so diverse that only a computer can cope with the scheduling. How and why these developments have occurred are the focus of the second section.

- *Preventing industrial disasters* – human ingenuity may have increased security in many ways, but it has also raised the stakes of failure. Bhopal is the most infamous example but there are each year many cases of fire and explosion that put workers and the surrounding community at risk. This section explains what can be done to minimise the risk, and also cope with those disasters which do occur.

Social protection in Eastern Europe and the former Soviet Union

Revolution brings its casualties, and the dramatic changes in Eastern Europe and the former Soviet Union have already exposed many people to the harsh realities of economic change. Upwards of 10 million unemployed, the old, the sick, the disabled – all may pay a high price for building a new and more dynamic economic system.

Universal social security was one of the strongest features of state socialism, providing a solid, if low, basis for survival. People may have been under-employed and underpaid but there was always some employment and some pay. With the transition to market economies, however, the social security systems will have to change as well – and will have to be funded from economies which are growing but slowly, if at all.

A recent study for the IMF and the World Bank has estimated that the costs of unemployment and the retraining of workers would be $1,250 per person per year in the former Soviet Union, and $2,500 in the rest of Eastern Europe. If, as the report also suggests, there are 52 million unemployed in five years' time, the total annual cost in the region could be 72 billion dollars per year – 3.4 per cent of GNP.

Many people in this region are attracted by the example of the industrial market economies – by the quality and quantity of material goods on offer. And most will still keep that vision ahead of them. But they may have underestimated how long it will take to obtain some of the fruits of reform. And as unemployment bites, and real wages fall, the social consensus may evaporate. This makes it increasingly urgent that governments develop strong and realistic forms of social security.

The starting point

A brief summary of the previous social security systems will give some indication of the changes needed.

First, the overall levels of expenditure: as a proportion of GDP the governments of Eastern Europe were spending roughly the same as the lower-income OECD countries – about 11 per cent. They had a full range of social benefits and services including health care, family benefits, maternity grants, sickness and disability benefits, as well as retirement and invalidity benefits.

But while the overall figure may be similar there are some crucial differences, including:

Unemployment benefits – in the OECD countries 1.6 per cent of GDP went on unemployment benefits. This was unnecessary in Eastern Europe since almost everyone had a job. The system encouraged enterprises to employ as many people as possible, whether or not there was work available. So enterprises were always willing to accept young people and school-leavers as well as a substantial number of retired older workers (who thus collected both a pension and a wage). Estimates of the extent of this "social employment" vary, but for countries like Poland, Czechoslovakia and the former Soviet Union it probably represented between 10 and 15 per cent of total employment.

- *Family allowances* – these were typically double the proportion of GDP common in the industrial market economies and for young families came to form an important part of household income.

- *Pensions* – these were fairly low. In the former Soviet Union, for example, over two-thirds of pensioners received a third or less than a third of the average industrial wage. Hence the incentive to carry on working.

- *Short-term benefits* – such as sick pay. These were relatively generous and earnings-related. In Czechoslovakia, for example, workers on sick pay would receive up to 85 per cent of previous earnings for a year.

- *Inflation* – since prices were almost all state-controlled, the need to keep up with inflation was not really an issue. But with inflation exploding now in many countries (200 per cent in Bulgaria in the first three months of 1990) the problem has become acute, not so much for the short-term

benefits, which are related to recent earnings, as for pensions whose values have dropped steeply.

People received all these benefits through some link with their employment. Everyone without valid exemption had the right and the obligation to work. And the enterprise they worked for also financed and administered most of the benefits. Even old-age pensions and family allowances, which were the responsibility of a state ministry, were also closely monitored by the trade union at the enterprise.

One further significant difference with market economies was the level of subsidy. Governments underpinned the general standard of living by subsidising commodities, food, energy and, above all, rents.

Managing the transition

Many of the characteristics of the former system clearly contradict the spirit of current reforms. How should governments manage this transition from old to new? Where, for example, are the resources for unemployment benefit or increased pensions to come from?

Increasing public expenditure is scarcely an option. The current economic crisis through which these countries are passing – with large external debts and public sector deficits, as well as a breakdown in both supply and distribution – effectively cut off this line of action. All that can be hoped for is that savings in some areas, such as subsidies to industry, might provide scope for some kind of very basic safety net.

Some may hope that a fairly immediate answer will come from systems which are self-financing – fully or partially funded pension schemes, for example, or contribution-based health care, or a system of unemployment compensation not financed from state budgets.

These may (or may not) be long-term answers but it would be illusory to consider that they can make an immediate contribution. In reality what lies ahead is a dramatic economic contraction. The issue, therefore, is not how to avoid the contraction but how best to share it.

Unemployment

The bulk of this contraction will appear as unemployment (see Chapter 2). And the way which social protection programmes address unemployment will determine not only how much poverty and social

Table 4.1. Unemployment benefits and minimum income, Eastern Europe and the former Soviet Union, 1991 (January)

	Bulgaria	Czecho-slovakia	Hungary	Poland	Romania	Former USSR
Labour force (millions)	4.5	8.0	5.1	18.4	11.0	127.0*
Average wage (local currency)	310	3 380	11 000	1 029 000	3 615	270
Minimum wage	80	2 000	5 017	—	3 000	130
Initial benefit (% of wage)	—	60	70	70	70	50
Duration (months)	—	6	48	3	9	6
Indexed?	—	No	No	Yes	Yes	No
Subsequent benefit (% of wage)	—	50	50	50/40	70	—
Duration (months)	—	6	48	6-12	3	—
Indexed?	—	No	No	Yes	Yes	—
Minimum income	—	1 300	5 050	5 107	3 000	—
Percentage of average wage	—	65	55	—	82	—
Percentage of minimum wage	—	65	100	95	100	—
Indexed?	—	No	Yes	Yes	Yes	—

* 1990. Source: ILO estimates.

dislocation will appear but also how successful the transition to a market economy will be.

The potential scale of unemployment is a matter for speculation. But from the perspective of social protection the *composition* of unemployment is just as important. One possibility is that many people will lose their jobs but then be retrained and rapidly take on new ones. Such a rapid outflow and rapid inflow might indeed be a good thing – and relatively easy to cope with. But if the unemployment is long term and concentrated on the young, the unskilled, the disadvantaged, or on older workers unable to adapt, then this would place different, probably greater, strains on any system of social protection.

The reforms so far

Most of the countries have already embarked on a series of reforms – at least in terms of legislation. And while there are significant differences between countries (in timing as well as in detail) there are also some common lines of approach.

Unemployment benefits and minimum income

The provisions made so far are summarised in table 4.1. The "minimum income" is a basic form of

safety net for those out of work. It appears, however, to have been set at a rather low level relative to the average wage – falling below (or at least at the bottom end of) the benefit required for the unemployed in ILO Convention No. 102. This is perhaps understandable. Smaller public expenditure budgets may make greater generosity impossible – given the potentially high levels of unemployment and the fact that most of those on minimum income will be the unemployed. And raising direct taxation (itself a relatively new phenomenon) might be unpopular with those who have kept their jobs or found new ones. Yet, setting the benefits too low may eventually weaken support for reforms.

For unemployment benefit the most important questions are also: how much, and for how long? These can be expressed as a proportion of a worker's previous wages – the "replacement rate" for a certain period. A high replacement rate for an initial period encourages workers to risk changing jobs, or seek retraining. But restricting this high rate to a short period quickly brings unemployed workers face to face with the prospect of minimum income and encourages them to seek work.

Indexation can also influence the decision of the unemployed. The minimum wage must of course be indexed – if it were not then in periods of high inflation the "safety net" would rapidly sink to the

Table 4.2. Retirement pensions in Eastern Europe and the former Soviet Union, 1990

	Bulgaria	Czecho-slovakia	Hungary	Poland	Romania	Former USSR
Percentage of population of working age (16-60)	60.8	60.2	61.2	60.3	61.1	59.8
Percentage of population over retirement age	19.2	16.6	19.0	14.8	15.6	14.7
Labour force (millions)	4.5	8.0	5.1	18.4	11.0	127.0
Pensioners (millions)	2.4	3.6	2.7	6.9	3.5	62.4
Retirement age: men	60	60	60	65	60	60
Retirement age: women	55	57	55	60	55	55
As a percentage of average wage:						
Average pension	45	50	51	—	53	41
Minimum pension	23	30	37	—	34	26

Source: ILO estimates.

ground. But unemployment benefits are another matter. If they are not indexed then inflation will so devalue benefits that they quickly approach the minimum income.

The new system in the former Soviet Union is relatively generous. Workers who are dismissed receive three months' full salary (from the enterprise) *before* they start to receive unemployment benefit. In Poland the replacement rate declines from 70 per cent of previous earnings to 40 per cent according to the duration of unemployment – but without falling below 95 per cent of the minimum salary. In Czechoslovakia the replacement rate is 60 per cent of previous earnings for the first six months and 50 per cent for the second. In Romania benefits are linked to the average national salary rather than previous earnings.

Pensions

Pensioners are going to feel the shock of the transition more than most – living on a fixed income at a time when price controls have been removed and inflation is rocketing. Unless adequate pensions are available, they will need to look for work and thus heighten unemployment problems.

Most countries are at present reassessing their pensions systems. The previous pension position is summarised in table 4.2. The actual levels of pension for each individual depended on years of service and on earnings – though there was a minimum level which served as a safety net.

- *Replacement rates* – as a proportion of average earnings the average pensions were low – between 40 and 50 per cent. Just what this has meant in practice compared with the industrial market economies, however, is difficult to judge. Pensions in the past were effectively supplemented by subsidies on items such as food and housing. On the other hand few people would have been able to supplement pensions from private savings.

  It is also difficult to estimate how many people survived on the minimum pension – set at 20 to 30 per cent of the average wage. It does seem, though, that a significant number of older pensioners were (and still are) exposed to hardship.

- *Retirement age* – the nominal ages have been quite low (except for Poland) compared with the OECD countries, for example, where they average 64.5 years for men and 63 years for women. But many pensioners actually carried on working and added the pension to their wages. A significant proportion of these must have been part of the "social employment" system, however, so will be at high risk as enterprises slim down.

- *Demographic balance* – demographically the region is very similar to OECD countries. However, the actual ratio of labour force members to pensioners appears quite low – around 2:1 in Bulgaria, Hungary and the former Soviet Union and 3:1 in Czechoslovakia and Poland.

- *Indexation* – pensions were not indexed. And even under the previous system inflation had eroded

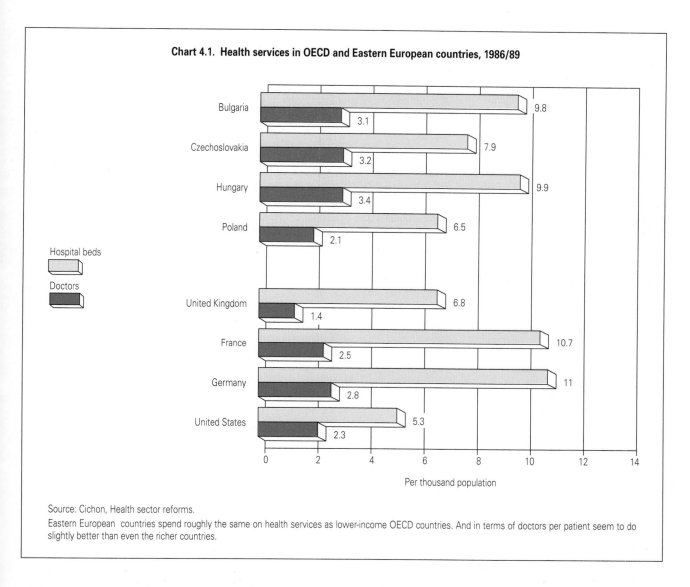

Chart 4.1. Health services in OECD and Eastern European countries, 1986/89

Hospital beds

Doctors

Country	
Bulgaria	9.8 / 3.1
Czechoslovakia	7.9 / 3.2
Hungary	9.9 / 3.4
Poland	6.5 / 2.1
United Kingdom	6.8 / 1.4
France	10.7 / 2.5
Germany	11 / 2.8
United States	5.3 / 2.3

Per thousand population

Source: Cichon, Health sector reforms.
Eastern European countries spend roughly the same on health services as lower-income OECD countries. And in terms of doctors per patient seem to do slightly better than even the richer countries.

their purchasing power. Most countries have in fact made ad hoc adjustments as part of the reform process, but it is difficult to know if these have restored pensions to an adequate level.

In the long run almost all the countries have set their sights on self-financing pension mechanisms, similar perhaps to those in Western Europe. Such new systems may involve full or partial funding, higher and more flexible retirement ages, full in-dexation, and a mixture of flat-rate, earnings-related or complementary benefits.

But the current generation of old people require much more immediate help. The rights they acquired

under the old system will be completely inadequate. And if they are not to live in harsh poverty, younger people will have to demonstrate inter-generational solidarity on a large scale – contributing not only to their own future pensions but also to the present-day pensions of their parents and grandparents.

Family allowances and other benefits

Family allowances currently contribute a high proportion of family incomes – around 20 per cent for a family with two young children. The State have had to support needy families directly since there have been few other ways of targeting them. Direct taxation, for example, was low so few concessions were available there.

Governments will clearly have to rethink such allowances. But they will find it difficult to dismantle them in the near future since they are an income on which so many poor families rely.

Health services

While comparisons are difficult to make, Eastern European countries spend roughly the same on health services as lower-income OECD countries and, in terms of doctors per patient, seem to do slightly better than even the richer countries (chart 4.1). Services are free to patients since the State finances them directly.

However, the queues are long and the quality and efficiency of delivery are poor. The services also have to perform cumbersome administrative functions (such as certificates for days off) which absorb a lot of the system's capacity.

Most countries are considering a major overhaul of their health care systems. This is unlikely to be immediate, however, unless industrial unrest within the system provokes an earlier breakdown.

Policies and implementation

The Eastern European countries have a massive challenge ahead – not easy, but not impossible. And the policies they choose will have to be quick and effective. Even providing the personnel and the offices to deliver benefits will be an immense task in itself and will probably involve cutting a few corners – sacrificing sophistication perhaps, for speed and volume.

But success is vital. Without adequate protection many people will not only suffer great hardship, they may lose faith in the reform process itself. Yet, if unemployment measures do not reflect some market discipline then the reforms themselves may be delayed, or even permanently stifled.

Flexible working time

One of the most significant changes in working life in industrialised countries in recent years has been the introduction of more flexible working time. Whether in the form of work-sharing, or flexitime, or hours averaging, or just compressing the working week, these new approaches are reshaping working life for millions of people in the industrialised world.

In Europe such schemes have often been linked with negotiations for a shorter working week. Unions here have been pressing for shorter hours for several decades. And hours have indeed fallen steadily since 1960. German employees have achieved the greatest reductions. Between 1960 and 1990 the average number of annual hours they worked fell from 2,080 to 1,589 – a drop of 24 per cent. By 1975 the unions had negotiated a 40-hour week with all employers' associations. And in 1990, they reached agreements which would cut the working week for four million engineering workers to 36 hours by 1993, and to 35 hours by 1995.

Employers have, in the past, accepted such reductions very reluctantly. But now, with the opportunity to couple these changes with flexible working patterns, employers are taking most of the initiatives. They see considerable advantages in moving away from rigid work patterns and in extending plant operating hours by "delinking" them from working hours.

In the United States flexible working patterns have often been introduced for a slightly different reason: to allow new people to enter the workforce. Working hours here have changed very little over the past 30 years – and are now substantially above the levels found in Europe. United States workers have, perhaps, been less concerned about overall hours than about their general standard of living; they expect this to rise steadily, but as real wages have remained static since 1975 the only way to make progress has been for more members of the family to go out to work. This has usually meant women, working first part time, and then full time. More flexible working patterns have helped them ease their way into the labour force.

Japanese workers have longer hours than their counterparts in Europe and North America (see chart 4.2). Official policy in Japan is, however, to reduce working hours. In 1988 the Government reduced official weekly hours from 48 to 46, and in April 1991 further reduced them to 44. And the aim is to reduce annual working hours to 1,800 (roughly North American levels) by the end of 1993. Perhaps at this stage there will be more pressure for innovations in working time arrangements, but so far there have been few changes except for the introduction of some part-time work.

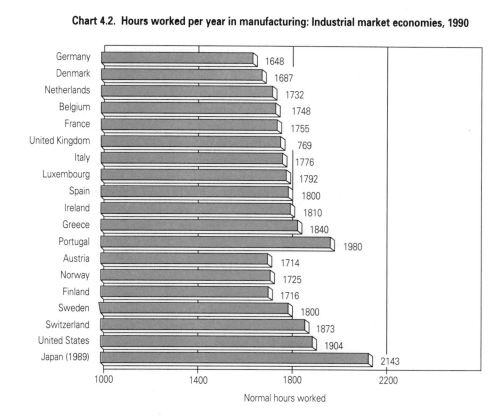

Chart 4.2. Hours worked per year in manufacturing: Industrial market economies, 1990

Country	Hours
Germany	1648
Denmark	1687
Netherlands	1732
Belgium	1748
France	1755
United Kingdom	769
Italy	1776
Luxembourg	1792
Spain	1800
Ireland	1810
Greece	1840
Portugal	1980
Austria	1714
Norway	1725
Finland	1716
Sweden	1800
Switzerland	1873
United States	1904
Japan (1989)	2143

Normal hours worked

Source: Social International, Feb. 1991.
Working hours tend to be shorter in Europe than in the United States or Japan – with German workers achieving the greatest reductions in recent years. Employers in many countries have conceded shorter hours for more flexible patterns of working time.

The employer's view

There are several clear advantages to employers in making such changes. Flexible time patterns allow them, for example, to:

- *Make better use of capital* – by extending working hours. The payback period for expensive equipment can be reduced and fewer workstations may be needed if they can be shared between different workers through a longer working day.

- *Make output more flexible* – by adapting to seasonal demand, perhaps, or to fluctuations in requirements at different times during the day.

- *Deal with complex staffing problems* – by integrating full-time and part-time workers more closely.

- *Give better customer satisfaction* – by allowing shops, banks and other services, for example, to extend their opening hours.

- *Improve productivity* – by having workers develop multiple skills, perhaps, or by improving morale and job satisfaction.

Employers face some disadvantages of course. They will have to cope with new shift patterns which can be difficult to plan and manage and may demand additional staff or computers. And since the new patterns may themselves require more staff (particularly part-time workers), they may have to spend more on non-wage items such as medical benefits, and canteen or transport subsidies.

The worker's point of view

From the point of view of workers and trade unions the picture looks somewhat different. On the whole they tend to be suspicious of such schemes. But they can see some advantages, including:

- *Shorter working hours* – the opportunity to bargain for a shorter working week is usually the main reason workers accept flexible work systems.

- *A more appropriate work pattern* – certain categories of workers such as those with family responsibilities, or the older or the disabled, may appreciate the greater possibilities for part-time work.

- *Greater job satisfaction* – some flexible schemes involve restructuring tasks and devolving responsibility to individuals or groups of workers, and thus offer workers greater independence and control.

Workers can, however, also find the new systems difficult – for reasons which will be familiar to many shift workers.

- *Strain on family life* – workers may find their leisure and working times different from those of partners or children. They have less time to spend with the family and have to adapt meals, household work and child-care to irregular working hours. This is particularly difficult if more than one family member is working to a flexible format but on different shifts.

- *Strain on social life* – those working on flexible shifts find it more complex to organise contacts with other people so they often have to spend their leisure time alone. Shift workers can also have problems with public transport, particularly in rural areas.

- *Erosion of union solidarity* – unions find that shifting the emphasis from collective to individual arrangements can diminish their bargaining strength.

Patterns of flexible working time

The patterns of working time at individual enterprises can be bafflingly complex. Each organisation uses a combination of techniques to achieve the desired result. Four-day work-weeks, for example, or ten-hour shifts, or hours averaging, or rotating days off, or flexitime, or part-time work, or jobsharing, or individual working hours. But most schemes include one or more of the following elements.

Part-time work

In its more traditional forms, this might include half-day working. But there are many other, more flexible, options. The Tokyu department stores in Japan, for example, have added what they call "free-time" employees to the full-time staff. Free-time workers can choose for themselves the hours and days they work – though they have to work at least eight hours a week and a minimum of two hours every day they appear. They also have to determine their work patterns in advance and not vary them from week to week.

This has proved a very popular idea (the company received eight times as many applications for such jobs as it expected). Married women who wanted to work as well as bring up children were keen to work in this way.

Their arrival did cause some problems, however. Older women did not like being supervised by younger, full-time staff. And few free-time employees wanted to work from 5 p.m. to 7 p.m. which is exactly when they are needed most.

But the company is happy with the scheme and plans to extend it to a new store opening in 1992. And now different kinds of people are joining the scheme. Some 15 per cent are men and more than half are students or new graduates – a reflection, perhaps, of young people's desire not to be bound by a nine-to-five job pattern.

Jobsharing

Jobsharing is another form of part-time work offering different kinds of flexibility. Here, two people agree to take responsibility for one job, and share the income accordingly. This has a number of advantages for the employer. Apart from increasing the range of skills and experience available within a single job title, it can also provide cover if one partner falls sick, and if the workload gets really heavy both people can be asked to work simultaneously.

Jobsharing, as one United States company discovered, can also significantly reduce absenteeism. The possibility was suggested in the "speak up" box of the Mid-Western Window Company by an employee who was a good worker but had a poor attendance record. The company is based in rural Iowa and makes high-quality windows and doors. They experimented with jobsharing and found it very successful. The average absenteeism rate for those who have started jobsharing has dropped from 5.8 per cent to 1.2 per cent. Before jobsharing, management had to overstaff the production lines to provide cover; now this is no longer necessary.

Jobsharers at Mid-Western have to find their own partners and are responsible for covering for each other's absences. They are expected to work approximately half-time each on an annual basis. They also agree to work extra hours when needed (mostly in the summer months). Full-time production-line employees were the first to share jobs, but now a number of clerical workers have formed teams – and the company nurse(s) now share a job.

Flexitime

This allows individual employees to choose their own starting and finishing times. While flexitime workers must normally all be present during "core times" around the middle of the day to ensure effective communication, there are more radical schemes tailored to particular kinds of workers where they do not even have to respect a core time.

The German software company Condat, for example, has 80 staff, mostly highly qualified. To make the job more attractive and retain its workers, Condat now allows them to choose their own working hours. It asks them, however, to plan to work between 30 and 40 hours a week. And although there is no core time, they have to inform the secretariat where they can be reached between 9 a.m. and 4 p.m. on workdays. Workers can raise or reduce their working hours and accumulate credit hours in a "time account" (though they cannot build up debits). Significantly, they can also build up enough credits to be able to take weeks, or even months, of sabbatical leave.

Compressed workweeks

The most common forms of compressed workweek are:

- four days of nine or ten hours
- three 12-hour days
- a week of four working days alternating with a week of five working days.

One of the largest banks in Belgium, the Belgische Arbeiders Cooperatie, has had a nine-hour, four-day working week since the late 1970s at its offices in Brussels and Antwerp. When it introduced the scheme the bank also reduced the working week from 38.45 hours to 36 hours. The new arrangement has proved very popular; of those entitled to work in this way, 90 per cent choose to do so. The lengthening of the working day has enabled employees to avoid rush hours and allowed the bank to make better use of its investment, since the company restaurant, for example, needs only to be geared to four-fifths of the personnel.

In general, however, compressed working weeks have the highest failure rate of all the new scheduling alternatives. The problem is usually the length of the working day, with the possibility of exhaustion and the risk of productivity falling towards the end of the shift. Unions, on the whole, are opposed to such schemes – concerned primarily about fatigue and the potential health problems.

Hours averaging

If workers agree to hours averaging they must work a fixed number of hours over a certain period – a week, say, or a month, or even a year – but must be prepared to change the actual hours they work each day or week to cope with fluctuating demand. At Elite, a French company which manages the stocks and returned empty bottles for Vittel, a mineral water producer, the levels of activity rise and fall with customer thirst which in turn rises and falls, not just seasonally, but daily, depending on the weather. Elite may know only 24 hours ahead what the volume of work will be. To cope with this, the workforce has accepted an average working week of 39 hours, though they will vary this between 34 and 44 hours, accumulating debits and credits depending on the hours they actually put in. There is a limit of 16 hours for debit, and 20 hours for credit – beyond which the company has to take remedial action. Workers also receive a form of overtime, but paid for in time credits rather than cash; employees who work more than 39 hours are credited with 1.25 hours for every extra hour worked – credits which they can later use whenever they choose.

Employers find that hours averaging allows them to adjust to demand and reduces the need to pay for overtime or take on temporary staff. Workers too may prefer this since they do not have to work more intensively during peak periods.

But there can be snags. If working hours are announced at very short notice, workers find it difficult to use their free time. And they may find that their wages fall if they earn less overtime. Trade unions argue, too, that individual annual hours schemes tend to erode worker solidarity.

Shift work

Shift work is, of course, nothing new in itself, but management can combine it with some of the newer flexible working patterns to remove some of the inconveniences to workers – altering shift hours to produce shorter night shifts, perhaps, or finishing Friday shifts early.

The Volvo truck components factory at Köping, in Sweden, has introduced a system of flexible working hours – juggling shifts which might be full time, part-time, night or weekend in various combinations to produce ten different shift schedules which both satisfy workers' needs and respond to fluctuating market demands.

The company has found that combining a two-shift system (6 a.m.-2 p.m. and 2 p.m.-11 p.m.) with a permanent night shift allows equipment to run 24 hours a day if necessary, and is more attractive to workers than a three-shift system.

Making the break

These new working practices are sometimes controversial. And they have often been introduced under pressure. Employers struggling to compete in a tough international environment have had to step up productivity just to survive. And workers may then have to choose between accepting work schedules they do not like and jobs they cannot afford to lose.

Employers and workers in such circumstances can have diametrically opposed interests. Employers emphasise the demands of production and of customer service. Trade unions emphasise the potential harm to health or family or social life and insist that inconvenient hours should be voluntary.

Control is another key question. Who will design and operate these new forms of flexibility? Trade unions will support arrangements which give workers greater choice. Employers may not wish to concede such freedom. The interests and needs of both workers and employers may coincide precisely, but this is unlikely.

Compromises have, however, appeared more commonly than one might have expected. High levels of unemployment have certainly contributed, putting trade unions under considerable pressure to reach

agreements. And the opportunity to bargain for shorter hours has also been a crucial lubricant in sticky negotiations.

But employers have also become more sophisticated in the way they introduce such schemes and have discovered that the chances of acceptance are much greater when workers' representatives have had early, active and influential participation.

Different regions of the world will always have different attitudes towards working hours. Shop opening hours are one of the clearest examples: you can easily buy a Swiss watch at midnight in New York, for example, but you would be hard pressed to do the same in Geneva.

Such contrasts are usually closely linked to both cultural patterns and social values. But although changes are likely to be slow, the differences may narrow over time. Demographic shifts will play a part; single-parent families are becoming much more common, as are households with more than one family member working. And if such workers are also working odd hours, they will want shopping hours to match the time they have available. Changes in one industry can thus spark off changes in another – and changes in one country can provide examples which employers and trade unions may be tempted to follow elsewhere.

Preventing industrial disasters

Chemically ignited fireballs spew into the night sky. Shanty town dwellers flee in terror as their homes are consumed by a raging inferno. A black cloud of smoke swirls up into an eerie pall visible for 20 miles around Bangkok.

The Klong Toey port explosion in Thailand on 2 March 1991 was a shocking experience for everyone involved; for the workers who saw sacks of phosphorus suddenly igniting, and 200-litre tanks of alcohol blowing up all around; for the terrified families of the nearby Koh Lao shanty town who escaped in panic, clutching their meagre possessions; for the troops and fire-fighters who struggled through the greasy black smoke, risking their lives to contain the blaze. Five people died immediately. Three thousand people lost their homes. About thirty thousand more breathed in the toxic fumes.

Nature once had a monopoly of spectacular disaster and the earthquakes in the former USSR last year, the cyclones in Bangladesh and the eruption of

Mount Pinatubo in the Philippines are yet another reminder of its raw power. But mankind has been steadily adding to the possibilities. The skill and ingenuity of scientists and engineers have brought enormous benefits. But the risks have increased too.

Some industrial installations are sites of potential major accidents. The Klong Toey fire in Thailand was on a relatively small scale. But it was reminder of the urgency of facing up to the risks which millions of people run (often unwittingly) by working with, or living around, large quantities of dangerous chemicals.

Two incidents in Europe in the mid-1970s first focused attention on industrial disasters. In 1974 a cyclohexane plant in Flixborough, United Kingdom, exploded, killing 28 workers, injuring 89 others and causing extensive property damage. And in 1976 a process malfunction at a chemical plant in Seveso, Italy, released clouds of a highly toxic chemical, dioxin, into the atmosphere, injuring people and animals.

But 1984 was the year which dramatised the potential horror of industrial hazards. An explosion of liquefied petroleum gas in Mexico City in November 1984 killed 650 people and injured thousands of others. A month later came Bhopal, a city in central India whose name will forever be associated with the hazards of industry. A choking cloud of methyl isocyanate gas from the Union Carbide plant swept through the makeshift houses of the shanty town that had settled around the plant. More than 2,000 people died, 200,000 more were injured – many of them permanently disabled.

The disasters have not abated since. In 1989 a chemical plant making polyethylene in Houston, Texas, exploded, killing 23 workers and injuring more than 130 others. And in Thailand in 1990 an accident with a truck carrying liquid petroleum gas killed 91 people and injured more than 100.

Such shocking incidents viewed on the nightly news may seem random, unconnected, almost arbitrary events. And they do differ in many respects: in location, in their causes and in the chemicals involved. But several common features stand out. All were uncontrolled events arising out of the storage and use of flammable, explosive or toxic substances – with the damage escalating according to the nature of the chemicals and the quantities involved. And the impact of all was felt way beyond the site itself.

The need for regulation

Most countries have safety and health laws to protect workers and the environment under normal conditions. Now, however, the problems can be of a scale and type which few regulatory authorities could ever have envisaged; new materials are being produced and stored in quantities that demand a new approach to control.

Most accidents are caused by unsafe working conditions or practices. So the first priority is always to ensure that the production process is as safe as possible and that the abnormal conditions which can lead to disaster can almost never occur. But no system can be fail-safe. A residual risk may still persist in spite of all the safety precautions, whether through operator error, system failure, or acts of mischief or sabotage. And external shocks, be they earthquakes, floods, heatwaves, even crashing aircraft or terrorist attack, are always a latent threat. Some of these can be anticipated, but many others cannot.

So any system for coping with major hazards must do two things: first, prevent accidents by taking appropriate safety measures; second, minimise the consequences of any accidents which do occur – by ensuring the plant is a safe distance from housing, for example, and drawing up effective emergency plans.

All this demands a high level of cooperation between the management of the enterprise, the workforce running the plant, the government and the regulatory authorities it appoints, and (not least) the community living within the danger zone. Everyone should be aware of the risks they run and of what to do should the worst happen.

The primary responsibility rests with the enterprise. No reputable company will knowingly expose its workers, or anyone else, to unnecessary hazards. So safety must be the prerequisite for the operation of any plant. And though safety does cost money a plant which is operating safely is also usually one where productivity is high.

Government too has an important role – not just providing the necessary legal framework but also ensuring that sufficient information is available and promoting the broadest possible forms of consultation.

Employers, workers, local authorities and members of the local community all need to have their views represented. Conflicts of interest may arise but they are better resolved in a free and open debate than exposed when a disaster has already happened.

The European Community and the Seveso Directive

The European Community has taken some significant steps here. In 1976, after a series of accidents and growing public concern for the protection of the environment, the countries of the EC initiated a study on this issue. They found many regulations for worker protection, product control and air and water pollution control, but very little allowance for the abnormal circumstances that can lead to disaster.

So in 1982 the EC adopted the "Seveso Directive". This classifies potentially hazardous installations into two types depending on the degree of risk, and it defines the measures which need to be taken. At the lower-risk sites, the management is effectively left to make its own arrangements but it must be able to prove to the authorities at any time that it has identified major accident hazards and provided the workers with information and training.

Higher-risk sites require a different approach. If an installation uses certain dangerous substances beyond a threshold quantity it has to notify the competent authority and give a report on the safety measures it is taking. The threshold quantities are defined in a list of 180 chemical substances, with threshold limits which vary between one kilogramme and 50,000 tonnes depending on the material and the degree of risk.

Each country in the European Community has enacted legislation implementing the Seveso Directive. In 1988 the number of sites subject to notification were as follows: Belgium (93), Denmark (68), France (322), the then Federal Republic of Germany (283), Greece (10), Ireland (50), Italy (351), Luxembourg (3), Netherlands (65), Spain (300) and the United Kingdom (283). In Germany the legislation was revised recently and over 3,000 installations are now covered.

Each EC country has, however, implemented the Directive in a slightly different fashion, either in terms of the authorities to be notified, for example, or the precise character of the safety report.

They also differ on the way that the public is notified. The overall safety plan has to be publicly available only in France. Elsewhere just the off-site emergency plans need be shown, and even then only for certain sites – as in Denmark, Germany, the Netherlands and the United Kingdom.

But even if the overall plans are not published there should still be some information available to the general public. There are two possible approaches

here – "passive" or "active". The passive approach is merely to make documents available for public inspection. The active alternative is announce the information in some way.

The United States

In the United States similar measures have been taken to face up to industrial hazards – bringing together government, industry, unions and many other interested groups. The framework for such efforts is the Emergency Planning and Community Right to Know Act which Congress passed in 1986. Based on this Act, two levels of supervision have been established. At the state level there are Emergency Response Commissions which coordinate Local Emergency Planning Committees. These committees examine reports from the management of major hazard installations in their area and require their participation in the preparation of emergency plans.

Government agencies, individual states, industry groupings and trade unions also take their own measures. The Occupational Health and Safety Administration, for example, has recently proposed new legislation for a comprehensive safety management programme. Several states, including New Jersey, California and Delaware, have developed, or are developing, legislation on this issue. The Chemical Manufacturers Associations has developed a Chemical Awareness and Emergency Response Program. And workers' organisations, such as the AFL-CIO, have produced a variety of training manuals on hazardous chemicals and emergency response.

However, there is some dissatisfaction in the United States with the current legislation. A coalition of trade unions and environmentalists is demanding legislation which would give them not just the "right to know" but a "right to act". They are concerned that many hazards are not being addressed; employers have found ways of withholding information and government standards are not high enough. There is also a problem with inspection personnel. Campaigners argue that a workplace in New Jersey, for example, would be inspected an average of once every 60 years. Following such pressure, right-to-act legislation has already been introduced in New Jersey. This would empower community organisations to inspect facilities with an expert of their choice and allow them to discuss with the owner or operator means of eliminating hazards. Similar legislation is also being drafted in Michigan.

Different approaches in other countries

Japan has several laws in this area enforced by different government authorities. The 1976 Accident Prevention Act for Petrochemical Complexes, for example, covered 901 establishments by 1989. Its requirements include notification of plant layout to the competent authorities, the establishment of a green buffer between the complexes and the local community, and the preparation of emergency plans in cooperation with local authorities.

In the former USSR the State Committee for Occupational Safety Supervision in Industry and in Nuclear Energetics approves a list of potentially hazardous chemicals as well as the safety rules and regulations which should be applied to them. Plant management, in coordination with local authorities, carries out emergency planning. And the enforcement of major hazard control measures is the primary responsibility of the State Commission for Emergency Situations of the Council of Ministers of the former USSR.

In other countries, including Australia and Finland, some elements of a major hazard control system are also in place. But in many industrialised countries (and most developing ones) there are no special regulations or standards covering the field of major hazard control as a system.

Developing countries

The greatest problems are probably faced by developing countries through a combination of factors:

- *Transfer of technology* – from industrialised countries, often involving very complex processes and dangerous materials.
- *Inadequate infrastructure* – while the investment in plant is made by the private sector, the public investment in terms of roads, communications and public welfare services often cannot keep pace.
- *Weak legislation* – which does not reflect the latest technology.
- *Low enforcement* – there are generally relatively few inspectors, even for major sites; indeed, there is a lack of skilled personnel in many important areas.

- *Lack of housing planning* – dangerous sites can be located in residential communities, or unplanned housing can spring up around the sites.

Many governments are aware of these problems, but they may not have the resources to tackle them. In many cases economic growth is the highest priority and health and safety matters may be regarded as something of a luxury. The lack of an adequate regulatory framework can even be an attraction for certain companies considering new plants.

However, many countries have now taken positive action. In Mexico, following the disaster in Mexico City, both Government and industry began in 1986 to establish new mechanisms and organisations to improve safety and increase the awareness of local people. The Government has now included requirements on major hazard control in federal labour laws and established a system of civil defence with a special section dealing with chemical and toxic threats.

India too is developing a more advanced system of hazard control. From 1985, following the Bhopal disaster, a task force was formed in each state to identify major hazard installations. This concluded that out of 100,000 or so factories, 599 could be considered major hazards. And in 1988 an ILO project was started with the Central Labour Institute in Bombay, involving the collection of data, training and the preparation of new technical guidelines.

ILO experts have also been working in cooperation with national authorities in a number of other countries. In Thailand about 60 installations have so far been identified (though there are thought to be up to 150) and draft legislation is being developed. A similar programme has just been started in Indonesia where 18 major hazard installations have been identified (out of 50 expected to exist) and a programme may also be developed in Pakistan.

Keeping hazards under control

The development of adequate hazard control systems may seem a daunting prospect for many countries. The lack of money, of personnel and of experience may appear to postpone such developments for the poorest countries into the indefinite future. It will certainly not be an easy task. But they could take heart from the fact that much wealthier countries took decades to develop systems of control to match the hazards that their people were facing.

And developing countries do at least have a body of international experience on which to draw.

In 1991 the ILO published a Code of Practice on the Prevention of Major Industrial Accidents. And in 1992 the International Labour Conference will consider new international instruments to lay down principles and policies that could help develop action at the national and enterprise levels.

Each country will in the end have to arrive at systems appropriate to its own needs. And even if it has to do so in a progressive manner, taking into account the resources available, this should not detract from a sense of urgency – a sense which the news headlines are likely to maintain and probably heighten in the years to come.

Bibliographical note

This report draws on a wide variety of sources including reports produced by the ILO and other international organisations, and a broad range of other journals and publications. Most of these are indicated below, except for those internal ILO documents which have not been published.

Selected sources — by chapter

Chapter 1

The chief sources for the section on freedom of association were ILO (1991a, 1991b and 1991c). For human rights in general: ILO (1988) and Davies (1988). For the section on child labour the chief general sources were ILO (1986), Bequele and Boyden (1988), Fyfe (1989), Myers (1991) and UNICEF (1986), with legislative information from ILO (1991d). Information for specific regions included, for Asia, CWA (1990) and for Latin America, ILO (1991e) and Myers (1989). Reports on individual countries included: Espínola et al. (1987); Golodner (1990); Ho (1988); ILO (1988b); MacLennan et al. (1985); Rialp (1992) and Schaule Jullens (1990). For the section on equal opportunities for women the chief sources were ILO (1990a), United Nations (1991), Henshall Momsen (1991), Lean Lim (1991). Information on individual countries included Armstrong (1990), Fierman (1990), McDermott (1989), Rao (1990) and Servais (1990).

Chapter 2

Main sources on employment include: for the industrial market economies, OECD (1991), United Nations/ECE (1991), UNDP (1991), Rodgers and Rodgers (1989) and Standing (1991): for Eastern Europe and the former Soviet Union, Standing and Sziráczki (1991); for Africa, ILO/JASPA (1990), van der Hoeven (1991) and World Bank (1991); for Asia, ILO (1991f), United Nations/ESCAP (1991), Edgren (1990) and Islam (1990); for Latin America and the Caribbean, ILO (1991g). The section on migration from Eastern Europe and the former Soviet Union includes information from Böhning (1991), Ipsos (1991), Kosmarsky (1990), Miller (1991), Okolski (1991) and Schmid (1991). For the section on migration in Asia the sources included Abella (1991), Balakrishnan (1991), Baum (1991), Eng Fong (1990), Fujiyasa (1991) and Shaw Myers (1991).

Chapter 3

For labour relations the principle sources were: industrial market economies, OECD (1991), Pankert (1991), and Standing (1991); for Eastern Europe and the former Soviet Union, Héthy (1991), and McShane (1991); for Africa, Mesfin Gabre, M. (1991); for Asia, Joon (1991), Velasco (1991) and Young Vae (1991); and for Latin America and the Caribbean, Ermida Uriarte (1991).

Chapter 4

The section on social protection in Eastern Europe and the former Soviet Union is based largely on Gillion (1991) and Holzmann (1991). For the section on flexible working hours the sources were ILO (1990b) and Bosch (1990). For the section on preventing industrial disasters the sources included ILO (1991h and 1991i) and Tobey (1990).

Selected sources

Abella, M. 1991. *Structural change and labour migration within the Asian region.* Bangkok, ILO; mimeographed.

Armstrong, P. 1990. "Is there still a chairman of the Board?", in *Journal of Management Development* (Bradford, United Kingdom), 8, 6.

Balakrishnan, N. 1991. "Under the hammer", in *Far Eastern Economic Review* (Hong Kong), 4 Apr.

Baum, J. 1991. "Taiwan's building block", in *Far Eastern Economic Review* (Hong Kong), 2 May.

Bequele, A.; Boyden, J. 1988. *Combating child labour.* Geneva, ILO.

Böhning, R. 1991. *International migration to Western Europe: What to do?* Seminar on International Security, The Graduate Institute of International Studies. Geneva, ILO; mimeographed.

Bosch, G. 1990. "From 40 to 35 hours", in *International Labour Review* (Geneva, ILO), 1990/5.

CWA (1990), in various issues of *Child Workers in Asia (CWA) 1990-91.* Bangkok.

Davies, P. 1988. *Human Rights.* London and New York, Routledge.

Edgren, G. "Employment adjustment and the unions: Case studies of enterprises in Asia", in *International Labour Review* (Geneva, ILO), 1990/5.

Eng Fong, P. 1990. *Foreign workers in Singapore: Policies, trends and implications.* Expert group meeting on cross-national migration in the Asian region. Nagoya, UNCRD.

Ermida Uriarte, O. 1991. "Las relaciones de trabajo en América Latina", in *Crítica & comunicación* (Lima, ILO).

Espínola, B.; Glauser, B.; Ortiz, R. M.; Ortiz de Carrizosa. 1987. *En la calle: Menores trabajadores de la calle en Asunción.* Asunción, Callescuela.

Fierman, J. 1990. "Why women still don't hit the top", in *Fortune International* (New York), 30 July.

Fujiyasa, M. 1991. "Japan pressed to open doors to more foreign workers", in *Tokyo Business Today.* Feb., Tokyo.

Fyfe, A. 1989. *Child labour.* Cambridge, Polity Press.

Gillion, C. 1991. *Social protection in East and Central European countries.* Geneva, ILO; mimeographed.

Golodner, L. 1990. "The children of today's sweatshops", in *Business and Society Review* (Darien, Connecticut, United States), No. 73.

Henshall Momsen, J. 1991. *Women and development in the Third World.* London and New York, Routledge.

Héthy, L. 1991. *Especially disadvantaged children in India: A literature survey.* Oxford, Children in Development; mimeographed.

van der Hoeven, R. 1990. "Adjustment with a human face: Still relevant or overtaken by events?", in *World Development*, Vol. 19, No. 12, Oxford.

Ho, C. 1988. *Especially disadvantaged children in India: A literature survey.* Oxford, Children in Development; mimeographed.

Holzmann, R. 1991. *Adapting to economic change: Reconciling social protection with market economies.* Geneva, ILO; mimeographed.

ILO. 1986. *Child labour: A briefing manual*, Geneva.

——. 1988a. *Human rights: A common responsibility.* Report of the Director-General, International Labour Conference, 75th Session, Geneva.

——. 1988b. "The emerging response to child labour", in *Conditions of Work Digest, 1/1988.* Geneva.

——. 1990a. Tripartite Symposium on Equality of Opportunity and Treatment for Men and Women in Employment in Industrialised Countries. Technical background paper. Geneva.

——. 1990b. "The hours we work: New work schedules in policy and practice", in *Conditions of Work Digest*, (Geneva, ILO), 2/1990.

——. 1991a. Reports of the Committee on Freedom of Association. (Reports 270-278).

——. 1991b. "Report on the situation of workers of the occupied territories", in *Report of the Director-General. Appendices (Vol. 2).* International Labour Conference, 78th Session, Geneva.

——. 1991c, *Report of the Committee of Experts on the Application of Conventions and Recommendations.* Report III (Part 4A). International Labour Conference, 78th Session, Geneva.

——. 1991d. "Child labour: Law and practice", in *Conditions of Work Digest* (Geneva, ILO) 1/1991.

——. 1991e. *Nota sobre las labores.* Latin American Regional Seminar on the Abolition of Child Labour and the Protection of Working Children. Geneva.

——. 1991f. *Report of the Director-General.* Eleventh Asian Regional Conference, Bangkok, Part I: "Growth and structural adjustment".

——. 1991g. *Employment policies in the economic restructuring of Latin America and the Caribbean.* Tripartite Symposium on Structural Adjustment, Employment and Training in Latin America and the Caribbean. Geneva.

——. 1991h. *Prevention of industrial disasters.* Report V(1), International Labour Conference, 79th Session. Geneva.

——. 1991i. *Code of practice on the prevention of major industrial accidents.* Geneva, ILO.

ILO/JASPA. 1990. *African Employment Report.* Addis Ababa.

IPSOS/World Media. 1991. Reported in "La gran escapada?", in *El País*, 3 June, Madrid.

Islam, R. 1990. "Rural poverty, growth and macroeconomic policies: The Asian experience", in *International Labour Review* (Geneva, ILO), 1990/6.

Joon, T. 1991. "Singapore country report". *ILO sub-regional seminar on the development of sound labour relations.* Kuala Lumpur, NTUC; mimeographed.

Kosmarsky, V. 1990. "How many Soviet citizens want to work abroad?", in *Izvestia* (Moscow). August 10.

Lean Lim, L. 1991. *The feminization of labour in the Asian Pacific Rim countries.* Bangkok, ILO; mimeographed.

MacLennan, E.; Fitz, J.; Sullivan, J. 1985. *Working Children.* London, Low Pay Unit.

McDermott, P.C. 1989. *From equal pay to pay equity: The Canadian experience*. Geneva, ILO; mimeographed.

McShane, D. 1990. "Eastern promise?" in *International Labour Reports* (Barnsley, United Kingdom), No. 40.

Mesfin Gabre, M. 1991. *Key issues for the promotion of sound labour relations in Africa*. National tripartite seminar for the promotion of sound labour relations in Zimbabwe. Geneva, ILO; mimeographed.

Miller, P. 1991. *The process of economic reform in Central and Eastern Europe: Its impact on the labour market and the international migration of workers*. Issues paper for informal meeting of Ministers of Labour. Geneva, ILO; mimeographed.

Myers, M.E. 1989. "Urban working children: A comparison of four surveys from South America", in *International Labour Review* (ILO). 1989/3.

Myers, W.E. (ed.). 1991. *Protecting working children*, London and New Jersey, Zed Books/UNICEF.

Okolski, M. 1991. *Migratory movements from countries of Central and Eastern Europe*. Conference of Ministers on the movement of persons coming from Central and Eastern European countries. Strasbourg, Council of Europe.

OECD. 1991. *Employment Outlook*. Paris.

Pankert, A. 1991. *Tendances et problèmes récents en matière de relations professionnelles dans les pays industrialisés à économie de marché*. Geneva, ILO; mimeographed.

Rao, M.H. 1990. "Employment of the wife and husband's participation in housework", in *Indian Journal of Social Work* (Bombay), No. 3.

Rialp, V. 1992. *Children in prostitution and fishing: Advocacy as a deterrent*. Geneva, ILO; forthcoming.

Rodgers, G. and Rodgers, J. (ed.). 1989. *Precarious jobs in labour market regulation*, Geneva, ILO.

Schaule Jullens, M.L. (ed.) 1990. *International child labour seminar*. Amsterdam, Delft.

Schmid, R. 1991. "L'Union soviétique entrouvre ses frontières", in *Journal de Genève* (Geneva). 21 May.

Servais, J.-M. 1990. "Las mujeres en el trabajo: Protección o igualdad?", in *INFORMA* (Lima, ILO), No. 4.

Shaw Myers, F. 1991. "Foreign labour: The approaching crunch, in *Mainichi Daily News*, 2 May.

Standing, G. 1991. *Labour insecurity through market regulation: Legacy of the 1980s, challenge for the 1990s*. Geneva, ILO; mimeographed.

Standing, G. and Sziráczki, G. (eds.) 1991. "Labour market transitions in Eastern Europe and the Soviet Union", in *International Labour Review*, Special Issue, 1991/2. Geneva.

Tobey, S. 1990. "Taking control: Workers and communities demand the right to act," in *Multinational Monitor* (Washington, DC), June.

UNDP. 1991. *Human Development Report*. New York.

UNICEF. 1986. *Exploitation of working children and street children*. Executive Board 1986 session, 14 Mar. E/ICEF/1986/CRP.3. New York, UNICEF.

United Nations. 1991. *The world's women 1970-1990: Trends and statistics*. New York, United Nations.

United Nations/ESCAP. 1991. *Economic and Social Survey of Asia and the Pacific 1990*. New York.

United Nations/ECE. 1991. *Economic Survey of Europe in 1990-91*. New York.

Velasco, P.B. 1991. *Industrial relations in the Philippines*. ILO subregional seminar to promote sound labour relations, Kuala Lumpur. Department of Labor; mimeographed.

World Bank. 1991. *World Development Report*. Washington DC.

Young Vae, K. 1991. *Several issues to promote sound labour relations in Korea*. ILO subregional seminar to promote sound labour relations, Hong Kong. Korea Employers' Federation; mimeographed.

Statistical appendix

This annex provides information on the main features of the social and labour scene in the world. Most of the indicators in this annex are collected by the ILO and published in its *Year Book of Labour Statistics.*

In this annex the term "country" does not imply political independence but may refer to any territory whose authorities produce separate social and labour statistics. The annex contains information on 128 countries, i.e. those with a population of more than one million inhabitants.

Although every effort has been made to standardise the data, they are not always comparable between countries. Thus, care must be taken in interpreting the indicators. For some countries that have recently been reunified, such as Germany and Yemen, statistics may refer to respectively the former Federal Republic of Germany and Democratic Yemen.

This annex consists of 8 main tables.

Table I. Socio-economic indicators

Real Gross Domestic Product per capita statistics give an indication of welfare levels, as GDP measures the total value added created within a country's territory. These statistics were taken from the World Bank and supplemented with estimates based on OECD-data.

The *annual rate of inflation* is measured by the general price index covering all consumption expenditure items. If such index is not available, the index excluding rent is taken. For some developing countries the index covers only the capital city or a group of major cities. The average annual rate of inflation for 1980-88 has been calculated on the basis of ILO statistics. The rates for 1989 and 1990 have in principle been selected from the ILO, but supplemented by data from the IMF for some countries.

The *poverty incidence* estimates are derived from a host of studies, the results of which are stored in ILO's compendium of data on the incidence of poverty in developing countries. Comparable estimates for industrialised countries were not available. The estimates are generally comparable over time and across (rural and urban) areas, since they are mostly based on country studies that use a common methodology and similar poverty lines. However, they may not be comparable between countries. The first observation refers to the mid-1970s, or to a year as close to that period as possible. The second observation refers to comparable figures for the latest year available for the 1980s.

The *dependency rates* measure the number of children (0-14) and elder people (65+) as a percentage of the potentially employable part of the population (15-64). They give some indication of the effort that working people in a country should undertake to bring up children and to care for the elderly. The rates are based on the most recent UN World Population Prospects.

The *adult literacy rates* measure the percentage of adults (persons of 15 years and older) that can read and write. They are based on UNESCO estimates and are given separately for men and women. These rates give an indication of the quality of the labour force and of the educational gap between men and women.

Table II. Ratification of basic ILO Conventions

By the end of 1991 the International Labour Organisation had formulated 172 labour Conventions, international legal instruments that impose on ratifying States binding obligations subjected to regular international supervision. The Conventions cover a wide area of labour and social issues, ranging from basic human rights to industrial relations, wages, hours of work, social security, and safety and health.

Table II shows the total number of ratifications per country and its ratification record on some basic ILO Conventions.

Table III. Labour force and employment trends

The average annual growth rates of *the population and the labour force* are shown for the 1980s and the 1990s. They are based on respectively the United Nations' and the ILO's most recent labour force projections.

The growth rates of *employment in and outside agriculture* are based on official estimates and statistics collected through labour force sample surveys and reported to the ILO. The data refer to total employment, including self-employment, wage employment and family labour.

The annual growth rates of *formal wage employment in manufacturing* are based on social insurance records and establishment surveys. Workers recorded by establishment surveys are considered to belong to the formal sector, since they are employed in establishments with more than five or ten people. The data collected by the ILO for its *Year Book* are supplemented by those collected by UNIDO.

Table IV. The structure of employment and the labour force

Most data in this table are taken from labour force sample surveys or official estimates, as they usually provide comparable data over time. Census data take second priority as they are generally carried out only at five- or ten-year intervals.

Activity rates measure the labour force participation of men and women. They are defined as the percentage of economically active persons in the 15 to 64 years age group.

This table includes three indicators of the changing employment structure over the past ten years: the *distribution by major sector*, the percentage of *wage employment in total employment* and the percentage of *women in wage employment outside agriculture*.

Table V. The structure of unemployment

Statistics on unemployment refer to all persons from a specific age group who during the reference period were without work, currently available for work and seeking work. These statistics are generally collected through labour force sample surveys. Where possible, the table shows the ILO estimates of unemployment rates since they are more comparable than the raw survey data.

Table VI. Real wages and compensation costs, and working time

The indicators on wage and compensation cost levels are given in real terms: they have been adjusted for consumer price changes over time.

The *legal minimum wage rates* were collected mainly from national publications. Wage rates refer only to payments in cash or in kind for adults working normal hours, that is, excluding overtime payments and other supplements. Where different legal minimum wage rates exist, the one covering (partially or completely) the manufacturing sector was chosen.

Statistics on *wages in manufacturing* are taken from payroll data supplied by a sample of establishments. They were taken from the OECD and PREALC for respectively the industrialised countries and Latin America, and from the ILO for all other countries. The wage data refer to earnings which are usually cash payments for normal working hours and overtime. They also include bonuses, cost-of-living allowances and special premiums, but exclude employers' contributions to social security. The earnings reported to the ILO are usually gross, that is, they include income taxes and workers' contributions to social security.

International comparable estimates on *hourly compensation costs* have been developed by the Bureau of Labor Statistics (BLS) in Washington, DC. They define compensation costs as the sum of gross earnings and the employers' contribution to social security.

The data on *normal annual working time* come from different sources. The data on OECD countries were taken from the Confederation of German Employers' Organisations. For the developing countries the data on normal weekly hours refer to a welder in the metal products manufacturing sector. They are usually based on information from collective agreements and are reported in ILO's October Inquiry. The information on annual leave represents the current provision for the national legal minimum. The information on public holidays was obtained from Swissair.

Table VII. Strikes and accidents at work

The ILO defines *strikes and lockouts* as "temporary work stoppages wilfully effected by a group of workers or by one or more employers with a view to enforcing or resisting a demand or expressing a grievance". In general, these statistics are the by-product of an administrative process, in which the notification of a work stoppage is often voluntary. For some countries, information is not compiled on political strikes, illegal strikes or strikes in certain branches of economic activity. The statistics on days not worked as a result of strikes and lockouts in manufacturing give some indication of labour unrest during the second half of the 1980s.

Statistics on *fatal accidents at work* are mainly obtained from compulsory accident reporting systems and work accident compensation schemes, and sometimes from establishment surveys. The use of these three sources may create some incomparability between countries, but the different definition of what constitutes an accident at work is the greatest source of incomparability. The ILO defines accidents at work as occurring in the course of work. But many countries also include in their statistics deaths resulting from commuting accidents or occupational illnesses. If countries use a wider definition of fatal accidents at work, then this is marked for each observation.

Table VIII. Social security

The statistics on social security are taken from the ILO's inquiry on the cost of social security. This inquiry takes place every three years, but will from 1991 onwards be supplemented by a much smaller annual survey on the scope of social security. For countries with the financial year from 1 July to 30 June and from 1 October to 30 September the figures are related to the ending year (e.g. figures for 1986/87 are reported as relating to 1987).

The percentages on *government contribution* and *benefit expenditure* in GDP give a broad indication of the macroeconomic importance of the social security system and the role of the government.

The percentage of *coverage of persons insured* measures the scope of different social security programmes. These percentages should refer to currently insured persons only. However, some countries could have reported registered persons, which will lead to an overestimation of these indicators. The coverage is measured against the total labour force as estimated by the ILO's labour force projections. It would be preferable to relate the coverage to total or non-agricultural wage employment, but those data are not systematically available for all countries. Wherever it is known that the whole population is protected by a particular scheme, the percentage of coverage has been set at 100 per cent.

The data on *benefits and benefit expenditure* measure the degree of protection that persons insured under various programmes can receive. The indicator on benefit expenditure on sickness benefits should refer to cash benefits only. If an unusually high figure is found, this may be due to the inclusion of medical benefits.

Signs and symbols used in the tables

On data

*   Data referring to an earlier year than defined in the heading
.   Data not available or not applicable
–   Data null or less than half of the unit employed
Estimates

On headings

/   Data refer to the most recently available year of the bracket (e.g. 1989/90)
–   Data cover the whole period indicated in the bracket (e.g. 1980-88)

I. Socio-economic indicators

	Gross Domestic Product per capita (1987 US$) 1990	Annual rate of inflation (%) 1980-1988	1989	1990	Population in poverty (%) Urban mid-1970s	Urban 1981-1990	Rural mid-1970s	Rural 1981-1990	Dependency rates (% of 15-64 population) (0-14 yrs) 1990	(65+) 1990	Adult literacy (% of 15+ population) Male 1990	Female 1990
Africa												
Algeria	2 690	8.9	9.3	16.6	20	.	.	.	83	7	70	46
Angola	770*	.	.	.	.	.	65	.	86	6	56	29
Benin	350	.	.	.	.	.	65	.	92	6	32	16
Botswana	1 480*	10.0	11.6	11.3	40	.	55	.	104	7	84	65
Burkina Faso	300	4.7	-0.5	-0.8	.	.	.	.	83	6	28	9
Burundi	230	7.1	11.6	7.0	55	.	85	.	88	6	61	40
Cameroon	910	10.6	-2.3	.	15	.	40	.	93	7	66	43
Central African Rep.	370	5.3	0.7	-0.2	.	.	91	.	87	7	52	25
Chad	160	3.1	-4.7	0.4	30	.	56	.	80	7	42	17
Congo	1 060	6.7	—	2.9	.	.	.	.	91	7	70	44
Côte d'Ivoire	800	6.4	1.3	.	.	30	.	26	98	5	67	40
Egypt	740	16.4	21.3	16.8	.	34	44	34	69	7	63	34
Ethiopia	110	3.9	7.8	5.1	60	.	65	.	88	6	.	.
Gabon	3 290	5.3	6.9	8.7	.	.	.	.	53	10	74	49
Ghana	390	46.1	25.2	37.3	.	59	43	54	88	5	70	51
Guinea	420	.	.	.	.	.	.	.	92	5	35	13
Kenya	380	10.4	9.8	11.8	10	.	55	.	106	6	80	59
Lesotho	260	14.1	14.7	9.6	50	.	55	.	81	7	.	.
Liberia	.	4.5	5.9	8.1	23	.	23	.	89	7	50	29
Libyan Arab Jamahiriya	5 340*	.	.	.	.	.	.	.	89	5	75	50
Madagascar	250	19.5	9.0	11.8	50	21	50	37	87	6	88	73
Malawi	160	17.1	12.4	11.8	25	.	85	.	99	5	.	.
Mali	250	.	-0.1	0.5	27	.	48	.	93	5	41	24
Mauritania	500	.	13.0	6.5	.	.	.	.	85	6	47	21
Mauritius	2 020	7.0	12.6	13.5	12	.	12	.	45	8	.	.
Morocco	860	7.8	3.1	6.7	38	28	45	32	72	6	61	38
Mozambique	100	.	.	.	.	.	.	.	83	6	45	21
Namibia	990*	.	.	.	.	.	.	.	90	6	.	.
Niger	290	3.1	-2.8	-0.8	.	.	35	.	96	5	40	17
Nigeria	240*	18.1	40.9	28.3	33	.	40	.	95	5	62	40
Rwanda	280	.	1.0	4.2	30	.	90	.	101	5	64	37
Senegal	670	7.3	0.4	0.3	.	.	.	.	88	6	52	25
Sierra Leone	150	63.8	62.8	111.0	65	.	66	.	85	6	31	11
Somalia	160	45.6	.	.	40	.	70	.	94	5	36	14
South Africa	2 500*	14.7	14.7	14.4	.	.	.	.	63	7	.	.
Sudan	590	32.8	66.1	81.4	.	.	85	.	87	5	43	12
Tanzania, United Rep. of	160	30.5	25.8	19.7	10	.	60	.	101	5	.	.
Togo	370	4.7	-1.2	1.0	42	.	.	.	88	6	56	31
Tunisia	1 330	8.4	7.4	6.8	34	16	43	31	66	7	74	56
Uganda	250	119.1	82.4	35.3	.	.	.	.	103	5	62	35
Zaire	210	.	.	.	.	.	80	.	90	5	84	61
Zambia	270	30.7	124.7	.	24	.	52	.	101	5	81	65
Zimbabwe	630	13.6	12.9	17.4	.	.	.	.	86	5	74	60
Americas												
Argentina	2 290	255.2	3 195	2 314	9	15	19	20	49	15	96	95
Bolivia	650	316.7	15.2	17.1	.	.	85	86	83	6	85	71
Brazil	2 000	178.7	1 201	2 901	34	38	68	66	59	8	83	80
Canada	16 798‡	6.2	5.0	4.8	.	.	.	.	31	17	.	.
Chile	1 730	20.0	17.0	26.0	12	.	25	.	48	9	94	93
Colombia	1 240	23.0	25.9	29.6	40	40	48	45	60	7	88	86
Costa Rica	1 840	27.6	16.5	19.0	18	24	28	30	61	7	93	93
Cuba	.	.	.	.	.	.	.	.	33	12	95	93
Dominican Republic	710	18.5	45.4	59.5	45	.	43	.	64	6	85	82
Ecuador	1 130	30.1	75.6	48.5	40	40	65	65	70	7	88	84
El Salvador	940	18.6	17.6	24.0	20	.	32	.	86	7	76	70
Guatemala	860	11.8	11.4	41.2	47	60	84	80	88	6	63	47
Haiti	320	4.9	7.5	20.9	55	65	78	80	72	7	59	47
Honduras	850	5.7	9.8	23.3	14	74	55	80	86	6	76	71
Jamaica	1 380	13.9	14.9	21.3	.	.	80	.	55	11	98	99
Mexico	1 780	77.6	20.0	26.7	20	23	49	43	63	7	90	85
Nicaragua	720	.	.	.	21	.	19	.	89	5	.	.
Panama	1 900	2.2	-0.1	0.6	36	36	50	52	58	8	88	88
Paraguay	1 010	19.3	26.0	38.2	19	.	50	.	72	6	92	88
Peru	980	132.5	3 399	7 482	38	52	80	72	64	6	92	79
Trinidad and Tobago	3 560	11.2	11.4	11.0	.	.	39	40	56	9	.	.
United States	19 207‡	4.6	4.8	5.4	.	.	.	.	33	19	.	.
Uruguay	2 400	52.8	80.4	112.5	13	19	27	29	41	19	97	96
Venezuela	2 480	15.3	84.5	40.7	20	30	43	42	66	6	87	90

	Gross Domestic Product per capita (1987 US$) 1990	Annual rate of inflation (%)			Population in poverty (%)				Dependency rates (% of 15-64 population)		Adult literacy (% of 15+ population)	
					Urban		Rural					
		1980-1988	1989	1990	mid-1970s	1981-1990	mid-1970s	1981-1990	(0-14 yrs) 1990	(65+) 1990	Male 1990	Female 1990
Asia and Oceania												
Afghanistan		15.8	71.5	47.4	18	.	36	.	76	5	44	14
Australia	13 332‡	8.3	7.6	7.2	.	.	.	.	33	16	.	.
Bangladesh	170	11.1	10.0	8.1	81	56	83	51	82	5	47	22
Bhutan	220	.	.	.	.	.	.	.	70	6	.	.
Cambodia	.	.	.	.	.	.	.	.	.	.	48	22
China	320	7.0	16.3	1.3	.	6	65	13	39	9	84	62
Hong Kong	9 260	7.6	10.1	9.7	.	.	.	.	29	13	.	.
India	360	9.2	7.1	8.8	46	38	59	49	62	8	62	34
Indonesia	510	9.0	6.4	12.5	39	20	40	16	59	7	84	68
Iran, Islamic Rep. of	2 820	19.0	22.4	7.6	13	.	38	.	84	7	65	43
Iraq	.	.	.	.	.	.	40	.	92	5	70	49
Israel	8 890	115.5	20.2	17.2	.	.	.	.	52	15	.	.
Japan	22 881‡	1.9	2.3	3.1	.	.	.	.	26	17	.	.
Jordan	1 720	4.1	25.8	16.1	14	.	17	.	84	5	89	70
Korea, Dem. People's Rep. of	.	.	.	.	.	.	.	.	42	6	.	.
Korea, Republic of	3 970	6.0	5.7	8.6	18	5	12	4	37	7	99	94
Kuwait	12 970*	3.2	3.3	.	.	.	.	.	56	2	77	67
Lao People's Dem. Rep.	320	.	.	.	.	.	.	.	82	6	.	.
Lebanon	.	.	.	.	.	.	.	.	61	9	88	73
Malaysia	2 310	3.3	2.8	3.1	18	8	48	25	66	6	87	70
Mongolia	.	.	.	.	.	.	.	.	74	6	.	.
Myanmar	.	8.7	27.2	17.6	40	.	40	.	63	7	89	72
Nepal	170	10.5	8.5	9.4	22	19	36	43	77	6	38	13
New Zealand	10 648‡	11.9	5.7	6.1	.	.	.	.	34	16	.	.
Oman	.	.	.	.	.	.	.	.	91	5	.	.
Pakistan	350	6.6	7.8	9.1	32	20	41	31	88	5	47	21
Papua New Guinea	790	5.8	4.5	6.9	10	.	75	.	71	4	65	38
Philippines	650	14.2	10.6	12.7	38	42	58	58	71	6	90	90
Saudi Arabia	5 470*	−0.4	1.1	2.1	.	.	.	.	87	5	73	48
Singapore	9 770	2.1	2.4	3.4	.	.	.	.	33	8	.	.
Sri Lanka	450	11.2	11.6	21.5	20	15	27	36	52	8	93	84
Syrian Arab Republic	1 110	23.4	11.4	19.4	.	.	60	54	98	5	78	51
Thailand	1 230	4.2	6.3	6.7	13	6	33	34	51	6	96	90
Turkey	1 380	41.4	69.6	63.6	.	.	.	.	57	7	90	71
United Arab Emirates	16 470*	.	.	.	.	.	.	.	45	3	.	.
Viet Nam	910	.	.	.	.	.	.	.	70	8	92	84
Yemen	460*	4.2	.	.	.	.	20	.	85	5	53	26
Europe and the former Soviet Union												
Albania	.	.	.	.	.	.	.	.	53	9	.	.
Austria	17 103‡	3.7	2.5	3.3	.	.	.	.	26	22	.	.
Belgium	15 659‡	4.9	3.1	3.5	.	.	.	.	27	22	.	.
Bulgaria	2 820	1.2	6.4	.	.	.	.	.	30	19	.	.
Czechoslovakia	3 320	1.3	1.3	10.0	.	.	.	.	36	18	.	.
Denmark	20 585‡	6.5	4.8	2.6	.	.	.	.	25	23	.	.
Finland	19 851‡	6.8	6.6	6.1	.	.	.	.	29	20	.	.
France	17 394‡	7.0	3.6	3.4	.	.	.	.	30	21	.	.
Germany	19 768‡	2.6	2.8	2.7	.	.	.	.	22	22	.	.
Greece	4 910	19.5	13.7	20.4	.	.	.	.	30	21	98	89
Hungary	2 380	7.9	17.0	28.9	.	.	.	.	30	20	.	.
Ireland	9 877‡	8.7	4.0	3.3	.	.	.	.	45	17	.	.
Italy	14 364‡	10.5	6.3	6.5	.	.	.	.	24	21	98	96
Netherlands	15 739‡	2.6	1.1	2.5	.	.	.	.	26	18	.	.
Norway	19 960‡	8.5	4.6	4.1	.	.	.	.	29	25	.	.
Poland	1 550	32.1	251.1	584.7	.	.	.	.	39	15	.	.
Portugal	4 050	18.2	12.6	13.4	.	.	.	.	32	20	89	82
Romania	1 420	3.7	0.5	4.8	.	.	.	.	35	15	.	.
Spain	8 596‡	10.0	6.8	6.7	.	.	.	.	30	20	97	93
Sweden	19 650‡	7.4	6.5	10.4	.	.	.	.	27	28	.	.
Switzerland	27 780‡	3.2	3.2	5.4	.	.	.	.	24	22	.	.
United Kingdom	13 406‡	6.0	7.8	9.5	.	.	.	.	29	23	.	.
ex-USSR	.	1.2	1.8	5.2	.	.	.	.	39	15	.	.
Yugoslavia	2 560	74.3	1 252	580.4	.	.	.	.	33	14	97	88

II. Ratification of basic ILO Conventions (as of 31 October 1991)

	Total number of ratifications	Freedom of Association		Rural Workers Organisations (No. 141)	Forced Labour		Discrimination		Child Labour Minimum Age (No. 138)	Employment Policy (No. 122)
		Right to Organise (No. 87)	Collective Bargaining (No. 98)		Forced Labour (No. 29)	Abolition (No. 105)	Employment & Occupation (No. 111)	Equal Remuneration (No. 100)		
Africa										
Algeria	52	×	×		×	×	×	×	×	×
Angola	30		×		×	×	×	×		
Benin	19	×	×		×	×	×	×		
Bostwana	2									
Burkina Faso	31	×	×		×		×	×		
Burundi	23				×	×				
Cameroon	47	×	×		×	×	×	×		×
Central African Rep.	35	×	×		×	×	×	×		
Chad	19	×	×		×	×	×	×		
Congo	17	×			×					
Côte d'Ivoire	31	×	×		×	×	×	×		
Egypt	58	×	×		×	×	×	×		
Ethiopia	15	×	×				×			
Gabon	34	×	×		×	×	×	×		
Ghana	45	×	×		×	×	×	×		
Guinea	53	×	×		×	×	×	×		×
Kenya	46		×	×	×	×			×	
Lesotho	11	×	×		×					
Liberia	20	×	×		×	×	×			
Libyan Arab Jamahiriya	27		×		×		×	×	×	×
Madagascar	30	×			×		×	×		×
Malawi	23		×				×	×		
Mali	21	×	×		×	×	×	×		
Mauritania	38	×			×		×			×
Mauritius	33		×		×	×			×	
Morocco	40		×		×	×	×	×		×
Mozambique	11					×	×	×		
Namibia	1									
Niger	30	×	×		×	×	×	×	×	
Nigeria	28	×	×		×	×		×		
Rwanda	25	×	×			×	×	×	×	
Senegal	34	×	×		×	×	×	×		×
Sierra Leone	33	×	×		×	×	×	×		
Somalia	16				×	×	×			
South Africa	12									
Sudan	12		×		×	×	×	×		×
Tanzania, United Rep. of	40		×		×	×				
Togo	19	×	×		×		×	×	×	
Tunisia	55	×	×		×	×	×	×		×
Uganda	25		×		×	×				×
Zaire	31		×		×			×		
Zambia	38			×	×	×	×	×	×	×
Zimbabwe	5							×		
Americas										
Argentina	66	×	×		×	×	×	×		
Bolivia	42	×	×			×	×	×		×
Brazil	66		×		×	×	×	×		×
Canada	27	×				×	×	×		×
Chile	40				×		×	×		×
Colombia	50	×	×		×	×	×	×		
Costa Rica	47	×	×	×	×	×	×	×	×	×
Cuba	86	×	×	×	×	×	×	×	×	
Dominican Republic	26	×	×		×	×	×	×		
Ecuador	56	×	×	×	×	×	×	×		×
El Salvador	6					×				
Guatemala	62	×	×	×	×	×	×	×	×	×
Haiti	23	×	×		×	×	×	×		
Honduras	20	×	×		×	×	×	×	×	×
Jamaica	25	×	×		×	×	×	×		×
Mexico	73	×		×	×	×	×	×		
Nicaragua	58	×	×	×	×	×	×	×	×	×
Panama	69	×	×		×	×	×	×		×
Paraguay	34	×	×		×	×	×	×		×
Peru	66	×	×		×	×	×	×		×
Trinidad and Tobago	13	×	×		×	×	×			
United States	11					×				
Uruguay	96	×	×	×		×	×	×	×	×
Venezuela	52	×	×	×	×	×	×	×	×	×

	Total number of ratifications	Freedom of Association			Forced Labour		Discrimination		Child Labour Minimum Age (No. 138)	Employment Policy (No. 122)
		Right to Organise (No. 87)	Collective Bargaining (No. 98)	Rural Workers Organisations (No. 141)	Forced Labour (No. 29)	Abolition (No. 105)	Employment & Occupation (No. 111)	Equal Remuneration (No. 100)		
Asia and Oceania										
Afghanistan	15			×		×	×	×		
Australia	48	×	×		×	×	×	×		×
Bangladesh	31	×	×		×	×	×			
Bhutan	1									
Cambodia	5				×					×
China	17							×		
Hong Kong	1									
India	35			×	×		×	×		
Indonesia	9		×		×			×		
Iran, Islamic Rep. of	11				×	×	×	×		×
Iraq	64		×		×	×	×	×	×	×
Israel	44	×	×	×	×	×	×	×	×	×
Japan	39	×	×		×			×		×
Jordan	17		×		×	×	×	×		×
Korea, Dem. People's Rep. of	1									
Korea, Republic of	1									
Kuwait	14	×			×	×	×			
Lao People's Dem. Rep.	4				×					
Lebanon	28		×		×	×	×	×		×
Malaysia	22		×		×					
Mongolia	8	×	×				×	×		×
Myanmar	21	×			×					
Nepal	4						×	×		
New Zealand	56				×	×	×	×		×
Oman	1									
Pakistan	30	×	×		×	×	×			
Papua New Guinea	19		×		×	×				×
Philippines	23	×	×	×		×	×	×		×
Saudi Arabia	13				×	×	×	×		
Singapore	20		×		×					
Sri Lanka	28		×		×					
Syrian Arab Republic	46	×	×		×	×	×	×		
Thailand	11				×	×				
Turkey	28		×			×	×	×		×
United Arab Emirates	4				×					
Viet Nam	22		×		×		×			×
Yemen	25	×	×		×	×	×	×		×
Europe and the former Soviet Union										
Albania	17	×	×		×			×		
Austria	47	×	×	×	×	×	×	×		×
Belgium	83	×	×		×	×	×	×		×
Bulgaria	80	×	×		×		×	×	×	
Czechoslovakia	65	×	×		×		×	×		×
Denmark	61	×	×	×	×	×	×	×		×
Finland	82	×	×	×	×	×	×	×	×	×
France	114	×	×	×	×	×	×	×	×	×
Germany	70	×	×	×	×	×	×	×	×	×
Greece	65	×	×	×	×	×	×	×	×	×
Hungary	52	×	×		×		×	×		×
Ireland	59	×	×		×	×	×	×	×	×
Italy	102	×	×	×	×	×	×	×	×	×
Netherlands	92	×		×	×	×	×	×	×	×
Norway	96	×	×	×	×	×	×	×	×	×
Poland	75	×	×		×	×	×	×	×	×
Portugal	65	×	×		×	×	×	×		×
Romania	39	×	×		×		×	×		×
Spain	123	×	×	×	×	×	×	×	×	×
Sweden	82	×	×	×	×	×	×	×	×	×
Switzerland	47	×		×	×	×	×	×		
United Kingdom	80	×	×	×	×	×		×		×
ex-USSR	49	×	×		×		×	×	×	×
Yugoslavia	76	×	×		×		×	×	×	×

III. Labour force and employment trends

	Annual growth rate (%)				Annual growth rates of employment (%)								
	Population		Labour force		Total Agriculture			Total Non-agriculture			Manufacturing (formal sector waged)		
	1981-1990	1991-2000	1981-1990	1991-2000	1988	1989	1990	1988	1989	1990	1988	1989	1990
Africa													
Algeria	2.9	2.8	3.7	3.7	.	.	.	.	.	.	.	.	.
Angola	2.6	2.9	1.8	2.1	.	.	.	.	.	.	.	.	.
Benin	3.0	3.2	2.1	2.6	.	.	.	.	.	.	5.6	4.7	.
Botswana	3.8	3.4	3.3	3.4	.	.	.	.	.	.	.	.	.
Burkina Faso	2.6	3.0	2.0	2.2	.	.	.	.	.	.	.	.	.
Burundi	2.8	3.0	2.1	2.5	.	.	.	.	.	.	.	.	.
Cameroon	3.2	3.5	1.9	2.3	.	.	.	.	.	.	.	.	.
Central African Republic	2.7	3.0	1.4	1.9	.	.	.	.	.	.	.	.	.
Chad	2.4	2.6	1.9	2.1	.	.	.	.	.	.	.	.	.
Congo	3.1	3.4	1.9	2.4	.	.	.	.	.	.	.	.	.
Côte d'Ivoire	3.9	3.9	2.6	2.6	.	.	.	.	.	.	.	.	.
Egypt	2.5	2.0	2.6	2.7	.	.	.	.	.	.	1.9	.	.
Ethiopia	2.4	3.0	1.9	2.2	.	.	.	.	.	.	.	.	.
Gabon	3.8	3.2	0.6	1.1	.	.	.	.	.	.	.	.	.
Ghana	3.4	3.2	2.7	3.0	.	.	.	.	.	.	.	.	.
Guinea	2.6	3.1	1.7	1.9	.	.	.	.	.	.	0.1	2.4	.
Kenya	3.7	3.8	3.5	3.7	.	.	.	.	.	.	.	.	.
Lesotho	2.9	2.9	2.0	2.2	.	.	.	.	.	.	.	.	.
Liberia	3.2	3.3	2.3	2.8	.	.	.	.	.	.	.	.	.
Libyan Arab Jamahiriya	4.1	3.6	3.6	3.5	.	.	.	.	.	.	.	.	.
Madagascar	3.2	3.3	2.0	2.3	.	.	.	.	.	.	.	.	.
Malawi	3.5	3.6	2.6	2.7	.	.	.	.	.	.	.	.	.
Mali	3.0	3.2	2.6	2.8	.	.	.	.	.	.	.	.	.
Mauritania	2.7	2.9	2.8	3.2	.	.	.	.	.	.	3.1	0.7	.
Mauritius	1.1	1.0	2.9	1.9	.	.	.	.	.	.	.	.	—
Morocco	2.6	2.3	3.2	3.0	.	.	.	.	.	.	6.8	.	.
Mozambique	2.6	2.7	2.0	2.0	.	.	.	.	.	.	.	.	.
Namibia	3.2	3.2	2.4	2.8	.	.	.	.	.	.	9.1	−2.7	.
Niger	3.3	3.4	2.4	2.7	.	.	.	.	.	.	.	.	.
Nigeria	3.3	3.3	2.7	2.9	.	.	.	.	.	.	.	.	.
Rwanda	3.4	3.5	2.8	3.0	.	.	.	.	.	.	.	.	.
Senegal	2.8	2.9	1.9	2.1	.	.	.	.	.	.	.	.	.
Sierra Leone	2.4	2.7	1.2	1.5	.	.	.	.	.	.	.	.	.
Somalia	3.4	2.6	1.7	1.9	.	.	.	.	.	.	0.7	0.4	0.1
South Africa	2.2	2.2	2.8	2.8	.	.	.	.	.	.	.	.	.
Sudan	3.0	2.9	2.9	3.2	.	.	.	.	.	.	.	.	.
Tanzania, United Rep. of	3.8	3.8	2.9	3.1	.	.	.	.	.	.	.	.	.
Togo	3.0	3.2	2.3	2.5	.	.	.	.	.	.	.	.	.
Tunisia	2.5	2.0	3.1	2.7	.	.	.	.	.	.	.	.	.
Uganda	3.7	3.7	2.8	3.0	.	.	.	.	.	.	.	.	.
Zaire	3.1	3.3	2.3	2.6	.	.	.	.	.	.	.	.	.
Zambia	3.9	3.8	3.3	3.6	.	.	.	.	.	.	0.5	0.5	.
Zimbabwe	3.1	3.1	2.8	3.1	.	.	.	.	.	.	1.8	.	.
Americas													
Argentina	1.4	1.2	1.1	1.6	.	.	.	.	.	.	.	.	.
Bolivia	2.8	2.9	2.8	2.6	2.9	−3.1	5.3	2.9	−3.1	5.3	3.0	.	.
Brazil	2.2	1.8	2.2	2.1	0.4	.	.	1.4	.	.	0.3	−0.7	.
Canada	1.0	0.7	1.2	0.8	−0.9	−1.7	−0.6	1.7	1.1	0.4	0.6	.	.
Chile	1.7	1.5	2.4	1.5	1.6	−0.5	0.1	3.5	3.6	−0.7	.	.	.
Colombia	2.1	1.8	2.7	2.3	0.8	−1.5	15.8	1.9	1.4	8.6	−1.3	.	.
Costa Rica	2.8	2.1	2.8	2.4	1.4	−1.6	1.0	1.5	3.2	1.7	.	.	.
Cuba	0.9	0.8	2.3	1.3	.	.	.	.	.	.	.	.	.
Dominican Republic	2.3	1.9	3.4	2.8	.	.	.	.	.	.	.	.	.
Ecuador	2.7	2.3	3.0	2.8	.	.	.	.	.	.	0.5	.	.
El Salvador	1.5	2.5	3.1	3.2	.	18.2	.	.	3.8	.	20.4	.	.
Guatemala	2.9	2.9	2.9	3.4	.	.	.	.	.	.	−2.7	.	.
Haiti	1.9	2.1	2.0	2.3	.	.	.	.	.	.	.	.	.
Honduras	3.4	2.9	3.9	3.9	.	.	.	.	.	.	.	.	.
Jamaica	1.4	1.1	2.8	2.2	−2.0	−2.5	.	3.2	1.8	.	.	.	.
Mexico	2.3	1.9	3.2	2.9	.	.	.	.	.	.	0.4	0.4	0.1
Nicaragua	3.4	3.1	3.8	4.0	.	.	.	.	.	.	−4.5	−10.2	0.1
Panama	2.1	1.8	2.9	2.4	5.1	1.0	.	−4.4	3.0	.	.	−2.9	.
Paraguay	3.1	2.6	3.0	2.8	.	.	.	.	.	.	.	.	.
Peru	2.2	2.0	2.9	2.8	.	.	.	.	.	.	−1.1	−5.2	.
Trinidad and Tobago	1.7	1.5	2.4	2.0	.	2.5	.	−0.9	−1.3	.	−0.3	.	.
United States	0.9	0.7	1.1	0.8	−1.1	0.8	−0.3.	1.2	1.0	0.3	.	0.2	−0.9
Uruguay	0.6	0.6	0.7	1.0	2.3	.	.	9.8	.	.	−2.4	.	.
Venezuela	2.8	2.3	3.3	2.9	0.1	−0.2	.	2.6	1.6	.	.	.	.

| | Annual growth rate (%) | | | | Annual growth rates of employment (%) | | | | | | | | |
| | Population | | Labour force | | Total Agriculture | | | Total Non-agriculture | | | Manufacturing (formal sector waged) | | |
	1981-1990	1991-2000	1981-1990	1991-2000	1988	1989	1990	1988	1989	1990	1988	1989	1990
Asia and Oceania													
Afghanistan	0.3	4.8	2.6	2.2	.	.	.	.	.	.	−2.3	.	.
Australia	1.4	1.1	1.7	1.2	3.2	−2.6	2.3	1.8	2.6	0.8	1.8	.	.
Bangladesh	2.7	2.7	2.9	3.0	.	.	.	.	.	.	−1.6	.	.
Bhutan	2.0	2.3	1.9	1.9	.	.	.	.	.	.	.	.	.
Cambodia	.	.	1.9	1.7	.	.	.	.	.	.	.	.	.
China	1.3	1.3	2.2	1.1	.	.	1.3	1.7	24.3	1.2	.	.	.
Hong Kong	1.5	0.8	2.1	1.2	−8.2	−6.2	−12.3	1.1	0.2	−	.	.	.
India	2.2	2.0	2.0	1.8	.	.	.	.	.	.	−0.1	−0.2	.
Indonesia	2.0	1.7	2.4	2.1	2.3	0.7	.	0.4	1.3	.	.	.	.
Iran, Islamic Rep. of	3.4	2.3	3.3	3.2	.	.	.	.	.	.	.	.	.
Iraq	3.6	3.4	3.7	4.1	.	.	.	.	.	.	.	.	.
Israel	1.7	1.5	2.2	2.0	−3.7	0.6	−4.5	2.0	0.2	1.3	−1.8	−3.8	.
Japan	0.6	0.4	0.9	0.3	−1.5	−1.2	−1.3	1.0	1.2	1.2	0.7	0.1	.
Jordan	3.2	3.3	4.4	4.1	.	.	.	.	.	.	.	.	.
Korea, Dem. People's Rep. of	1.8	1.8	2.9	2.8	.	.	.	.	.	.	.	.	.
Korea, Republic of	1.2	0.8	2.4	1.8	−1.3	−1.0	−1.9	2.4	2.6	2.3	2.3	−0.1	.
Kuwait	4.0	2.6	5.2	3.2	.	.	.	.	.	.	.	.	.
Lao People's Dem. Rep.	2.6	2.8	2.0	2.2	.	.	.	.	.	.	.	.	.
Lebanon	0.1	2.1	2.1	2.6	.	.	.	.	.	.	.	.	.
Malaysia	2.7	2.1	2.9	2.6	.	.	.	.	.	.	5.5	.	.
Mongolia	2.8	2.7	2.9	2.8	.	.	.	.	.	.	.	.	.
Myanmar	2.1	2.1	.	.	0.8	0.8	0.8	1.3	0.5	−9.2	.	.	.
Nepal	2.6	2.3	2.3	2.3	.	.	.	.	.	.	.	.	.
New Zealand	0.9	0.8	1.6	1.0	−1.6	−1.8	1.9	−1.7	−1.3	0.2	−4.6	−5.1	.
Oman	4.3	3.8	3.8	2.9	.	.	.	.	.	.	.	.	.
Pakistan	3.7	2.8	2.9	3.0	2.4	1.5	1.5	−1.4	1.5	1.5	.	.	.
Papua New Guinea	2.3	2.3	2.1	2.0	.	.	.	.	.	.	.	.	.
Philippines	2.6	2.2	2.5	2.4	−0.1	−0.3	1.7	3.3	1.8	1.4	.	.	.
Saudi Arabia	4.2	3.9	4.0	3.4	.	.	.	.	.	.	.	.	.
Singapore	1.2	1.0	1.5	0.6	−27.8	3.1	−17.5	2.1	1.5	1.9	8.3	.	.
Sri Lanka	1.5	1.2	1.6	1.6	.	.	.	.	.	.	.	.	.
Syrian Arab Republic	3.6	3.6	3.6	4.1	.	.	.	.	.	.	.	.	.
Thailand	1.8	1.3	2.3	1.6	4.9	.	.	0.3	.	.	.	.	.
Turkey	2.3	1.8	2.2	2.0	.	2.0	.	.	0.4	.	2.2	.	.
United Arab Emirates	4.6	2.1	4.0	1.8	.	.	.	.	.	.	.	.	.
Viet Nam	2.2	2.1	2.8	2.6	.	.	.	.	.	.	.	.	.
Yemen	3.6	3.6	2.9	3.5	.	.	.	.	.	.	.	.	.
Europe and the former Soviet Union													
Albania	2.0	1.6	2.8	2.2	.	.	.	.	.	.	1.4	.	.
Austria	−	−	0.6	−	−2.7	−0.8	.	0.4	0.7	.	−1.1	−	.
Belgium	−	−	0.5	−	−1.1	−0.7	.	−	1.7	.	.	.	.
Bulgaria	0.2	0.1	−	0.3	.	.	.	.	.	.	0.9	.	.
Czechoslovakia	0.2	0.3	0.4	0.8	−0.6	−1.4	.	0.3	0.1	.	−0.1	−0.4	.
Denmark	−	−	0.5	0.1	.	.	.	.	.	.	−1.5	−0.1	−0.1
Finland	0.4	0.2	0.7	0.2	−2.6	.	−2.6	0.5	.	0.1	−1.5	−1.1	.
France	0.4	0.4	0.8	0.4	−1.8	−1.8	−1.8	0.5	0.8	.	−0.9	0.1	.
Germany	−0.1	−0.1	0.4	−0.5	−1.1	−5.2	.	0.6	0.9	.	.	.	.
Greece	0.4	0.1	0.5	0.2	0.1	.	.	1.1	.	.	0.5	.	.
Hungary	−0.1	−	0.1	0.4	−1.4	−1.4	.	.	.	.	−1.4	−1.6	−5.4
Ireland	0.9	0.9	1.6	1.5	0.5	−0.8	.	0.5	.	.	1.3	.	.
Italy	0.1	−	0.6	−	−2.6	−2.8	−1.3	1.0	−	1.8	−0.1	.	.
Netherlands	0.6	0.6	1.2	0.3	0.5	0.4	0.5	1.5	1.0	1.7	0.2	.	.
Norway	0.3	0.3	0.8	0.6	.	−0.7	−1.1	.	−1.6	−0.4	−3.3	−0.6	.
Poland	0.8	0.5	0.6	0.8	−1.3	−2.0	.	−	0.3	.	−1.0	−1.9	−2.2
Portugal	0.5	0.3	0.9	0.8	.	.	−1.8	.	.	1.8	1.4	.	.
Romania	0.5	0.5	0.7	0.7	0.1	−0.2	.	0.6	1.0	.	0.2	1.3	.
Spain	0.4	0.4	1.1	0.7	−0.8	−2.9	−3.6	2.2	2.8	2.0	0.4	.	.
Sweden	0.2	0.1	0.4	0.2	−0.9	−2.7	−3.2	0.8	0.9	0.6	0.6	−	.
Switzerland	0.4	0.2	0.5	−0.2	−0.6	−3.1	2.9	0.7	0.6	0.7	.	.	.
United Kingdom	0.2	0.2	0.4	0.1	−0.9	−1.2	.	1.7	1.5	0.4	1.2	0.8	.
ex-USSR	0.8	0.7	0.7	0.6	.	.	.	.	.	.	−1.0	−1.3	−1.4
Yugoslavia	0.7	0.4	0.9	0.7	.	.	.	.	.	.	.	.	.

IV. Labour force and employment structure

	Activity rate (%) Male		Female		Structure of total employment (%) Agriculture		Industry		Services		Wage employment (as % of total) Agriculture		Non-agriculture		Women as % of non-agricultural wage employment	
	1979/ 1981[1]	1988/ 1990	1979/ 1981[1]	1988/ 1990	1979/ 1984[1]	1985/ 1990	1979/ 1984[1]	1985/ 1990	1979/ 1984[1]	1985/ 1990	1979/ 1984[1]	1985/ 1990	1979/ 1984[1]	1985/ 1990	1979/ 1980	1988/ 1990
Africa																
Algeria	.	.	.	.	.	18	.	33	.	49	.	36	.	84	.	.
Angola	.	.	.	.	.	.	.	.	.	.	.	.	.	.	.	.
Benin	87.4	.	40.1	.	.	.	.	.	.	.	.	.	.	.	.	.
Botswana	82.7	.	47.4	.	56	58	13	11	32	31	5	.	93	.	24[2]	31[2]
Burkina Faso	.	.	.	.	.	.	.	.	.	.	.	.	.	.	.	.
Burundi	94.0	.	94.8	.	93	.	2	.	5	.	1	.	69	.	10	.
Cameroon	77.3	.	56.2	.	.	79	.	7	.	14	.	.	.	.	.	.
Central African Republic	.	.	.	.	.	.	.	.	.	.	.	.	.	.	.	.
Chad	91.8	92.1	26.4	26.5	.	.	.	.	.	.	.	.	.	.	.	.
Congo	.	.	.	.	.	.	.	.	.	.	.	.	.	.	.	.
Côte d'Ivoire	.	.	.	.	.	.	.	.	.	.	.	.	.	.	.	.
Egypt	74.9	.	6.5	.	43	41	22	22	36	38	.	46	.	78	13	.
Ethiopia	91.4	.	59.8	.	89	.	2	.	9	.	.	.	.	.	.	.
Gabon	.	.	.	.	.	.	.	.	.	.	.	.	.	.	.	.
Ghana	.	.	.	.	61	.	13	.	26	.	5	.	34	.	.	.
Guinea	.	.	.	.	85	.	2	.	12	.	.	.	.	.	.	.
Kenya	.	.	.	.	.	.	.	.	.	.	.	.	.	.	17[2]	21[2]
Lesotho	.	.	.	.	.	.	.	.	.	.	.	.	.	.	.	.
Liberia	.	.	.	.	75	.	6	.	19	.	8	.	41	.	.	.
Libyan Arab Jamahiriya	.	.	.	.	19	20	34	30	47	50	.	.	.	.	.	.
Madagascar	.	.	.	.	.	.	.	.	.	.	.	.	.	.	.	.
Malawi	.	.	.	.	.	87	.	5	.	8	.	6	.	66	9[2]	10[2]
Mali	.	.	.	.	.	.	.	.	.	.	.	.	.	.	.	.
Mauritania	.	.	.	.	.	.	.	.	.	.	.	.	.	.	.	.
Mauritius	.	87.2	.	47.5	25	.	29	.	46	.	.	.	.	.	26[2]	37[2]
Morocco	.	.	.	.	.	.	.	.	.	.	.	.	.	.	.	.
Mozambique	87.6	.	87.0	.	85	.	7	.	8	.	.	.	.	.	.	.
Namibia	.	.	.	.	.	.	.	.	.	.	.	.	.	.	.	.
Niger	.	.	.	.	.	.	.	.	.	.	.	.	.	.	4[2]	9[2]
Nigeria	.	.	.	.	45	48	11	7	44	45	7	2	43	33	.	.
Rwanda	.	.	.	.	.	.	.	.	.	.	.	.	.	.	.	.
Senegal	.	87.6	.	25.1	.	.	.	.	.	.	.	.	.	.	.	.
Sierra Leone	.	.	.	.	.	.	.	.	.	.	.	.	.	.	.	.
Somalia	.	.	.	.	.	.	.	.	.	.	.	.	.	.	.	.
South Africa	85.6	.	43.4	.	17	15	36	36	47	48	.	.	.	.	.	.
Sudan	.	.	.	.	72	.	8	.	19	.	.	.	.	.	.	22[2]
Tanzania, United Rep. of	.	.	.	.	.	.	.	.	.	.	.	.	.	.	.	.
Togo	83.9	.	56.4	.	68	.	9	.	22	.	1	.	35	.	.	.
Tunisia	85.5	79.3	20.6	21.7	36	26	34	34	30	40	37	36	78	77	.	18
Uganda	.	.	.	.	.	.	.	.	.	.	.	.	.	.	.	.
Zaire	.	.	.	.	.	.	.	.	.	.	.	.	.	.	.	.
Zambia	81.7	.	39.9	.	55	.	14	.	31	.	44	.	82	.	14	.
Zimbabwe	.	.	.	.	.	71	.	8	.	21	.	.	.	.	13[2]	15[2]
Americas																
Argentina	83.6	85.7	33.2	33.4	13	.	34	.	53	.	53	.	74	.	.	.
Bolivia	82.0	85.4	24.1	25.1	47	47	21	13	32	40	.	36	.	52	.	34
Brazil	86.0	89.8	31.9	47.7	.	24	.	23	.	52	39	39	79	75	36	.
Canada	81.9	85.5	55.5	67.5	6	4	29	25	65	71	38	40	93	93	41	46
Chile	74.7	79.9	28.7	34.9	17	19	24	25	59	55	43	55	64	72	.	37
Colombia	80.7	83.1	24.0	49.9	1	1	33	31	66	68	.	58	.	70	.	41
Costa Rica	93.1	87.3	31.2	35.9	35	26	22	26	43	48	55	56	82	76	.	38
Cuba	77.8	81.4	36.6	48.0	.	.	.	.	.	.	81	.	99	.	36[2]	42[2]
Dominican Republic	79.1	.	26.8	.	31	.	24	.	45	.	20	.	76	.	.	.
Ecuador	85.4	79.3	31.0	33.7	35	.	21	.	44	.	30	.	64	.	.	.
El Salvador	86.1	82.9	39.7	53.8	44	8	21	30	35	62	58	61	64	65	34	39
Guatemala	87.5	92.0	14.6	29.7	51	50	19	18	30	32	44	38	56	61	.	.
Haiti	88.5	80.8	70.6	49.8	74	68	7	9	18	23	6	.	42	.	.	.
Honduras	88.8	.	17.8	.	60	50	16	17	24	33	.	.	.	.	.	.
Jamaica	83.5	80.4	54.4	59.9	28	26	19	24	53	50	.	.	.	.	.	.
Mexico	78.5	83.9	26.1	36.5	37	.	29	.	34	.	30	25	69	59	31	.
Nicaragua	.	88.5	.	41.7	46	.	17	.	37	.	.	.	.	.	.	.
Panama	84.4	84.0	38.3	42.4	30	31	18	15	52	55	28	29	80	76	39	46
Paraguay	85.5	87.1	24.1	53.7	47	2	21	28	32	69	15	.	65	.	.	.
Peru	80.6	77.6	32.3	50.7	39	1	18	26	43	73	19	.	70	.	.	.
Trinidad and Tobago	85.9	75.7	40.3	44.6	10	12	38	32	51	56	.	50	.	82	.	37
United States	83.4	81.5	57.4	66.1	4	3	32	26	65	71	47	56	93	92	44	47
Uruguay	.	.	.	.	3	4	27	30	70	66	.	57	.	79	.	.
Venezuela	82.3	83.4	31.3	36.7	15	13	28	27	57	60	37	40	74	71	.	37

	Activity rate (%)				Structure of total employment (%)						Wage employment (as % of total)				Women as % of non-agricultural wage employment	
	Male		Female		Agriculture		Industry		Services		Agriculture		Non-agriculture			
	1979/ 1981[1]	1988/ 1990	1979/ 1981[1]	1988/ 1990	1979/ 1984[1]	1985/ 1990	1979/ 1984[1]	1985/ 1990	1979/ 1984[1]	1985/ 1990	1979/ 1984[1]	1985/ 1990	1979/ 1984[1]	1985/ 1990	1979/ 1980	1988/ 1990
Asia and Oceania																
Afghanistan	88.3	.	7.4	.	.	.	.	.	.	.	.	.	.	.	.	.
Australia	85.5	85.1	52.8	61.9	7	5	31	26	61	69	33	33	88	83	.	43
Bangladesh	85.3	.	4.5	.	63	59	12	13	26	28	39	38	47	36	.	.
Bhutan	.	.	.	.	.	.	.	.	.	.	.	.	.	.	.	.
Cambodia	.	.	.	.	.	.	.	.	.	.	.	.	.	.	.	.
China	.	.	.	.	74	.	16	.	10	.	.	.	.	.	35	38
Hong Kong	83.5	85.2	48.4	52.7	1	1	51	37	48	62	17	51	86	89	.	.
India	89.3	.	35.1	.	71	.	13	.	16	.	44	.	58	.	11[2]	13[2]
Indonesia	81.9	82.6	38.2	53.4	56	56	13	13	30	30	16	11	44	47	24	29
Iran, Islamic Rep. of	.	.	.	.	9	30	34	26	57	44	.	11	.	68	.	.
Iraq	.	.	.	.	.	14	.	19	.	67	.	.	.	.	.	.
Israel	76.0	68.1	42.8	46.9	6	4	32	28	62	68	25	29	81	82	39	43
Japan	84.4	82.8	52.3	57.1	11	7	35	34	54	58	7	9	79	83	34	38
Jordan	79.3	.	7.0	.	11	.	26	.	63	.	22	.	81	.	10	.
Korea, Dem. People's Rep. of	.	.	.	.	.	.	.	.	.	.	.	.	.	.	.	.
Korea, Republic of	71.9	76.1	41.5	50.0	36	18	30	35	34	47	13	8	67	72	31	38
Kuwait	86.7	.	20.7	.	2	1	32	25	66	74	91	90	90	94	15	.
Lao People's Dem. Rep.	.	.	.	.	.	.	.	.	.	.	.	.	.	.	.	.
Lebanon	.	.	.	.	.	.	.	.	.	.	.	.	.	.	.	.
Malaysia	83.2	.	41.4	.	41	31	19	22	39	47	32	29	77	78	29	.
Mongolia	.	.	.	.	.	.	.	.	.	.	.	.	.	.	.	.
Myanmar	.	.	.	.	67	70	10	9	23	21	.	.	.	.	.	.
Nepal	88.8	.	45.7	.	93	.	1	.	7	.	.	.	.	.	.	.
New Zealand	86.2	82.0	45.8	62.9	11	11	32	25	56	65	47	44	91	86	.	52
Oman	.	.	.	.	.	.	.	.	.	.	.	.	.	.	.	.
Pakistan	89.5	87.2	7.3	11.8	53	51	20	20	27	29	8	11	40	43	.	.
Papua New Guinea	.	.	.	.	.	.	.	.	.	.	.	.	.	.	.	.
Philippines	.	83.3	.	49.1	52	45	15	15	33	40	15	20	70	67	.	40
Saudi Arabia	.	.	.	.	.	.	.	.	.	.	.	.	.	.	.	.
Singapore	83.6	84.2	44.2	54.2	1	−	35	36	63	64	23	54	84	86	37	42
Sri Lanka	78.1	82.2	28.3	49.4	49	49	20	21	31	30	47	44	76	70	18[2]	.
Syrian Arab Republic	78.2	.	14.0	.	33	23	31	29	36	48	20	24	75	68	.	14
Thailand	88.7	90.5	76.6	81.3	74	66	8	11	18	22	4	11	60	60	35	40
Turkey	87.6	84.0	48.3	39.2	61	50	16	20	24	30	5	4	76	70	13	15
United Arab Emirates	94.9	.	16.3	.	5	.	38	.	57	.	85	.	93	.	6	.
Viet Nam	.	.	.	.	.	.	.	.	.	.	.	.	.	.	.	.
Yemen	.	.	.	.	.	.	.	.	.	.	.	.	.	.	.	.
Europe and the former Soviet Union																
Albania	.	.	.	.	.	.	.	.	.	.	.	.	.	.	.	.
Austria	80.9	79.8	48.2	54.1	11	8	41	37	48	55	13	14	91	92	38	40
Belgium	83.7	.	47.1	.	3	3	35	28	62	69	9	.	86	.	34	39
Bulgaria	.	.	.	.	.	16	.	47	.	37	.	99	.	98	.	.
Czechoslovakia	84.3	.	73.6	.	13	11	46	45	41	43	44	.	99	.	47	.
Denmark	85.8	87.4	69.0	77.8	7	6	33	27	60	67	25	38	90	92	46	49
Finland	77.5	80.0	65.4	72.6	12	8	35	31	54	61	23	26	95	91	48	50
France	81.1	75.5	51.0	58.8	9	6	36	30	55	64	17	15	90	89	40	44
Germany	84.5	82.2	49.7	55.5	5	4	44	40	50	56	.	.	.	.	37	39
Greece	76.3	.	35.2	.	31	25	29	28	40	47	3	4	68	68	.	34
Hungary	83.7	.	61.7	.	19	.	44	.	38	.	75	.	94	.	45	.
Ireland	84.9	81.1	34.8	36.8	20	15	33	29	48	56	12	14	89	86	35	39
Italy	87.0	82.8	38.9	46.7	11	9	40	32	49	59	38	42	77	74	32	36
Netherlands	78.7	80.0	34.4	53.1	5	5	33	26	62	69	33	36	91	91	30	38
Norway	90.0	83.4	65.1	70.7	9	6	30	24	61	69	23	27	93	90	43	47
Poland	.	79.1	.	64.1	30	26	38	38	32	36	.	21	.	96	.	46
Portugal	87.1	80.6	53.8	57.8	24	18	35	34	41	48	21	19	85	82	37	42
Romania	.	.	.	.	.	.	.	.	.	.	.	.	.	.	.	.
Spain	83.4	78.6	33.1	41.8	20	12	36	34	44	54	31	40	81	81	27	33
Sweden	79.8	86.9	67.5	82.6	6	3	33	29	62	68	36	40	95	93	47	50
Switzerland	89.9	.	51.4	.	6	.	39	.	54	.	56	.	92	.	38	.
United Kingdom	87.9	85.0	55.9	63.7	3	2	39	29	59	69	53	.	95	.	43	48
ex-USSR	82.5	81.3	73.8	70.7	.	20	.	47	.	34	.	.	.	.	.	.
Yugoslavia	86.2	.	51.9	.	31	.	34	.	35	.	12	.	97	.	.	.

[1] In these brackets, data refer to the earliest available year. [2] Formal wage employment.

V. Unemployment structure (percentages)

	Total	Male	Female	Age Youth (15-24) Male	Youth (15-24) Female	Adult (25+) Male	Adult (25+) Female	Level of education None	First	Second	Third
	1989/1990	1989/1990	1989/1990	1989/1990	1989/1990	1989/1990	1989/1990	1989/1990	1989/1990	1989/1990	1989/1990
Africa											
Algeria	.	.	.	.	.	.	.	9	24	29	6
Angola	.	.	.	.	.	.	.	.	.	.	.
Benin	.	.	.	.	.	.	.	.	.	.	.
Botswana	.	.	.	.	.	.	.	.	.	.	.
Burkina Faso	.	.	.	.	.	.	.	.	.	.	.
Burundi	.	.	.	.	.	.	.	.	.	.	.
Cameroon	.	.	.	.	.	.	.	.	.	.	.
Central African Republic	.	.	.	.	.	.	.	.	.	.	.
Chad	.	.	.	.	.	.	.	.	.	.	.
Congo	.	.	.	.	.	.	.	.	.	.	.
Côte d'Ivoire	.	.	.	.	.	.	.	.	.	.	.
Egypt	.	.	.	.	.	.	.	.	.	.	.
Ethiopia	.	.	.	.	.	.	.	.	.	.	.
Gabon	.	.	.	.	.	.	.	.	.	.	.
Ghana	.	.	.	.	.	.	.	.	.	.	.
Guinea	.	.	.	.	.	.	.	.	.	.	.
Kenya	.	.	.	.	.	.	.	.	.	.	.
Lesotho	.	.	.	.	.	.	.	.	.	.	.
Liberia	.	.	.	.	.	.	.	.	.	.	.
Libyan Arab Jamahiriya	.	.	.	.	.	.	.	.	.	.	.
Madagascar	.	.	.	.	.	.	.	.	.	.	.
Malawi	.	.	.	.	.	.	.	.	.	.	.
Mali	.	.	.	.	.	.	.	.	.	.	.
Mauritania	.	.	.	.	.	.	.	.	.	.	.
Mauritius	.	.	.	.	.	.	.	.	.	.	.
Morocco	.	.	.	.	.	.	.	.	.	.	.
Mozambique	.	.	.	.	.	.	.	.	.	.	.
Namibia	.	.	.	.	.	.	.	.	.	.	.
Niger	.	.	.	.	.	.	.	.	.	.	.
Nigeria	.	.	.	.	.	.	.	.	.	.	.
Rwanda	.	.	.	.	.	.	.	.	.	.	.
Senegal	.	.	.	.	.	.	.	.	.	.	.
Sierra Leone	.	.	.	.	.	.	.	.	.	.	.
Somalia	.	.	.	.	.	.	.	.	.	.	.
South Africa	7.9	7.9	7.8	.	.	.	.	.	.	.	.
Sudan	.	.	.	.	.	.	.	.	.	.	.
Tanzania, United Rep. of	.	.	.	.	.	.	.	.	.	.	.
Togo	.	.	.	.	.	.	.	.	.	.	.
Tunisia	13.4	.	.	.	.	.	.	11	20	17	5
Uganda	.	.	.	.	.	.	.	.	.	.	.
Zaire	.	.	.	.	.	.	.	.	.	.	.
Zambia	.	.	.	.	.	.	.	.	.	.	.
Zimbabwe	.	.	.	.	.	.	.	.	.	.	.
Americas											
Argentina	7.3	7.0	7.7	.	.	.	.	.	.	.	.
Bolivia	19.0	.	.	.	.	.	.	.	.	.	.
Brazil	.	.	.	6	8	2	2	1	3	.	.
Canada	8.1	8.1	8.1	14	12	6	6	.	11	9	5
Chile	5.6	5.6	5.7	13	12	3	—	.	.	.	.
Colombia	10.2	8.1	13.2	.	.	5	8	8	8	13	8
Costa Rica	4.6	4.2	5.9	8	10	3	.	5	4	6	3
Cuba	.	.	.	.	.	.	.	.	.	.	.
Dominican Republic	.	.	.	.	.	.	.	.	.	.	.
Ecuador	8.0	.	.	.	.	.	.	.	.	.	.
El Salvador	8.3	9.5	6.8	.	.	.	.	.	.	.	.
Guatemala	7.2	.	.	3	6	1	1	—	2	7	2
Haiti	.	.	.	.	.	.	.	.	.	.	.
Honduras	7.7	8.9	6.2	.	.	.	.	2	4	8	6
Jamaica	16.8	9.5	25.2	34	99	6	21	.	.	.	.
Mexico	2.6	2.4	2.9	3	7	2	3	.	.	.	.
Nicaragua	12.0	9.7	16.6	.	.	.	.	.	.	.	.
Panama	16.3	13.7	21.6	29	44	10	15	—	2	6	6
Paraguay	6.6	.	.	.	.	.	.	.	5	8	4
Peru	7.9	6.0	10.7	.	.	.	.	.	.	.	.
Trinidad and Tobago	22.0	20.8	24.5	37	46	9	14	11	21	25	5
United States	5.4	5.4	5.4	11	10	4	4	.	.	7	3
Uruguay	9.2	7.3	11.8	.	.	.	.	3	6	11	7
Venezuela	8.7	9.2	7.5	17	16	7	5	6	12	13	6

	Total	Male	Female	Age				Level of education			
				Youth (15-24)		Adult (25+)		None	First	Second	Third
				Male	Female	Male	Female				
	1989/ 1990	1989/ 1990	1989/ 1990	1989/ 1990	1989/ 1990	1989/ 1990	1989/ 1990	1989/ 1990	1989/ 1990	1989/ 1990	1989/ 1990
Asia and Oceania											
Afghanistan	.	.	.	.	.	.	.	.	.	.	.
Australia	6.9	6.7	7.2	13	13	4	4	10	.	9	4
Bangladesh	.	.	.	.	.	.	.	.	.	.	.
Bhutan	.	.	.	.	.	.	.	.	.	.	.
Cambodia	.	.	.	.	.	.	.	.	.	.	.
China	2.5	0.9	1.2	.	.	.	.	.	.	.	.
Hong Kong	1.3	1.3	1.3	4	3	1	1	1	1	2	1
India	.	.	.	.	.	.	.	2	3	9	12
Indonesia	2.8	2.8	2.8	14	11	1	—	1	1	10	10
Iran, Islamic Rep. of	.	.	.	.	.	.	.	.	.	.	.
Iraq	.	.	.	.	.	.	.	.	.	.	.
Israel	9.6	8.4	11.3	21	23	7	10	9	9	11	5
Japan	2.1	2.0	2.2	5	4	2	1	.	.	.	.
Jordan	.	.	.	.	.	.	.	.	.	.	.
Korea, Dem. People's Rep. of	.	.	.	.	.	.	.	.	.	.	.
Korea, Republic of	2.3	2.7	1.7	9	6	1	—	.	1	3	4
Kuwait	.	.	.	.	.	.	.	.	.	.	.
Lao People's Dem. Rep.	.	.	.	.	.	.	.	.	.	.	.
Lebanon	.	.	.	.	.	.	.	.	.	.	.
Malaysia	7.9	.	.	.	.	.	.	.	.	.	.
Mongolia	.	.	.	.	.	.	.	.	.	.	.
Myanmar	.	.	.	.	.	.	.	.	.	.	.
Nepal	.	.	.	.	.	.	.	.	.	.	.
New Zealand	7.7	8.1	7.2	15	14	9	8	12	.	7	5
Oman	.	.	.	.	.	.	.	.	.	.	.
Pakistan	3.1	3.4	0.9	.	.	.	.	2	3	6	4
Papua New Guinea	.	.	.	.	.	.	.	.	.	.	.
Philippines	9.2	8.1	11.1	.	.	.	.	.	.	.	.
Saudi Arabia	.	.	.	.	.	.	.	.	.	.	.
Singapore	1.8	2.1	1.4	3	3	2	1	2	2	2	2
Sri Lanka	.	.	.	.	.	.	.	.	.	.	.
Syrian Arab Republic	.	.	.	.	.	.	.	3	7	8	8
Thailand	.	.	.	5	6	1	1	1	3	6	.
Turkey	8.5	8.4	8.8	17	17	5	1	4	8	17	9
United Arab Emirates	.	.	.	.	.	.	.	.	.	.	.
Viet Nam	.	.	.	.	.	.	.	.	.	.	.
Yemen	.	.	.	.	.	.	.	.	.	.	.
Europe and the former Soviet Union											
Albania	.	.	.	.	.	.	.	.	.	.	.
Austria	3.1	2.8	3.6	11	12	4	5	.	4	3	2
Belgium	7.3	4.6	11.6	.	.	.	.	.	15	9	3
Bulgaria	.	.	.	.	.	.	.	.	.	.	.
Czechoslovakia	.	.	.	.	.	.	.	.	.	.	.
Denmark	.	.	.	.	.	.	.	.	.	.	.
Finland	3.4	4.0	2.8	7	5	4	5	.	6	5	1
France	9.0	6.7	12.0	.	.	.	.	.	14	9	3
Germany	5.1	4.4	6.1	5	8	10	14	.	.	8	4
Greece	.	.	.	.	.	.	.	3	4	12	9
Hungary	.	.	.	.	.	.	.	.	.	.	.
Ireland	14.0	14.8	15.5	26	22	13	15	20	23	14	5
Italy	11.0	7.3	17.1	26	38	3	3	.	7	13	5
Netherlands	7.5	5.4	10.7	10	12	5	11	.	20	7	6
Norway	5.2	5.6	4.8	12	11	8	6	.	8	6	2
Poland	.	.	.	.	.	.	.	.	.	.	.
Portugal	4.6	3.1	6.6	7	13	3	2	2	5	7	2
Romania	.	.	.	.	.	.	.	.	.	.	.
Spain	15.9	11.7	23.9	26	40	9	9	15	13	19	12
Sweden	1.5	1.5	1.5	4	3	1	2	.	2	1	1
Switzerland	.	.	.	.	.	.	.	.	.	.	.
United Kingdom	6.9	7.2	6.4	.	.	.	.	.	.	.	.
ex-USSR	.	.	.	.	.	.	.	.	.	.	.
Yugoslavia	.	.	.	.	.	.	.	.	.	.	.

VI. Real wages and hourly compensation costs, and working time

	Legal minimum wage rates (1985=100)			Manufacturing wages (1985=100)			Hourly compensation costs (production workers) in manuf.		Normal working time (manufacturing)			
							(1985=100)	% of non-wage costs	Weekly hours	Annual leave (days)	Public holidays	Normal annual hours
	1988	1989	1990	1988	1989	1990	1990	1990	1990	1990	1990	1990
Africa												
Algeria	.	.	.	.	.	.	.	.	44	20	10	2 033
Angola	.	.	.	.	.	.	.	.	44*	23	7	2 056*
Benin	.	.	.	.	.	.	.	.	40*	18	12	1 848*
Botswana	102.2	100.4	.	101.5	116.6	.	.	.	.	.	.	.
Burkina Faso	116.0	.	.	.	.	.	.	.	.	.	.	.
Burundi	.	.	.	.	.	.	.	.	45	12	8	2 185
Cameroon	.	.	.	.	.	.	.	.	.	.	.	.
Central African Republic	.	.	.	.	.	.	.	.	.	.	.	.
Chad	.	.	.	.	.	.	.	.	40	18	13	1 840
Congo	.	.	.	.	.	.	.	.	.	.	.	.
Côte d'Ivoire	86.7	.	.	.	.	.	.	.	.	.	.	.
Egypt	.	.	.	.	.	.	.	.	.	.	.	.
Ethiopia	.	.	.	.	.	.	.	.	.	.	.	.
Gabon	.	.	.	.	.	.	.	.	.	.	.	.
Ghana	76.1	.	.	185.0	.	.	.	.	.	.	.	.
Guinea	.	.	.	.	.	.	.	.	.	.	.	.
Kenya	.	.	.	108.2	111.6	.	.	.	45	12	13	2 144
Lesotho	.	.	.	.	.	.	.	.	45	12	13	2 144
Liberia	.	.	.	.	.	.	.	.	.	.	.	.
Libyan Arab Jamahiriya	.	.	.	.	.	.	.	.	.	.	.	.
Madagascar	.	.	.	.	.	.	.	.	40*	18	12	1 848*
Malawi	.	.	.	80.2	.	.	.	.	.	.	.	.
Mali	.	.	.	.	.	.	.	.	40*	19	11	1 869*
Mauritania	.	.	.	.	.	.	.	.	.	.	.	.
Mauritius	127.4	.	.	.	.	.	.	.	.	.	.	.
Morocco	101.7	105.4	109.4	.	.	.	.	.	.	.	.	.
Mozambique	.	.	.	.	.	.	.	.	.	.	.	.
Namibia	.	.	.	.	.	.	.	.	.	.	.	.
Niger	112.4	.	.	.	.	.	.	.	.	.	.	.
Nigeria	.	.	.	.	.	.	.	.	.	.	.	.
Rwanda	.	.	.	.	.	.	.	.	45	15	12	2 106
Senegal	.	.	.	.	.	.	.	.	.	.	.	.
Sierra Leone	.	.	.	.	.	.	.	.	.	.	.	.
Somalia	.	.	.	.	.	.	.	.	.	.	.	.
South Africa	.	.	.	99.1	101.1	.	.	.	.	.	.	.
Sudan	.	.	.	.	.	.	.	.	48	5	10	2 374
Tanzania, United Rep. of	.	.	.	.	.	.	.	.	.	.	.	.
Togo	.	.	.	.	.	.	.	.	.	.	.	.
Tunisia	.	.	.	.	.	.	.	.	40	5	10	1 968
Uganda	.	.	.	.	.	.	.	.	.	.	.	.
Zaire	.	.	.	.	.	.	.	.	.	.	.	.
Zambia	.	.	.	.	.	.	.	.	45	5	7	2 250
Zimbabwe	.	.	.	98.2	98.0	.	.	.	44*	16	11	2 080*
Americas												
Argentina	82.7	37.2	35.5	91.7	72.6	67.8	.	.	.	.	.	.
Bolivia	112.0	101.5	.	.	.	.	.	.	48	15	11	2 256
Brazil	75.4	81.8	.	101.8	109.8	98.7	205	32	.	.	.	.
Canada	.	.	.	98.1	98.6	98.9	122	13	.	.	.	.
Chile	97.3	108.2	115.6	109.8	113.5	115.5	.	.	.	.	.	.
Colombia	100.5	101.4	97.9	102.6	104.2	101.3	.	.	48*	15	18	2 166*
Costa Rica	102.5	98.2	.	96.5	.	.	.	.	48*	10	17	2 246*
Cuba	.	.	.	.	.	.	.	.	44*	23	7	2 033*
Dominican Republic	109.0	97.0	.	.	.	.	.	.	.	.	.	.
Ecuador	88.0	71.9	.	.	.	.	.	.	.	.	.	.
El Salvador	66.2	56.3	.	.	.	.	.	.	44	5	10	2 165
Guatemala	80.7	72.4	.	80.2	.	.	.	.	.	.	.	.
Haiti	105.0	96.8	.	.	.	.	.	.	.	.	.	.
Honduras	89.5	81.5	.	.	.	.	.	.	44	10	10	2 121
Jamaica	.	.	.	.	.	.	.	.	.	.	.	.
Mexico	73.6	70.0	.	.	92.4	87.2	95	30*	.	.	.	.
Nicaragua	.	.	.	.	.	.	.	.	.	.	.	.
Panama	98.7	98.8	.	.	.	.	.	.	.	.	.	.
Paraguay	135.1	136.4	.	110.8	134.4	.	.	.	.	.	.	.
Peru	83.9	44.6	39.5	63.2	44.7	.	.	.	48*	18	12	2 218*
Trinidad and Tobago	.	.	.	.	.	.	.	.	40	14	17	1 840
United States	91.0	86.8	89.6	97.4	95.5	93.9	94	20	40	12	11	1 904
Uruguay	90.2	83.5	72.9	120.1	123.7	125.2	.	.	.	.	.	.
Venezuela	97.4	80.8	.	.	.	.	.	.	44	15	14	2 042

	Legal minimum wage rates (1985=100)			Manufacturing wages (1985=100)			Hourly compensation costs (production workers) in manuf.		Normal working time (manufacturing)			
							(1985 =100)	% of non-wage costs	Weekly hours	Annual leave (days)	Public holidays	Normal annual hours
	1988	1989	1990	1988	1989	1990	1990	1990	1990	1990	1990	1990
Asia and Oceania												
Afghanistan	.	.	.									
Australia	.	.	.	91.3	91.2	.	131	15	38	20	10	1 756
Bangladesh												
Bhutan	.	.	.						.	.	.	.
Cambodia	.	.	.	.	.	.	.	.	.	.	.	.
China	.	.	.	114.2	110.2	.			.	.	.	.
Hong Kong	.	.	.				152	3	.	.	.	.
India	.	.	.					9*	48	17	22	2 164
Indonesia	.	.	.				.	.	.	.	.	.
Iran, Islamic Rep. of	.	.	.	.	.	.	.	.	.	.	.	.
Iraq	.	.	.	.	.	.			.	.	.	.
Israel	.	.	.				156*	18*	.	.	.	.
Japan	.	.	.	106.5	109.9	112.3	164	13		8	14	2 143
Jordan	.	.	.	98.7	82.2	.	.	.	52*	18	17	2 409*
Korea, Dem. People's Rep. of	.	.	.	.	.	.	.	.				
Korea, Republic of	.	.	.	128.4	152.1	168.3	254	16	43*	8	18	2 050*
Kuwait	.	.	.	.	.	.	.	.	.	.	.	.
Lao People's Dem. Rep.	.	.	.	.	.	.	.	.	.	.	.	.
Lebanon	.	.	.	.	.	.	.	.	.	.	.	.
Malaysia	.	.	.	.	.	.	.	.	.	.	.	.
Mongolia	.	.	.	.	.	.	.	.	.	.	.	.
Myanmar	.	.	.	.	.	.	.	.	.	.	.	.
Nepal	.	.	.	.	.	.	.	.	48	18	22	2 184
New Zealand	.	.	.	97.6	96.4	94.7	153	6	40	15	11	1 880
Oman	.	.	.	.	.	.	.	.	.	.	.	.
Pakistan	.	.	.	.	.	.	.	11*	.	.	.	.
Papua New Guinea	.	.	.	.	.	.	.	.	.	.	.	.
Philippines	106.7	115.4	.	.	.	.	.	.	.	.	.	.
Saudi Arabia	.	.	.	.	.	.	.	.	.	.	.	.
Singapore	.	.	.	.	.	.	126	14	.	.	.	.
Sri Lanka	.	.	.	97.7	99.2	.	.	14*	.	.	.	.
Syrian Arab Republic	46.1	51.9	.	.	.	.	.	.	.	.	.	.
Thailand	.	.	.	.	91.4	.	.	.	.	.	.	.
Turkey	.	.	.	.	.	.	.	17*	.	.	.	.
United Arab Emirates	.	.	.	.	.	.	.	.	.	.	.	.
Viet Nam	.	.	.	.	.	.	.	.	.	.	.	.
Yemen	.	.	.	.	.	.	.	.	.	.	.	.
Europe and the former Soviet Union												
Albania	.	.	.						.	.	.	.
Austria	.	.	.	99.9	103.0	104.2	192	28	39	27	13	1 714
Belgium	.	.	.	100.9	103.4	104.5	174	26	38	20	11	1 748
Bulgaria	.	.	.				.	.				
Czechoslovakia	.	.	.	105.0	105.9		.	.	40	10	8	1 944
Denmark	.	.	.	108.3	108.4	110.6	190	6	37	25	8	1 687
Finland	.	.	.	109.2	111.7	116.2	210	23	40	38	9	1 716
France	102.8	103.1	104.5	101.1	102.1	103.1	167	30	39	25	11	1 755
Germany	.	.	.	111.6	113.1	115.8	183	21	38	30	13	1 648
Greece	.	.	.	89.8	95.2	.	124*	18*	40	22	9	1 840
Hungary	.	.	.				.	.	.	.	.	.
Ireland	.	.	.	107.9	109.0	.	162	15	39	21	8	1 810
Italy	.	.	.	101.3	101.8	102.4	183	32	40	31	8	1 776
Netherlands	.	.	.	103.9	104.7	105.1	172	22	39	32	7	1 732
Norway	.	.	.	108.6	110.0	111.5	169	22	38	21	10	1 725
Poland	.	.	.	116.4	128.6		.	.	.	.	.	.
Portugal	.	.	.	96.6	.	.	192	22	44	22	14	1 980
Romania	.	.	.	.	.	.	.	.	40	15	5	1 911
Spain	98.7	98.0	98.4	105.8	106.1	108.2	199	29	40	22	14	1 800
Sweden	.	.	.	107.0	111.2	110.3	178	30	40	25	11	1 800
Switzerland	.	.	.				176	16	41	24	8	1 873
United Kingdom	.	.	.	111.5	112.5	112.4	165	15	39	25	8	1 769
ex-USSR	.	.	.				.	.	.	.	.	.
Yugoslavia	.	.	.	92.8	120.0	.	.	.	42	18	8	1 974

VII. Strikes and accidents at work

| | Days not worked as a result of strikes and lockouts in manufacturing (per 1,000 workers) | | | | | Deaths as a result of accidents at work (annual average per 100,000 workers) | | | | | | | |
| | | | | | | Mining | | Manufacturing | | Construction | | Transport | |
	1986	1987	1988	1989	1990	1981-1985	1986-1990	1981-1985	1986-1990	1981-1985	1986-1990	1981-1985	1986-1990
Africa													
Algeria	.	.	.	.	.	.	.	.	.	.	.	.	.
Angola	.	.	.	.	.	.	.	.	.	.	.	.	.
Benin	.	.	.	.	.	.	.	.	.	.	.	.	.
Botswana	.	.	.	.	.	.	.	.	14[1]	.	9[1]	.	.
Burkina Faso	.	.	.	.	.	89[3]	52[3]	62[3]	15[3]	32[3]	22[3]	30[3]	25[3]
Burundi	.	.	.	.	.	433[3]	.	52[3]	.	66[3]	55[3]	80[3]	110[3]
Cameroon	.	.	.	.	.	.	.	.	.	.	.	.	.
Central African Republic	.	.	.	.	.	.	.	.	.	.	.	.	.
Chad	.	.	.	.	.	.	.	.	.	.	.	.	.
Congo	.	.	.	.	.	.	.	.	.	.	.	.	.
Côte d'Ivoire	.	.	.	.	.	.	.	.	.	.	.	.	.
Egypt	.	.	.	.	.	60[4]	20[4]	18[4]	14[4]	36[4]	29[4]	38[4]	25[4]
Ethiopia	.	.	.	.	.	.	.	4[1]	.	.	.	.	.
Gabon	.	.	.	.	.	.	.	.	.	.	.	.	.
Ghana	107	16	.	.	.	.	.	.	.	.	.	.	.
Guinea	.	.	.	.	.	.	.	.	.	.	.	.	.
Kenya	523	.	.	.	.	157[1]	35[1]	26[1]	24[1]	65[1]	55[1]	66[1]	72[1]
Lesotho	.	.	.	.	.	.	.	.	.	.	.	.	.
Liberia	.	.	.	.	.	.	.	.	.	.	.	.	.
Libyan Arab Jamahiriya	.	.	.	.	.	.	.	.	.	.	.	.	.
Madagascar	.	.	.	.	.	.	.	.	.	.	.	.	.
Malawi	.	.	.	.	.	.	.	11[1]	.	36[1]	.	38[1]	.
Mali	.	.	.	.	.	.	.	.	.	.	.	.	.
Mauritania	.	.	.	.	.	.	.	.	.	.	.	.	.
Mauritius	5	70	169	28	4	.	.	9[4]	3[4]	59[4]	16[4]	22[4]	23[4]
Morocco	.	.	.	.	.	.	.	.	.	.	.	.	.
Mozambique	.	.	.	.	.	.	.	.	.	.	.	.	.
Namibia	.	.	.	.	.	.	.	.	.	.	.	.	.
Niger	.	.	.	.	.	64[4]	23[4]	73[4]	81[4]	81[4]	45[4]	212[4]	190[4]
Nigeria	.	.	.	.	.	.	.	.	.	.	.	.	.
Rwanda	.	.	.	.	.	.	.	.	.	.	.	.	.
Senegal	.	.	.	.	.	.	.	.	.	.	.	.	.
Sierra Leone	.	.	.	.	.	.	.	.	.	.	.	.	.
Somalia	.	.	.	.	.	.	.	.	.	.	.	.	.
South Africa	432	643	425	610	.	.	.	.	.	.	.	.	.
Sudan	.	.	.	.	.	.	.	.	.	.	.	.	.
Tanzania, United Rep. of	.	.	.	.	.	.	.	.	.	.	.	.	.
Togo	.	.	.	.	.	48[4]	57[4]	47[4]	60[4]	27[4]	30[4]	27[4]	34[4]
Tunisia	.	.	.	.	.	.	.	.	.	.	.	.	.
Uganda	.	.	.	.	.	.	.	.	.	.	.	.	.
Zaire	.	.	.	.	.	.	.	.	.	.	.	.	.
Zambia	39	42	85	145	.	.	.	.	.	.	.	.	.
Zimbabwe	.	.	.	.	.	75[2]	67[2]	14[2]	9[2]	38[2]	33[2]	95[2]	72[2]
Americas													
Argentina	.	.	.	.	.	45[2]	17[2]	8[2]	6[2]	54[2]	21[2]	18[2]	12[2]
Bolivia	.	.	.	.	.	38[1]	29[1]	2[1]	1[1]	6[1]	.	4[1]	2[1]
Brazil	.	.	.	.	.	.	.	.	.	.	.	.	.
Canada	310	476	234	208	.	71[2]	64[2]	8[2]	6[2]	30[2]	26[2]	19[2]	15[2]
Chile	.	.	.	.	.	.	.	.	.	.	.	.	.
Colombia	.	.	.	.	.	.	.	.	.	.	.	.	.
Costa Rica	41	.	4	141	.	91[4]	125[4]	13[4]	9[4]	45[4]	18[4]	62[4]	29[4]
Cuba	.	.	.	.	.	.	.	11[1]	14[1]	19[1]	20[1]	27[1]	28[1]
Dominican Republic	.	.	.	.	.	.	.	1[1]	.	.	.	.	.
Ecuador	1 765	1 430	3 241	.	.	234[3]	248[3]	48[3]	45[3]	.	.	.	.
El Salvador	.	.	.	.	.	164[1]	.	81[1]	.	104[1]	.	90[1]	.
Guatemala	.	.	.	.	.	125[1]	173[1]	·86[1]	48[1]	178[1]	122[1]	192[1]	96[1]
Haiti	.	.	.	.	.	.	.	.	3[2]	.	.	.	.
Honduras	.	.	.	.	.	.	.	.	.	.	.	.	.
Jamaica	.	.	.	.	.	.	.	7[2]	4[2]	.	.	2 797[2]	809[2]
Mexico	.	.	.	.	.	.	40[1]	.	23[1]	.	65[1]	.	33[1]
Nicaragua	.	.	.	.	.	90[4]	101[4]	22[4]	19[4]	43[4]	70[4]	47[4]	36[4]
Panama	.	.	782	.	.	.	.	16[1]	9[1]	18[1]	25[1]	11[1]	12[1]
Paraguay	.	.	.	.	.	.	.	.	.	.	.	.	.
Peru	11 866	4 773	10 408	5 640	.	32[1]	53[1]	27[1]	7[1]	17[1]	39[1]	6[1]	24[1]
Trinidad and Tobago	.	.	.	.	.	.	18[1]	6[1]	4[1]	4[1]	.	3[1]	7[1]
United States	329	138	121	143	28	35[2]	22[2]	4[2]	4[2]	18[2]	15[2]	18[2]	14[2]
Uruguay	.	.	.	.	.	.	.	.	.	.	.	.	.
Venezuela	.	.	.	.	.	.	.	.	.	.	.	.	.

	Days not worked as a result of strikes and lockouts in manufacturing (per 1,000 workers)					Deaths as a result of accidents at work (annual average per 100,000 workers)							
						Mining		Manufacturing		Construction		Transport	
	1986	1987	1988	1989	1990	1981–1985	1986–1990	1981–1985	1986–1990	1981–1985	1986–1990	1981–1985	1986–1990
Asia and Oceania													
Afghanistan													
Australia	378	373	405	365									
Bangladesh								4[1]				21[1]	
Bhutan													
Cambodia													
China													
Hong Kong						117[4]	169[4]	5[4]	4[4]	104[4]	95[4]	56[4]	37[4]
India	4 741	5 015	4 553	3 141				8[1]				—[1]	
Indonesia													
Iran, Islamic Rep. of													
Iraq													
Israel	315	66	473			28[4]		29[4]		38[4]		23[4]	
Japan	10	9				174[1]	74[1]	5[1]	4[1]	26[1]	24[1]	11[1]	11[1]
Jordan						26[4]	21[4]	53[4]	255[4]	28[4]	122[4]	20[4]	87[4]
Korea, Dem. People's Rep. of													
Korea, Republic of	11	1 826				331[4]	456[4]	18[4]	17[4]	52[4]	30[4]	68[4]	60[4]
Kuwait													
Lao People's Dem. Rep.													
Lebanon													
Malaysia						50[3]	33[3]	13[3]	11[3]				
Mongolia													
Myanmar								7[1]	4[1]				
Nepal													
New Zealand	4 504	523	941			32[4]	30[4]	5[4]	7[4]	15[4]	9[4]	18[4]	13[4]
Oman													
Pakistan						62[3]	76[3]	24[3]	48[3]				
Papua New Guinea													
Philippines	4 011	1 869				19[2]	29[2]	1[2]	2[2]	1[2]	1[2]	2[2]	
Saudi Arabia													
Singapore								8[1]	7[1]	69[1]	34[1]	1[1]	
Sri Lanka	4							11[1]	12[1]	36[1]	13[1]	4[1]	
Syrian Arab Republic													
Thailand						27[4]	24[4]	7[4]	6[4]	8[4]	9[4]	17[4]	10[4]
Turkey						277[1]		18[1]		68[1]		115[1]	
United Arab Emirates													
Viet Nam													
Yemen													
Europe and the former Soviet Union													
Albania													
Austria	—	2		—		46[1]	23[1]	8[1]	8[1]	37[1]	28[1]	36[1]	22[1]
Belgium						41[1]	13[1]	7[1]	6[1]	24[1]	26[1]	32[1]	26[1]
Bulgaria													
Czechoslovakia						39[1]	24[1]	7[1]	6[1]	16[1]	15[1]	13[1]	12[1]
Denmark	190	191	198	101	169	52[1]		3[1]	3[1]	6[1]	7[1]	5[1]	7[1]
Finland	602	214	294	214		27[2]	25[2]	4[2]	4[2]	11[2]	9[2]	9[2]	9[2]
France	89	82						7[1]	6[1]	27[1]	24[1]	33[1]	31[1]
Germany	3	4	5	7		38[3]	29[3]	10[3]	7[3]	27[3]	19[3]		
Greece													
Hungary						41[3]	30[3]	12[3]	12[3]	27[3]	29[3]	22[3]	22[3]
Ireland						39[1]	21[1]	30[1]	3[1]	9[1]	20[1]		
Italy						26[1]	21[1]	5[1]	4[1]	22[1]	22[1]	19[1]	16[1]
Netherlands									2[1]		4[1]		4[1]
Norway	1 135	3	7	10	37	14[1]	6[1]	4[1]	5[1]	10[1]	8[1]	19[1]	13[1]
Poland			69	142	18	26[1]	24[1]	7[1]	7[1]	16[1]	14[1]	18[1]	15[1]
Portugal	228	63				52[3]	84[3]	17[3]	23[3]	50[3]	63[3]	35[3]	34[3]
Romania													
Spain	342	426	559	869	258	66[1]	70[1]	11[1]	13[1]	29[1]	34[1]	37[1]	35[1]
Sweden													
Switzerland						44[2]	61[2]	4[2]	4[2]	22[2]	16[2]	10[2]	13[2]
United Kingdom	206	116	318	146	209	18[1]	39[1]	2[1]	2[1]	10[1]	10[1]	3[1]	3[1]
ex-USSR													
Yugoslavia						31[1]	19[1]	6[1]	5[1]	17[1]	13[1]		

[1] Accidents at work. [2] Accidents at work and occupational illnesses. [3] Accidents at work and commuting accidents. [4] Accidents at work, occupational illnesses and commuting accidents.

VIII. Social security

	Government in total contribution (%) 1989	Benefit expenditure in GDP (%) 1989	Coverage of persons insured (% of labour force) Old age 1989	Sickness 1989	Maternity 1989	Real benefit expenditure per insured person (in US$) Medical care 1989	Sickness 1989	Employ-ment injury 1989	pensioner 1987=100 Old age 1989	Benefit per pensioner (in US$) Old age 1989
Africa										
Algeria										
Angola										
Benin		0.6							4	
Botswana										
Burkina Faso										
Burundi		0.7						16	89	182
Cameroon										
Central African Republic										
Chad										
Congo										
Côte d'Ivoire		0.5	4.9	4.9		7		30	92	844
Egypt	3.0	1.1								
Ethiopia		1.4								
Gabon	3.2	2.0								
Ghana		–	33.7							
Guinea			0.8	0.8	0.8		13*	10		
Kenya		0.6	0.9							
Lesotho										
Liberia										
Libyan Arab Jamahiriya										
Madagascar										
Malawi										
Mali										
Mauritania										
Mauritius	42.5*	5.6*								
Morocco	16.3	1.5	8.6	8.6				4	102	911
Mozambique										
Namibia										
Niger										
Nigeria										
Rwanda		0.3	9.2					4		256
Senegal										
Sierra Leone										
Somalia										
South Africa										
Sudan		–								
Tanzania, United Rep. of										
Togo										
Tunisia	2.2	3.6	41.4	41.4	41.4	52				
Uganda										
Zaire										
Zambia										
Zimbabwe										
Americas										
Argentina										
Bolivia										
Brazil	20.9	–	5.1	1.1			993	1 995	84	289
Canada	71.2*	17.3*	100	100	100	2 257*	22*	289*	102*	6 114*
Chile	51.6	9.9	83.0			95		37		
Colombia		1.5	24.9	25.7		109	9	8	100*	1 308
Costa Rica										
Cuba										
Dominican Republic										
Ecuador										
El Salvador										
Guatemala										
Haiti										
Honduras										
Jamaica	63.5	1.2	32.9							329
Mexico										
Nicaragua										
Panama	5.0	9.4	43.9	37.4		379	33	71		
Paraguay										
Peru			42.2	42.2	42.2	93		2	17	636
Trinidad and Tobago	52.3	2.1	62.7	62.7	62.7					
United States	37.4	12.6	97.6	18.0		3 414	4		77	7 239
Uruguay										
Venezuela										

	Government in total contribution (%)	Benefit expenditure in GDP (%)	Coverage of persons insured (% of labour force)			Real benefit expenditure per insured person (in US$)			pensioner	Benefit per pensioner (in US$)
			Old age	Sickness	Maternity	Medical care	Sickness	Employment injury	1987=100 Old age	Old age
	1989	1989	1989	1989	1989	1989	1989	1989	1989	1989
Asia and Oceania										
Afghanistan	.	.	.	.	.	.	.	.	.	.
Australia	89.2	8.0	.	1.0*	.	.	5 355	.	.	.
Bangladesh	.	2.1	.	.	.	.	.	.	.	.
Bhutan	.	.	.	.	.	.	.	.	.	.
Cambodia	.	.	.	.	.	.	.	.	.	.
China	.	3.4	23.9	20.6	.	37	.	.	.	378
Hong Kong	.	.	.	.	.	.	.	.	.	.
India	.	.	.	.	.	.	.	.	.	.
Indonesia	49.2	–	.	.	.	.	.	.	.	.
Iran, Islamic Rep. of	.	.	.	.	.	.	.	.	.	.
Iraq	.	.	.	.	.	.	.	.	.	.
Israel	.	.	.	.	.	.	.	.	.	.
Japan	.	.	.	.	.	.	.	.	.	.
Jordan	.	.	.	.	.	.	.	.	.	.
Korea, Dem. People's Rep. of	.	.	.	.	.	.	.	.	.	.
Korea, Republic of	.	.	.	.	.	.	.	.	.	.
Kuwait	.	.	.	.	.	.	.	.	.	.
Lao People's Dem. Rep.	.	.	.	.	.	.	.	.	.	.
Lebanon	.	.	.	.	.	.	.	.	.	.
Malaysia	.	.	.	.	.	.	.	.	.	.
Mongolia	.	.	.	.	.	.	.	.	.	.
Myanmar	.	.	.	.	.	.	.	.	.	.
Nepal	.	.	.	.	.	.	.	.	.	.
New Zealand	100	12.0	.	.	.	.	.	.	.	.
Oman	.	.	.	.	.	.	.	.	.	.
Pakistan	.	.	.	.	.	.	.	.	.	.
Papua New Guinea	.	.	.	.	.	.	.	.	.	.
Philippines	.	0.7	57.5	52.3	52.3	7	1	1	98	728
Saudi Arabia	.	1.4	.	.	.	.	.	.	.	.
Singapore	0.1	7.1	.	.	.	.	.	.	.	.
Sri Lanka	6.2	2.0	.	.	.	.	.	.	.	.
Syrian Arab Republic	.	.	.	.	.	.	.	.	.	.
Thailand	.	–	.	.	.	.	.	.	.	.
Turkey	35.0	4.5	.	.	.	63	.	5	112	3 358
United Arab Emirates	.	.	.	.	.	.	.	.	.	.
Viet Nam	.	.	.	.	.	.	.	.	.	.
Yemen	.	.	.	.	.	.	.	.	.	.
Europe and the former Soviet Union										
Albania	.	.	.	.	.	.	.	.	.	.
Austria	19.1	21.5	79.5	80.4	92.5	831	147	114	102	17 224
Belgium	.	.	.	.	.	.	.	.	.	.
Bulgaria	.	.	.	.	.	.	.	.	.	.
Czechoslovakia	96.1	.	98.1	98.1	98.1	146	89	.	110	1 160
Denmark	90.5	27.8	100	100	100	.	.	.	93	6 641
Finland	47.5	20.6	100	100	100	2 380	283	200	102	8 470
France	.	.	.	.	.	.	.	.	.	.
Germany	26.9	23.0*	100	100	.	2 342	125	118	95	13 245
Greece	20.2*	11.9	.	.	.	.	.	.	.	.
Hungary	.	.	.	.	.	.	.	.	.	.
Ireland	58.6	19.9*	.	.	.	.	.	.	.	.
Italy	.	.	.	.	.	.	.	.	.	.
Netherlands	22.0	27.7	100	100	100	1 280	565	.	101	7 311
Norway	27.4	17.6	100	100	100	.	.	.	.	.
Poland	21.7	11.5	.	.	.	.	.	.	.	.
Portugal	14.2	10.4	17.9	85.3	85.3	.	71	5	110	4 346
Romania	51.1	.	68.1	68.1	.	.	64	1	.	1 150
Spain	.	.	.	.	.	.	.	.	.	.
Sweden	55.5	33.7	100	100	100	1 947	1 118	284	117	16 548
Switzerland	27.5	13.3	100	100	100	877	128	615	.	.
United Kingdom	54.1	17.0	.	.	.	.	.	.	.	.
ex-USSR	57.9	.	.	.	.	.	.	.	.	.
Yugoslavia	.	.	.	.	.	.	.	.	.	.